GLOBAL POLITICAL STUDIES

GLOBAL GOVERNANCE

PERSPECTIVES, CHALLENGES AND OUTLOOK

GLOBAL POLITICAL STUDIES

Additional books in this series can be found on Nova's website
under the Series tab.

Additional e-books in this series can be found on Nova's website
under the eBooks tab.

GLOBAL POLITICAL STUDIES

GLOBAL GOVERNANCE

PERSPECTIVES, CHALLENGES AND OUTLOOK

SAGARIKA DUTT

EDITOR

nova
science publishers
New York

NOTICE TO THE READER

Library of Congress Cataloging-in-Publication Data

ISBN: 978-1-53612-969-4

Published by Nova Science Publishers, Inc. † New York

CONTENTS

Contents

PREFACE

Interest in global governance has been growing over the years. This is reflected in the academic literature as well as the work of international institutions like the United Nations. The Commission on Global Governance that published its report entitled 'Our Global Neighbourhood' in 1995 noted that with the end of the cold war, the world community seemed to be uniting around the idea that it should assume greater collective responsibility in a wide range of areas, including security, sustainable development, the promotion of democracy, equity and human rights, and humanitarian action. This is, however, not a new idea as the UN system was created, after the Second World War, for the same purpose. What has happened since then is that the global agenda has grown and now covers many vital areas of life that in the past were left to individual states and their governments. An example is the Sustainable Development Goals adopted by the UN in 2015. There are seventeen of them ranging from the eradication of poverty and good health and well-being to responsible consumption and production, climate action and partnerships for the goals. But the UN itself is a subject of debate. Is it just a forum and a 'talking shop', or can it bring about real change in the world?

This book begins with an introduction to the concept of global governance including the views expressed by different authors and scholars, as well as the Commission on Global Governance, and then goes on to present chapters written by different authors on various topics and aspects of global governance such as the United Nations and sustainable development, multilateralism and the management of international trade, and counterterrorism in a globalised world. All the contributors to this volume are academics who teach courses on International Relations or Global Studies. Their chapters are based on their specialisms and research interests. They are written from different perspectives and discuss some of the challenges facing the global community such as terrorism, or those facing individual communities, for example, the small island developing states that are threatened as a result of rising sea levels. International trade is another area in which there are many challenges and the future of multilateral trade negotiations does not seem good. In this chapter, the author expresses his personal opinion about the outlook for international trade, suggesting that the World Trade Organization (WTO) is not the only option that countries have for promoting trade.

The book provides a flavour of the kinds of global issues the world is interested in. Some of them have been around for a long time, such as development, but have evolved over time. Others, like global Islamism, are new issues, but may well have their roots in old issues like poverty, social exclusion and marginalisation. If governance is an important part of national life, and indeed life in local communities, governance at the international or global level is equally important as individual countries and states cannot isolate themselves from the rest of the world, especially in the age of globalisation, and neither do they want to. As many scholars have pointed out, globalisation has increased the need for governance at all levels, and better governance can ensure that globalisation leads to a better life for all citizens.

Sagarika Dutt
1 October 2017

LIST OF CONTRIBUTORS

Blavoukos, Spyros: Dr. Spyros Blavoukos is Associate Professor in the Department of International and European Economic Studies, Athens University of Economics and Business, Greece. Email: sblavo@aueb.gr

Bourantonis, Dimitris: Dimitris Bourantonis is Professor of International and European Studies in the Department of International and European Economic Studies, Athens University of Economics and Business, Greece. Email: bouranto@aueb.gr

Dutt, Sagarika: Dr. Sagarika Dutt has a PhD in International Relations from the University of Kent and is a Senior Lecturer at the Nottingham Trent University, UK. She is also the Subject Leader for International Relations. Email: sagarika.dutt@ntu.ac.uk

Farrands, Christopher: Dr. Christopher Farrands is Principal Lecturer in International Relations at the Nottingham Trent University, UK. Email: chrisfarrands@outlook.com

Mukherjee, Kunal: Dr. Kunal Mukherjee is Lecturer in International Relations at Lancaster University, UK. Email: k.mukherjee1@lancaster.ac.uk

Smith, Roy: Dr. Roy Smith is Principal Lecturer in International Relations and Subject Leader for Global Studies at the Nottingham Trent University, UK. Email: roy.smith@ntu.ac.uk

Underhill, Natasha: Dr. Nastasha Underhill is a Lecturer in International Relations at the Nottingham Trent University, U.K. She is also the course leader for the BA Hons (International Relations) degree programme. Email: natasha.underhill@ntu.ac.uk

In: Global Governance
Editor: Sagarika Dutt

ISBN: 978-1-53612-969-4
© 2018 Nova Science Publishers, Inc.

Chapter 1

FROM GOVERNANCE TO GLOBAL GOVERNANCE: AN INTRODUCTION

Sagarika Dutt

Senior Lecturer in International Relations and Subject Leader,
Nottingham Trent University, Nottingham, UK

ABSTRACT

The concept of global governance has grown in importance since the 1990s, and in diverse fields and academic disciplines. In the field of international relations, the importance of the concept lies in the fact that the world we live in has changed and traditional theories like Realism may no longer be sufficient for analysing world politics. There are different kinds of power and organising principles that form patterns of global governance, for example, powers deriving from global finance or information technologies, as well as the organising principle of globalisation. The crux of the matter is that authority is being relocated in multiple directions. This chapter engages with the understandings and definitions of governance and global governance found in the academic literature in order to provide a theoretical framework for the rest of the chapters in this book.

WHAT IS GOVERNANCE?

The word 'governance' has always been part of the vocabulary in the western, English-speaking world. According to the Oxford Dictionary it means the 'act or manner or function of governing', while govern means 'to rule with authority'. It could also mean 'to conduct policy and affairs' of the state or some other entity. Governance is not synonymous with government, although the state has traditionally had a role to play in governance by providing direction to society.[1] James Rosenau argues that 'both refer to purposive behaviour, to goal-oriented activities, to systems of rule; but government suggests activities that are backed by formal authority, by police powers to insure the implementation of duly constituted policies, whereas governance refers to activities backed by shared goals that may or may not derive from legal and formally prescribed responsibilities and that do not necessarily rely on police powers to overcome defiance and attain compliance' (Rosenau 1992, 4). This goes well with the view that governance is about producing public goods (Ruggie 2010, xv). Explaining it in another way Lynn (2012, 52) writes that 'societal steering is viewed as having three primary wellsprings': government; the firms of the proprietary private sector; and civil society organisations, prominently including non-governmental organisations (NGOs). These three sources of societal direction may operate in virtual independence from one another, but that is rare. Normally governments contract with NGOs or firms for the delivery of services. Both NGOs and the private sector are generally subject to various forms of regulation by different levels and agencies of government. Interactions between the three sectors can take different forms such as contracts, subsidies, self-organising networks, independent regulatory authorities and so on. As Bevir (2011) argues, 'governance arrangements are often hybrid

---

[1] Bevir (2012) argues that 'Governance stands in contrast to elder concepts of the state as monolithic and formal. For a start, theories of governance typically open up the black box of the state. Policy network theory, rational choice theory and interpretive theory undermine reified concepts of the state as a monolithic entity, interest, or actor. These theories draw attention to the processes and interactions through which all kinds of social interests and actors combine to produce the policies, practices and effects that define current patterns of governing'.

practices…Novel forms of mixed public-private or entirely private forms of regulation are developing'. Lynn argues that this analytic framework helps us to consider how societies differ from each other in patterns of steering, how they change over time, and whether the boundaries between the sectors are being redrawn. The framework is also useful for comparing different definitions of governance. The concept of governance has grown in importance since the 1990s (Levi-Faur 2012, 5), and in diverse fields and academic disciplines, such as business, economics, environmental studies, political science, public administration, and so on (Levi-Faur 2012, 5; Bevir 2011).

In the field of international relations, the importance of the concept lies in the fact that the world we live in has changed and traditional theories like Realism may no longer be sufficient for analysing world politics. Hewson and Sinclair (1999, 3) write that 'Realism came to supremacy in the Cold War by providing a potent way of accounting for the great contest between East and West. Subsequently neorealism sought to universalise a Cold War conception of the state', but times have changed. Politics today is not just about the power of the state or politics among nations (Morgenthau 2006). There are different kinds of power and organising principles that form patterns of global governance which need to be given more thought, and taken into account in both theoretical and empirical research on global governance. For example, 'the powers deriving from global finance or information technologies as well as the organising principle of globalisation' (Hewson and Sinclair 1999, 3-4). The crux of the matter is that authority is 'being relocated in multiple directions. The Westphalian or territorial state system is no more than one form or element of contemporary global governance. Numerous other forms of governance seep through the fabric of global life, proliferating and diversifying' (Ibid., 7). Ruggie (2010, xviii) argues that 'a postmodern overlay on the modern territorial system of global governance has emerged. It is characterised by an extensive transnationalization of issues, transaction flows, and actors that cuts across familiar national jurisdictions, blurs the boundaries between external and internal spaces, and intermingles the public, private, and civic spheres in novel ways.' Bevir (2011) also argues that a' distinctive feature of governance is that it is multijurisdictional and often transnational. Current patterns of governance combine people and institutions across different policy sectors and different levels of government (local, regional, national and international)'. For example, the practice of regulating food safety operates simultaneously at international, national and local levels.

SHIFTS IN GOVERNANCE: A NEW ONTOLOGY?

In the *Oxford Handbook of Governance*, Levi-Faur (2012, 7) writes that 'The rise of governance coincided with the widespread consensus that ours is…an era of change, of shifts, and even of transformation and paradigm change. In the governance literature this was best captured in the observation of "shifts" in governance and controversies about their directions and implications… The shifts are conceptualised in three different directions: upward (to the regional, transnational, intergovernmental, and global), downward (to the local, regional, and the metropolitan), and horizontally (to private and civil spheres of authority)'. This argument is supported by other scholars as well.[2] The significance of the shifts in governance lies in the suggestion that authority can be institutionalised, and in different spheres, 'and by implication these arenas can compete, bargain, or coordinate among themselves or ignore each other' (Levi-Faur 2012, 7).

Levi-Faur (2012, 7) goes on to say that 'some of the most dominant ways to think about shifts in governance include a shift from politics to markets, from community to markets, from politicians to experts, from political, economic, and social hierarchies to decentred markets, partnerships and networks; from bureaucracy to *regulocracy*, from service provision to regulation; from the positive state to the regulatory state; from Big Government to small government; from the national to the regional;

---

[2] See James Rosenau. 1999. "Toward an ontology for global governance." In *Approaches to Global Governance Theory*, edited by Martin Hewson and T.J. Sinclair, 287-301. Albany: State University of New York Press.

from the national to the global; from hard power to soft power, and from public authority to private authority'. For Political Scientists, and Social Scientists in general, this means that a shift away from government is not necessarily a shift away from the state, as the state itself is more than government. For example, Ofcom is the communications regulator in the UK. It operates under a number of Acts of Parliament, and is accountable to Parliament. It sets and enforces regulatory rules for the sectors for which it has responsibility. Its main responsibility is to 'further the interests of citizens and of consumers, where appropriate by promoting competition' (Ofcom website). Secondly, governments are not static, and can adapt or reorganize themselves in horizontal or decentred forms. This would indicate a shift away from hierarchy and towards decentred governance (Zumbansen 2012, 86). However, the hybridization of modes of control both within and beyond the state can lead to a fragmented order, or what Rosenau (1999, 293) calls *fragmegration*, 'the interactions of globalizing and localizing forces, of tendencies toward integration and fragmentation' that are simultaneous and interactive processes which have implications for citizens, democracies and international relations, in general.[3]

GOVERNANCE AS STRUCTURE, PROCESS, MECHANISM AND STRATEGY

As this chapter goes on to discuss global governance, it is worth noting some of the ways in which the academic literature on governance has used the concept. Much of this is relevant to a discussion of global governance. Studies on governance have focused on governance as structure, as process, as mechanism, and as strategy. The distinctions are explained by Levi-Faur (2012, 8) as follows: 'As a structure governance signifies the

---

[3] Amitav Acharya (2016, 453-4) writes that some see the fragmentation of global governance as 'producing a sub-optimal or "good enough" global governance' while others see it 'in starkly negative terms.' His own view is that 'fragmentation is inevitable and may even be creative because it reflects broader forces of change in world politics.' Amitav Acharya. 2016. "The Future of Global Governance: Fragmentation may be inevitable and creative". *Global Governance* 22: 453-460.

architecture of formal and informal institutions; as a process it signifies the dynamics and steering functions involved in lengthy never-ending processes of policy-making; as a mechanism it signifies institutional procedures of decision-making, of compliance and of control (or instruments); finally, as a strategy it signifies the actors' efforts to govern and manipulate the design of institutions and mechanisms in order to shape choice and preferences'. He also observes that most of the literature on governance focuses on governance as structure, 'probably as a reflection of the dominance of institutionalism in the social sciences'.

Similarly, in the study of international relations, global governance has always been associated with institutions and processes of institutionalization, including the activities of world organisations (Hewson and Sinclair 1999, 15; Sinclair 2013, 31). Armstrong et al. (2004, 12) write that the concept of 'governance' has 'become increasingly popular as a means of denoting a world order in which, even in the absence of formal government, enduring structures of rules, norms and institutions have emerged in many areas of international life'. For example, the Universal Postal Union sets the rules for international mail exchanges and the World Trade Organisation (WTO) promotes trade rules which are actually agreements that governments negotiate (respective websites). But business corporations may also make rules (Sinclair 2012, 23). Other IR scholars have similar understandings and definitions of governance and global governance. Thakur and Weiss (2010, 6) describe it as the 'sum of laws, norms, policies, and institutions that define, constitute, and mediate relations among citizens, society, markets and the state in the international arena – the wielders and objects of international public power'. Their definition of 'governance' and 'global governance' is exactly the same, except that the latter occurs in the international arena. In the foreword to their book Ruggie (2010, xv) argues that 'Governance, at whatever level of social organization it occurs, refers to the workings of the system of authoritative rules, norms, institutions, and practices by means of which any collectivity manages its common affairs'. The instruments of global governance take the form of treaties, customary international law, formal organisations such as the UN or the WTO, and embedded norms such as those legitimizing certain uses of force but not others, for example. But there is always a 'tension between the need to internationalize rules and the desire to assert and retain national control' (Ibid.). In general, laws at both the national and international level underpin governance, as well as order. Hedley Bull (1995, 135) observes that one of the functions of international law in relation to international order is 'to state the basic rules of coexistence among states and other actors in international society'. While another function is to help mobilize compliance with the rules of international society. Rosenau is widely regarded as the seminal theorist on governance within the academic discipline of IR. Rosenau (1992, 4-5) defines governance as 'a system of rule' but points out that it is 'a system of rule that is as dependent on intersubjective meanings as on formally sanctioned constitutions and charters. Put more emphatically, governance is a system of rule that works only if it is accepted by the majority (or, at least, by the most powerful of those it affects), whereas governments can function even in the face of widespread opposition to their policies. In this sense governance is always effective in performing the functions necessary to systemic persistence, else it is not conceived to exist…Thus it is possible to conceive of governance without government – of regulatory mechanisms in a sphere of activity which function effectively even though they are not endowed with formal authority'. In addition to structure, the conceptualization of governance as a process, a mechanism, and a strategy, also has a lot of relevance for the study of international relations. Governance refers to the process 'whereby an organization or society steers itself, and the dynamics of communication and control are central to that process' (Rosenau 2005, 46). Similarly, the conduct of international relations by states and other actors is 'an ongoing process of steering, or enhancing the institutional capacity to steer and coordinate' (Levi-Faur 2012, 7). Processes of policy making are just as important at the international/global level as they are at the local, national, and regional levels. Similarly, decision making is integral to the conduct of international relations, and mechanisms of decision making at the international level could be conceptualised as forms of global governance. Here, we could also ask what kind of decision-making mechanisms are most suitable at the international/global level. For example, according to the *Oxford Handbook of Governance*, 'Command is a decision-making mechanism that involves rule-making with the expectation of compliance from the subject being commanded. It is an authoritative and hierarchical mechanism of decision-making which often is associated with the state but of course is not confined to it' (Levi-Faur 2012, 9). However, Rosenau (2005, 46) cautions us that the concept of commands can be misleading. It implies that hierarchy, perhaps even, authoritarian rule, characterises governance systems. While this may be true of many forms of governance, 'hierarchy is certainly not a necessary prerequisite to the framing of goals, the issuing of directives, and the pursuit of policies...often the practices and institutions of governance can and do evolve in such a way as to be minimally dependent on hierarchical, command-based arrangements'.

A less hierarchical and more democratic mechanism of decision-making is persuasion. It 'involves the elaboration of values, preference, and interest as well as the rationalization and framing of options for action and the exchange of ideas and information in a deliberative manner' (Levi-Faur 2012, 9). This is how the UN works and this is reflected in the views of the Commission on Global Governance discussed later in this chapter. In the field of trade, on the other hand, monetized exchange is a more appropriate mechanism of decision-making. 'Monetized exchanges are usually market exchanges and are characterized by minimal or moderate transaction costs' (Ibid.). Finally, solidarity is yet another mechanism of decision-making. It 'rests on loyalty rather than voice, love rather than interest, faith rather than critical thinking, and group identity rather than individualism' (Ibid). In some areas of national/global concern, this may be the most suitable mechanism of decision making.

MECHANISMS OF GLOBAL GOVERNANCE

Rosenau's (2005) chapter in 'The Global Governance Reader', edited by Rorden Wilkinson, is devoted to a discussion of the mechanisms of global governance. It also provides an opportunity to clarify his understanding of global governance. It doesn't just refer to formal institutions and organisations through which international affairs are managed, such as the UN system and the national governments of its member states, which actually implement UN decisions. Global governance, according to Rosenau (2005, 45) includes 'systems of rule at all levels of human activity – from the family to the international organization – in which the pursuit of goals through the exercise of control has transnational repercussions'. He favours this broad formulation on account of the ever growing interdependence in the world 'where what happens in one corner or at one level may have consequences for what occurs at every other corner and level' (Ibid., 45-6). This, in turn, requires control or steering mechanisms, which proliferate, as some actors 'seek to modify the behaviour and/or orientations of other actors…the resulting patterns of interaction between the former and the latter can properly be viewed as a system of rule sustained by one or another form of control'.

It is interesting that Rosenau does not give much importance to whether the controlees resist or comply with the efforts to control them. He argues that it is only when the attempts to control become increasingly successful and 'compliance with them increasingly patterned that a system of rule founded on mechanisms of control can be said to have evolved. Rule systems and control mechanisms, in other words, are founded on a modicum of regularity, a form of recurrent behaviour that systematically links the efforts of controllers to the compliance of controlees through either formal or informal channels' (Ibid., 46-7). There is, therefore, an element of power involved in all systems of rule (this is reminiscent of David Easton's discussion about the political system and the authoritative allocation of values for a society[4]). But elsewhere he argues, as we saw

---

[4] However, Czempiel (1992, 250) writes that he understands "governance" to mean 'the capacity to get things done without the legal competence to command that they be done. Where governments, in the Eastonian sense, can distribute values authoritatively, governance can distribute them in a way which is not authoritative but equally effective. Governments exercise rule, governance uses power. From this point of view the international system is a system of governance.' He also writes that 'Conflicts are systems of governance with each party trying to induce, or to force, the other party to do certain things it otherwise would not have done'. (Czempiel, Ernst-Otto. 1992. "Governance and Democratization." In *Governance without government: order and change in world politics*, edited by James N. Rosenau and Ernst-Otto Czempiel, 250-271. Cambridge: Cambridge University Press)

earlier, that governance is a system of rule that is dependent on intersubjective meanings and works only if it is accepted by the majority, or at least, the most powerful of those it affects. At any rate, as far as global governance is concerned he concludes that 'there is no single organizing principle on which global governance rests, no emergent order around which communities and nations are likely to converge. Global governance is the sum of myriad – literally millions of – control mechanisms driven by different histories, goals, structures and processes.' (Ibid., 48).

The world is characterised by disaggregation and the absence of global coherence. However, it is possible to identify pockets of coherence at different levels and in different parts of the world that can serve as bases for assessing the contours of global governance in the future. This is on account of control mechanisms which tend to evolve, and can be conceptualised as evolving along a continuum 'that runs from nascent to fully institutionalised mechanisms, from informal modes of framing goals, issuing directives, and pursuing policies to formal instruments of decision-making, conflict resolution, and resource allocation' (Ibid., 49). They may also decline and cease to exist. Successful mechanisms of governance are more likely to evolve out of bottom-up, rather than top-down, processes, argues Rosenau. Given the disaggregation of modern governance and the process of evolution it undergoes, it can fluctuate between order and disorder as conditions change. Rosenau further argues that although 'Global governance in the twenty-first century may not take the form of a single world-order, but it will not be lacking in activities designed to bring a measure of coherence to the multitude of jurisdictions that are proliferating on the world stage' (Ibid., 50). The work of the UN, the conferences hosted by it, and the multilateral treaties and conventions sponsored by it could provide examples of such activities.

The world is full of challenges, as Wilkinson points out in the introduction to the *Global Governance Reader*. Conflict, poverty, environmental degradation, disease, and human insecurity are just some of the problems the world has to solve. At the same time, the world has to respond to change, for example, the end of the cold war, and the rise of new powers. And it is not just in the sphere of international politics that change is occurring. Societies are changing, all over the world, as are economic relations, often leading to 'shifts in the location of authority and the site of control mechanisms' (Ibid., 50). The growth of the EU can be cited as an example of this, while the Brexit vote (2017) can be seen as a political backlash against these shifts. Both social and economic relations are affected by new technologies, for example, the social media, and of course, the internet. Globalisation is eroding the power of the state and its ability to control the lives of its citizens, for better or for worse (Commission on Global Governance 1995, 11). Rosenau (2005, 50) writes that 'the numerous shifts in the loci of governance stem from interactive tensions whereby processes of globalization and localization are simultaneously unfolding on a worldwide scale. In some situations these foregoing dynamics are fostering control mechanisms that extend beyond national boundaries, and in others... is leading to the diminution of national entities and the formation or extension of local mechanisms. The combined effect of the simultaneity of these contradictory trends is that of lessening the capacities for governance located at the level of sovereign states and national societies'. This makes global governance, or the control mechanisms that add up to it, as conceptualised by Rosenau, all the more important. A few words about steering/control mechanisms is therefore in order. As Rosenau (2005, 51) argues, steering mechanisms of global governance may be sponsored by states, or come into existence as a result of the efforts of non-state actors at the transnational or subnational levels, or 'through states and other types of actors jointly sponsoring the formation of rule systems'.

Transnational governance may take a variety of forms. Using Rosenau's typology, transnational nascent control mechanisms can be identified. For example, 'NGOs may serve as the basis for, or actually become, nascent forms of transnational governance'. Rosenau explains that this is because 'in an ever more interdependent world, the need for control mechanisms outstrips the capacity or readiness of national governments to provide them' (Rosenau 2005, 52). NGOs work at both the national and international levels. They may supplement the service provided by the government, for example the British Red Cross aims to provide social/community care in the UK, and responds to humanitarian crises overseas. During a war or armed conflict, as in Syria and Iraq (repossession of Mosul on 19. 2. 17), and hunger and starvation in East Africa in March 2017, numerous INGOs, such as Save the Children and Oxfam, may provide humanitarian assistance, often alongside UN agencies, like UNICEF. NGOs/INGOs also have consultative status at the UN and attend UN sponsored conferences. They have become influential actors in international relations and have a role to play in global governance. In his famous book, *The Conscience of the World: The influence of Non-governmental organisations in the UN System* (1996), Peter Willetts argues that NGOs have come to exert considerable influence on the UN's agenda setting, decision-making, and policy implementation. 'Global civil society, expressed through the NGOs, is as much a part of UN politics as pressure group activity is a part of the domestic politics of a democracy'. Chapters Two and Three in this book discuss the UN and sustainable development. This is a field in which NGOs/INGOs have a significant contribution to make.

Profit making organisations in the private sector, including multinational corporations, are also important non-state actors that have a role to play in global economic governance. Although neoliberal theories suggest that they have a preference for a free market (subjected to minimal regulation) as opposed to an over regulated market, Sinclair (2012, 23) argues that they often lobby government for better regulation and government oversight of markets. In addition, regulation, or self-regulation, is often undertaken by market agents themselves. But there are other perspectives on this issue. According to Willetts (2011b, 332), there has been a shift from domestic deregulation to global re-regulation. He writes that 'in some areas of economic policy, governments have lost sovereignty and regulation now has to be exercised at the global level rather than by governments acting independently'. There are also good examples of voluntary and informal regulation aimed at developing more effective governance (Held 2014, 64-5), such as the UN Global Compact and its principles that companies are accepting voluntarily. The UN Global

Compact seeks to implement ten principles of corporate social responsibility and corporate sustainability on human rights, labour standards, the environment, and anti-corruption (https://www. unglobal compact.org/about). Business corporations are the force behind modern/21st century capitalism and are conscious of their growing power. Not only do they meet the needs of people/consumers, they work alongside states to build modern economies, bring in much needed investment, promote trade, create jobs, in short lay the foundations of a liberal economic order and promote economic growth.

One of the best examples of state-sponsored mechanisms of global governance is the UN system. Rosenau (2005, 60) writes that the 'United Nations system is an obvious case of a steering mechanism that was sponsored by states and that took an institutional form from its founding. To be sure, its processes of institutionalization have continued to evolve since 1945 to the point where it is now a complex system of numerous associate agencies and subunits that, collectively, address all the issues on the global agenda and that amount to a vast bureaucracy. The institutional histories of the various agencies differ in a number of respects, but taken as a whole they have become a major center of global governance. They have been a main source of problem identification, information, innovation, and constructive policies in the fields of health, environment, education, agriculture, labour, family, and a number of other issues that are global in scope'. Weiss and Thakur (2010) also argue that the UN has a major role in global governance but that there are gaps in global governance. These gaps will be discussed later in this chapter. There is a vast literature on the UN and its agencies, including on its reform (Bourantonis and Wiener 1995; Gordenker 2014; Hassler 2013; Mingst and Karns 1995; Mingst and Karns 2012; Taylor and Groom 2000; Weiss and Daws, 2007; Weiss and Thakur 2010; Weiss 2012). Chapter 6 contributes to this literature.

THE COMMISSION ON GLOBAL GOVERNANCE

It is therefore, appropriate to examine the UN's views on global governance. The Commission on Global Governance was set up in the early 1990s, as a result of the Stockholm Initiative on Global Security and Governance, and published its report entitled *Our Global Neighbourhood* in 1995. The report begins by observing that 'The world community seemed to be uniting around the idea that it should assume greater collective responsibility in a wide range of areas, including security – not only in a military sense but in economic and social terms as well – sustainable development, the promotion of democracy, equity and human rights, and humanitarian action' (Commission on Global Governance 1995, 1). But following the Gulf War, ethnic cleansing in the Balkans, brutal violence in Somalia, and genocide in Rwanda, the world seemed in danger of losing its way. Twenty years on, nobody can argue that we now live in a more peaceful world. The war in Syria is a testament to that. Yet the UN and the international community cannot give up and that is what this book is about. There are challenges that have to be met and it is the role of the UN to provide leadership in meeting these challenges.

The UN Commission defines governance as 'the sum of the many ways individuals and institutions, public and private, manage their common affairs. It is a continuing process through which conflicting or diverse interests may be accommodated and co-operative action may be taken. It includes formal institutions and regimes empowered to enforce compliance, as well as informal arrangements that people and institutions either have agreed to or perceive to be in their interest' (Ibid., 2). This definition emphasises that there are many actors in global governance, and that these actors aren't just states. 'At the global level, governance has been viewed primarily as intergovernmental relationships, but it must now be understood as also involving non-governmental organizations (NGOs), citizens' movements, multinational corporations, and the global capital market. Interacting with these are global mass media of dramatically enlarged influence' (Ibid., 2-3). The plurality of actors and agendas makes global governance a far more complex process than inter-governmentalism. It can be broken down into different issue areas, some of which are reflected in the chapters in this book, notwithstanding the conceptual distinctions made between regimes and global governance.[5] It may also give rise to different forms of global governance and charges of hegemonic control by dominant actors – states and institutions. For example, Cox (1997, xxvii) cited in O'Brien et al. (2000, 3) argues that old forms of multilateralism were based on a hegemonic or top down approach whereas the 'new' or emerging multilateralism is an attempt to 'reconstitute civil societies and political authorities on a global scale, building a system of global governance from the bottom up'.

The Commission on Global Governance also argues that 'governance must take an integrated approach to questions of human survival and prosperity'. They envisage that it will foster global citizenship and be more inclusive and participatory – that is more democratic – than in the past. It will include poorer, marginalized and alienated segments of national and international society in decision-making. It will seek peace and progress for all people (Commission on Global Governance 1995, 4-5). This conception clearly envisages a normative order. As Rosenau (1992, 10) puts it, 'normative concerns are bound to intensify as questions about global order – about the fundamental arrangements for coping with conflicts and moving towards goals – surface in the political arena'. Concerns about the protection or advancement of human rights, for example, become enmeshed in problems of normative order 'as one focuses on the ways in which the prevailing global arrangements impact on individuals and how their freedom to speak, organize, and worship is or might be curtailed by the practices and institutions through which their lives are governed' (Ibid., 11). However, the Commission insists that the UN must continue to play a central role in global governance. 'With its universality, it is the only forum where the governments of the world come

---

[5] Rosenau (1992, 8-9) writes that 'Like governance, regimes are conceived as arrangements – "as sets of implicit or explicit principles, norms, rules, and decision-making procedures around which actors' expectations converge" (Krasner, 1982) – for sustaining and regulating activities across national boundaries', in 'a given issue-area', for example whaling or the conservation of polar bears. These actors may be both governmental and non-governmental actors who have shared interests and benefit from cooperation. As a result they are prepared to accept the principles, norms, rules, and decision-making procedures that facilitate multilateral cooperation. On the other hand, global governance, is an all-encompassing concept covering the activities of potentially all the members of international society over a wide range of specific issues.

together on an equal footing and on a regular basis to try to resolve the world's most pressing problems. Every effort must be made to give it the credibility and resources it requires to fulfil its responsibilities' (Commission on Global Governance 1995, 6). These sentiments are echoed by other authors and organisations.

The report of the Commission on Global Governance is divided into seven chapters. The first chapter, entitled 'A New World' defines the concept of global governance and discusses what it involves, in the contemporary era of change, 'on such a global scale, and with such global visibility', as well as uncertainty. The report argues that a vision is needed, 'Our common future will depend on the extent to which people and leaders around the world develop the vision of a better world and the strategies, the institutions, and the will to achieve it. Our task as a Commission is to enlarge the probability of their doing so by suggesting approaches to the governance of the global, increasingly interdependent human society' (Ibid., 12). The rest of the chapter discusses topics that affect the work of the UN: Military Transformations, including a new arms race that includes biological and chemical weapons, in addition to nuclear ones; the rise in civil conflict; and widespread violence. The following sections discuss Economic Trends, including persistent poverty, and the private sector; and Social and Environmental Change. It is interesting to note that 22 years on our global concerns are still the same. The chapter concludes that the challenges facing the world today are vastly more complicated than those that confronted the delegates at the UN's founding conference in San Francisco in 1945 'They demand co-operative efforts to put in place a system of global governance better suited to present circumstances – a system informed by an understanding of the important transformations of the past half-century and guided by enlightened leadership' (Ibid., 39).

The second chapter is on *Values for the Global Neighbourhood*. This in some ways is one of the most important chapters of the Commission's report. It argues that the world is a 'global village'. Technology has made the world smaller, while trade, transnational firms, and investment have linked the world's different parts much more closely than before in a multitude of ways, and contributed to global interdependence which requires countries to work together. In the global neighbourhood, 'citizens have to co-operate for many purposes: to maintain peace and order; expand economic activity; tackle pollution; halt or minimize climate change; combat pandemic diseases; curb the spread of weapons; prevent desertification; preserve genetic and species diversity; deter terrorists; ward off famine, defeat economic recession; share scarce resources; arrest drug traffickers, and so on' (Ibid., 42). The authors of the report argue that 'action to improve global governance to cope with contemporary challenges would be greatly helped by a common commitment to a set of core values that can unite people of all cultural, political, religious, or philosophical backgrounds. These values must be appropriate to the needs of an increasingly crowded and diverse planet' (Ibid., 48).

While accepting that 'states remain the single most important set of international actors' and that 'norms of interstate relations will provide a critical source of stability', the Commission argues that 'there is a need now to adapt some of these norms to new circumstances. It is fundamentally important that governance should be underpinned by democracy at all levels and ultimately by the rule of enforceable law'. The core values that humanity should uphold are respect for life, liberty, justice and equality, mutual respect, caring, and integrity. 'These provide a foundation for transforming a global neighbourhood based on economic exchange and improved communications into a universal moral community in which people are bound together by more than proximity, interest, or identity. They all derive in one way or another from the principle, which is in accord with religious teachings around the world, that people should treat others as they would themselves wish to be treated. It is this imperative that was reflected in the call made in the UN Charter for recognition of "the inherent dignity and equal and inalienable rights of all members of the human family"' (Ibid., 48-49).

Since the establishment of the UN, the international community has made great progress in the elaboration of human rights. This process began with the drafting of the UN Charter and has been furthered by the Universal Declaration of Human Rights; the International Covenant on Civil and Political Rights, 1966; and the International Covenant on

Economic, Social and Cultural Rights, 1966. But rights need to be accompanied by responsibilities. The Commission argues that 'The tendency to emphasise rights while forgetting responsibilities has deleterious consequences. Over the long run, rights can only be preserved if they are exercised responsibly and with due respect for the reciprocal rights of others' (Ibid., 56). In the global civil society everyone has a responsibility to contribute to the common good; consider the impact of their actions on the security and welfare of others; promote equity, including gender equity; protect the interests of future generations by pursuing sustainable development and safeguarding the global commons; and preserving humanity's cultural and intellectual heritage (Ibid., 57). These responsibilities are based on the liberal values mentioned above and underpin the work of many NGOs/INGOs around the world, and UN specialised agencies such as UNESCO. The Commission comments that 'An important consequence of the emergence of a global neighbourhood is that national civil societies have begun to merge into a broader global civil society. Groups of many kinds are reaching out and establishing links with counterparts in other parts of the world. Without the objectives and limits that a global ethic would provide, however, global civil society could become unfocussed and even unruly. That could make effective global governance difficult' (Ibid., 55).

The rest of the report deals with critical issues such as the promotion of security, managing economic interdependence, and protecting the environment. The report also considers the reform of the UN; and the strengthening of the rule of law worldwide. It ends with a summary of the Commission's proposals. Commenting on the changing nature of global security, the report argues that 'global security must be broadened from its traditional focus on the security of states to include the security of people and the planet' (Ibid., 78). This is a significant shift in our approach to security and has led to the development of the concept of human security and environmental security (Dutt and Bansal, 2012). The former includes the right to be protected from chronic threats such as hunger, disease, and repression, as well as violence of all kinds (ranging from domestic violence to war and terrorism). On the security of the planet the report notes that

'Vast increases in the amounts of carbon dioxide and other greenhouse gases being emitted to the atmosphere from human sources are affecting the atmospheric processes that determine the world's climate, giving rise to the prospect of climate change that could drastically reduce the habitability of the planet'. The international community needs to take steps to deal with this problem. 'The Framework Convention on Climate Change, the Convention on Biodiversity, and the protocol on ozone depletion and its amendments, to name a few – must be rapidly and substantially strengthened' (Ibid., 82-3).

Of course, this issue is related to economic activities and economic growth, and the adoption of the new Sustainable Development Goals by the UN in 2015 emphasises this. For example, goal 7 is on access to affordable and clean energy, while goal 12 is on responsible, i.e., sustainable, consumption and production. The UN's initiative on promoting sustainable development is discussed in chapter Three. On the subject of managing economic interdependence, the Commission's report notes that the international community 'faces enormous challenges in dealing with economic governance – challenges related to the growing interdependence of economies and civil society, the continued impoverishment of much of the world and the unused human potential that entails, and the increased realization of the threats to the environment and thus to planetary survival' (Ibid., 135). It argues that stability requires a carefully crafted balance between the freedom of markets and the provision of public goods. By international public goods it means 'the rules and sense of order that must underpin any stable and prosperous system' (Ibid., 150). This is similar to Rosenau's definition of global governance and serves the purposes of this book very well. Both states and other actors, including MNCs/TNCs, need to take cognizance of this argument and participate in global economic governance. As the Commission's report notes, 'a sophisticated, globalized, increasingly affluent world currently co-exists with a marginalized global underclass' (Ibid., 139), and this is a challenge for many countries and their governments.

GOOD GOVERNANCE

The concept of global governance can be used as a heuristic device (Weiss 2005, 80-1), 'a means of capturing and describing the way in which authority in the international system is transforming' (Wilkinson 2005, 10). However, most of the theoretical and empirical research done on governance (and global governance) is concerned with good governance. Governance, at any level of human activity, it is argued, can be 'good, bad or indifferent'. Good governance, therefore, 'can be considered a normative concept – concerned with standards that most would agree are laudable' (Weiss and Thakur 2010, 6). Bo Rothstein (2012) writes that good governance is a relatively new concept that has made a strong impact in some of the highest policy circles since the mid-1990s. In the beginning it was used mainly in circles dealing with developing countries and the so-called transition countries. In 1996, the IMF declared that 'promoting good governance in all its aspects, including by ensuring the rule of law, improving the efficiency and accountability of the public sector, and tackling corruption, are essential elements of a framework within which economies can prosper' (cited in Rothstein 2012, 143). But after the developed countries were affected by various economic and financial crises, the use of the concept was extended to the examination and analysis of governance in these countries as well. Rothstein argues that good governance is about the enactment and implementation of policies that can be broadly understood as 'public goods'. They are needed because they will not be supplied by standard market operations. 'Instead, some forms of binding and enforceable regulations are needed'. For example, the preservation of scarce natural resources, or protection of property rights cannot be left to the market alone. In some cases, good governance requires collaboration with business and/or voluntary organisations (Ibid., 143-4).

From the point of view of this book and its authors, the rise of the good governance agenda is important because without it, it will not be possible to achieve the international goals adopted and promoted by the UN, for example, the Sustainable Development Goals, or make progress on (slowing down) global warming and climate change. Rothstein (2012, 145) writes that 'in development policy circles, the good governance agenda has to a large extent replaced what was known as the Washington Consensus. This approach stated that economic growth could be created by massive deregulation of markets, tightening of public spending, guarantees for property rights, and large-scale privatizations. The reason why this strategy did not work, according to many observers, was that poor countries lacked the necessary type of institutions that were "taken for granted" in neoclassical economics'.

Empirical research has shown that good governance can have a positive impact on human well-being, and can prevent violent inter-state conflicts and civil wars. However, good governance is not synonymous with, or simply another name for, democracy. On the contrary, authors such as Larry Diamond have warned that in many countries, democracy is 'haunted by the spectre of bad governance', which he defines as 'governance that is drenched in corruption, patronage, favouritism, and abuse of power' (cited in Rothstein 2012, 149-50). In the opinion of former Secretary-General of the UN, Kofi Annan, good governance is 'ensuring respect for human rights and the rule of law; strengthening democracy; promoting transparency and capacity in public administration' (Weiss 2005, 70). Measures have been developed for various aspects of good governance, like government effectiveness, levels of corruption, and the quality of legal systems (Rothstein 2012, 145).[6] However, Menocal and Wild (2013) have pointed out that 'current international measures of "good governance" (such as the World Bank's Worldwide Governance Indicators) show a weak causal relationship with progress on MDGs... This suggests that the good governance agenda may not necessarily capture those governance factors that seem most important to development'.

---

[6] The Ibrahim Index of African Governance ranks countries on the basis of data collected on African governance, classified within four categories: safety and rule of law; participation and human rights; sustainable economic opportunity; and human development. (Alina Rocha Menocal and Leni Wild. 2013. "The relationship between governance and progress." In *Global Development Goals, Leaving no one behind*, edited by Natalie Samarasinghe, UNA-UK, 30-32. London: UNA-UK.).

Good governance is usually associated with good government, which means an accountable, efficient, lawful, representative and transparent government (Weiss 2005, 80). As Rothstein (2012, 150-1) remarks, 'It would certainly be strange to argue that a government that is very inefficient or ineffective could produce good governance'. But a definition of good governance should be based in a normative theory 'that gives some orientation for what should be regarded as "good" in this context'. While there are different conceptions of good governance, the UN's ideas are now in the forefront. Weiss (2005, 78) writes that 'the forces of democratisation and globalisation are pressuring good governance proponents to reorient their priorities from the exigencies of economic growth and efficiency to those governance policies and institutions that best promote greater freedom, genuine participation and sustainable human development. It is on this fundamental point that thinking at the UN is currently ahead of the curve, compared with the conventional wisdom in the corridors of the Washington-based IFIs.'

GAPS IN GLOBAL GOVERNANCE

While the literature on good governance mostly addresses the issue of governance at the domestic level of the state, the literature on global governance skirts around the issue. Weiss (2005, 83) writes that 'we should think creatively about ways to pool the collective strengths and avoid the collective weaknesses of governments, intergovernmental organisations, NGOs and global civil society'. Elsewhere he writes that "good" global governance implies 'an optimal partnership among the state, regional, and global level of actors, and among state, intergovernmental, and nongovernmental categories of actors' (2012, 36). However, Sinclair (2012, 34) argues that discussions about global governance depend on the approach we adopt. For example, Institutionalism's approach to global governance has a problem-solving rather than a critical purpose. Using this approach, Weiss and Thakur (2010) identify five gaps in global governance that can potentially prevent a problem from being solved. These are as follows:

- knowledge gaps
- normative gaps
- policy gaps
- institutional gaps
- compliance gaps

When a problem is identified, before we can deal with it we need to understand the problem and its causes. But there may not be any theoretical explanations, or empirical data, available, which does not help. Social and scientific research, including the collection of empirical information, may thus be necessary to suggest the best remedies and solutions. Sometimes ideological positions adopted by certain interests don't help and can prevent progress. At the global level, both the UN and civil society institutions such as universities, think tanks, research institutes and NGOs can play a crucial role in filling knowledge gaps and are engaged in generating data in many fields. Although there can sometimes be different interpretations of available data. Global warming and climate change is one area in which there are still knowledge gaps. When there are knowledge gaps, they will also lead to normative, policy, institutional and compliance gaps as in the absence of a body of knowledge on a given issue, policies cannot be adopted. Norms in the context of global governance refer to the moral code of a society, a generally accepted standard of proper behaviour. The Universal Declaration of Human Rights is a good example of such norms. In many fields, the UN (and its member states) has adopted resolutions and declarations (soft law) and conventions and treaties (hard law). Thus the international community deals with normative gaps in global governance as and when necessary.

A policy is a principled stand on any particular issue. In the context of global governance it refers to 'an interlinked set of governing principles and goals and the agreed programs of action to implement those principles and achieve those goals' (Weiss and Thakur 2010, 12). The Kyoto

Protocol, the Nuclear Non-Proliferation Treaty (NPT) and the Comprehensive Test Ban Treaty (CTBT) are examples of policies designed to combat the threats of global warming and nuclear weapons respectively. Policy making can be broken down into policy formulation, adoption and implementation. As the UN is not a world government or even a supranational system, like the EU, policy implementation is problematic. Why? Because policies made by or under the auspices of the UN need to be implemented by individual member states (Ibid., 15).

Then there are institutional gaps. Weiss and Thakur (2010, 15) write that 'if policy is to escape the trap of being ad hoc, episodic, judgmental, and idiosyncratic, it must be housed within an institution that has resources and autonomy'. They argue that even the most powerful institutions such as the Security Council, the World Bank, and the International Monetary Fund (IMF) often lack appropriate resources or authority or both. On the other hand, the UN has made a valuable contribution. Global conferences organised under the auspices of the UN have often led to the creation of new institutions for implementing and monitoring compliance with the new norms. The Stockholm conference led to UNEP and the Rio Summit to the UNFCCC and the CSD. But the UN needs to be properly funded. This was pointed out in March 2017 by a spokesman for the UN Secretary-General, Antonio Guterres. For example, the World Food Program and the UN High Commissioner for Refugees which receive the most funding from the US, need long term support to address global humanitarian crises. President Trump's plan to reduce US contributions to UN initiatives 'could hurt long term reform projects' (UN Wire, 17 March 2017, 'Guterres: UN funding cuts could hurt long-term efforts').

Finally, there are compliance gaps which could be related to the problem of implementing policies and decisions. It has three aspects: implementation, monitoring, and enforcement. As mentioned before, some states may not be willing to implement certain policies, for example, relating to the acquisition of nuclear technology and material. The second problem relates to the monitoring of the implementation records of states that have signed international treaties such as the Kyoto Protocol or the NPT. The third problem relates to the enforcement of treaty obligations.

What can be done to persuade, even force, a party/state to comply? Weiss and Thakur argue that while more political will is needed from states, as well as knowledge to solve problems, global governance needs a form of institutionalism that works so that the solution of problems are not obstructed by politics (or left to the vagaries of politics).

CONCLUSION

Global governance, therefore, implies the emergence of a normative order. As Latham (1999, 30) argues, 'we want global governance to be effective, and we want it to be just, to lead to a just world order'. Rosenau writes that 'to suggest that governance is always effective is to posit a close link between governance and order' (Rosenau 1992, 5). Both states and markets contribute to 'system-wide orderly arrangements.' But he argues that there is a significant difference between empirically tracing the underlying arrangements and analysing their potential consequences, on the one hand, and making value judgements about these arrangements, on the other. Empirical orders refer to arrangements that govern global affairs. They can produce stability and coherence, but they can also be a form of hegemonic order/control, which is undesirable. Additionally, they may not be able to bring about change (because it threatens the status quo or order itself) even when the system is crying out for change. Empirical orders may give rise to normative concerns, for example, where there are human rights violations, exploitation and conflict. But an order that has its roots in shared norms will be a normative order. Rosenau writes that 'the distinction between empirical and normative orders is also manifest whenever analysis focuses on policy questions…Those who link forms of systemic order with policy goals necessarily work with images of normative orders…orders that are constructed or reinforced so as to enhance or thwart the establishment of specific values'(Rosenau 1992, 11). It is this conception of global governance that this book seeks to apply in various areas of international relations.

REFERENCES

Armstrong, David., Lorna Lloyd. & John Redmond. 2004. *International Organisation in World Politics*. Basingstoke and New York: Palgrave Macmillan.

Bevir, Mark. (ed). 2011. *The Sage Handbook of Governance*. London, Thousand Oaks, New Delhi and Singapore: Sage Publications Ltd.

Bourantonis, D. & J. Wiener. (eds). 1995. *The United Nations in the New World Order, The World Organization at fifty*. Basingstoke: Palgrave Macmillan.

Bull, Hedley. 1995. *The Anarchical Society*. Basingstoke and London: Macmillan Press Ltd.

Cox, Robert. (ed). 1997. *The New Realism: Perspectives on Multilateralism and World Order*. Basingstoke: Macmillan/United Nations University Press.

Diamond, L. J. 2007. "A quarter-century of promoting democracy." *Journal of Democracy 18*: 118-120.

Dutt, Sagarika. & Alok Bansal. (eds). 2012. *South Asian Security: 21st century discourses*. Abingdon, Oxon and New York: Routledge.

Dutt, Sagarika. 2012. "The UN and Global Governance: Do ideas alone help?" *India Quarterly 68* (2): 187-194.

Easton, David. 1971. *The Political System – An Inquiry into the state of Political Science*. New York: Alfred A. Knopf.

Fitzgerald, Amber. 2000. "Security Council reform: Creating a more representative body of the entire UN membership". *Pace International Law Review 12* (2): 321-364.

Gordenker, Leon. 2014. "The UN System" In *International Organization and Global Governance*, edited by T. G. Weiss and R. Wilkinson, 209-222. Abingdon, Oxon and New York: Routledge.

Hassler, Sabine. 2013. *Reforming the UN Security Council Membership*. Abingdon, Oxon and New York: Routledge.

Held, David. 2014. "The Diffusion of Authority" In *International Organization and Global Governance*, edited by T. G. Weiss and R. Wilkinson, 60-72. Abingdon, Oxon and New York: Routledge.

Hewson, Martin. & T. J. Sinclair. 1999. "The emergence of global governance theory." In *Approaches to global governance theory*, edited by Martin Hewson and T. J. Sinclair, 3-22. Albany: State University of New York Press.

Kenealy, Daniel., John Peterson. & Richard Corbett. 2015. *The European Union: How does it work?* 4th edition, Oxford: Oxford University Press.

Krasner, Stephen D. 1982. "Structural causes and regime consequences: Regimes as intervening variables." *International Organization 36*(2), Spring 1982.

Latham, R. 1999. "Politics in a floating world – Toward a critique of global governance." In *Approaches to global governance theory*, edited by Martin Hewson and T. J. Sinclair, 23-53. Albany: State University of New York Press.

Levi-Faur, David. (ed). 2012. *The Oxford Handbook of Governance*, New York: Oxford University Press.

Levi-Faur, David. 2012. Chapter 1, "From 'Big Government' to 'Big Governance' ?" In *The Oxford Handbook of Governance*, edited by David Levi-Faur, 3-18. New York: Oxford University Press.

Lynn, Jr. Lawrence. 2012. "The Many Faces of Governance: Adaptation? Transformation? Both? Neither?" In *The Oxford Handbook of Governance*, edited by David Levi-Faur, 49-64. New York: Oxford University Press.

Menocal, A. R. and L. Wild. 2013. "The relationship between governance and progress." In *Global Development Goals, Leaving no one behind*, edited by Natalie Samarasinghe, UNA-UK, 30-32. London: UNA-UK.

Mingst, Karen A. & M. P. Karns. 1995. *The United Nations in the Post-Cold War Era.* Boulder, CO and Oxford: Westview Press.

Mingst, Karen A. & M. P. Karns. 2012. *The United Nations in the 21st Century*, Boulder, CO: Westview Press.

Morgenthau, Hans J., revised by Kenneth W. Thompson. & David Clinton. 2006. *Politics among nations, The struggle for power and peace*, New York: McGraw Hill Higher Education. Seventh edition.

O'Brien, Robert, A. M. Goetz, Jan Aart Scholte. & Marc Williams. 2000. *Contesting Global Governance, Multilateral Economic Institutions and Global Social Movements*. Cambridge: Cambridge University Press.

Rosenau, James N. & Ernst-Otto Czempiel. (eds). 1992. *Governance without government: order and change in world politics*. Cambridge: Cambridge University Press.

Rosenau, James N. 1999. "Toward an ontology for global governance." In *Approaches to global governance theory*, edited by Martin Hewson and T. J. Sinclair, 287-301. Albany: State University of New York Press.

Rosenau, James N. 2005. "Governance in the twenty-first century." In *The Global Governance Reader*, edited by Rorden Wilkinson, 45-67. Abingdon and New York: Routledge.

Rothstein, Bo. 2012. "Good Governance." In *The Oxford Handbook of Governance*, edited by David Levi-Faur, 143-154. New York: Oxford University Press.

Ruggie, John Gerrard. 2010. "Foreword". In *Global Governance and the UN, An Unfinished Journey*, by Thomas G. Weiss and Ramesh Thakur, xv-xx. Bloomington and Indianapolis: Indiana University Press.

Sinclair, Timothy J. 2012. *Global Governance*, Cambridge and Malden: Polity Press.

Taylor, Paul. & A. J. R. Groom (eds). 2000. *The United Nations at the Millennium*. London and New York: Continuum.

The Commission on Global Governance. 1995. *Our Global Neighbourhood*. Oxford: Oxford University Press.

Wallace, Helen., Mark A. Pollack. & Alasdair R. Young. 2010. *Policy making in the European Union*, Oxford: Oxford University Press, 6th edition.

Weiss, Thomas G. 2005. "Governance, good governance and global governance: Conceptual and actual challenges" In *The Global Governance Reader*, edited by Rorden Wilkinson, 68-88. Abingdon and New York: Routledge.

Weiss, Thomas G. & Sam Daws (eds). 2007. *The Oxford Handbook on the United Nations*. Oxford and New York: Oxford University Press.

Weiss, Thomas G. 2012. *What's wrong with the UN and how to fix it.* Cambridge: Polity.

Weiss, Thomas G. 2013. *Global Governance, Why? What? Whither?* Cambridge and Malden: Polity Press.

Weiss, Thomas G. & Ramesh Thakur. 2010. *Global Governance and the UN, An Unfinished Journey.* Bloomington and Indianapolis: Indiana University Press.

Willetts, Peter. (ed). 1996. *The Conscience of the world: The influence of non-governmental organisations in the UN system.* London: C. Hurst & Company Ltd.

Willetts, Peter. 2011a. *Non-governmental organizations in world politics, The construction of global governance.* Abingdon, Oxon and New York: Routledge.

Willetts, Peter. 2011b. Chapter 20, "Transnational actors and international organizations in global politics." In *The Globalization of World Politics, An introduction to international relations*, edited by John Baylis, Steve Smith and Patricia Owens, 326-342. Oxford and New York: Oxford University Press.

Zumbansen, P. 2012. "Governance: An Interdisciplinary Perspective" In *The Oxford Handbook of Governance*, edited by D. Levi-Faur, 83-96. Oxford and New York: Oxford University Press.

In: Global Governance
Editor: Sagarika Dutt

ISBN: 978-1-53612-969-4
© 2018 Nova Science Publishers, Inc.

Chapter 2

THE UNITED NATIONS AND SUSTAINABLE DEVELOPMENT: THE MILLENNIUM DEVELOPMENT GOALS

Sagarika Dutt
Senior Lecturer in International Relations and Subject Leader,
Nottingham Trent University, Nottingham, UK

ABSTRACT

In 1992, the United Nations Conference on Environment and Development was held in Rio de Janeiro, Brazil which paved the way for the adoption of the Millennium Development Goals (MDGs) in 2000, to be achieved by 2015. In 1997 the UN adopted the *Agenda for Development* which considered economic development, social development and environmental protection to be interdependent and mutually reinforcing components of sustainable development. The UN claims that a lot of progress has been made in achieving these goals but also says that they did not focus enough on reaching the very poorest and most excluded people. This chapter discusses the lessons learnt by the international community from the results that have been achieved.

INTRODUCTION

The United Nations was established in 1945 'to save succeeding generations from the scourge of war', 'to reaffirm faith in fundamental human rights' and 'to promote social progress and better standards of life'.[7] Thus development has become one of its main priorities (Agenda for Development, 1997). The establishment of the UN, argues Emmerij, Jolly and Weiss (2001), led to the emergence of 'four powerful sets of ideas', peace; independence; development; and human rights (Jolly, Emmerij and Weiss, 2009). UN General Assembly resolution 1710 (XVI), adopted during its 16th session in December 1961, designated the 1960s as the UN development decade. It noted that 'in spite of the efforts made in recent years the gap in per capita incomes between the economically developed and less developed countries has increased and the rate of economic and social progress in the developing countries is still far from adequate'. It argued that the 'economic and social development of the economically less developed countries is not only of primary interest to those countries but is also basic to the attainment of international peace and security' and an increase in world prosperity. The resolution stressed the need for international economic cooperation on a bilateral and multilateral basis to accelerate progress in achieving higher rates of economic growth and social advancement in developing countries. This was followed by three more development decades. The United Nations Development Programme (UNDP) was created in 1965 and makes a significant contribution to the UN's work in the field of development (Murphy 2006; UNDP website). In 1986 the UN General Assembly adopted the Declaration on the right to development (A/RES/41/128) which declares that it is 'an alienable human right by virtue of which every human person and all peoples are entitled to participate in, contribute to, and enjoy economic, social, cultural and political development...'

---

[7] UN Charter.

Thérien (2005, 218) writes that for more than a generation, the North-South divide was central to the explanation of world inequality and poverty. But today, the gap between the rich and the poor countries no longer has the resonance it once had. He also makes a distinction between the Bretton Woods paradigm and the UN paradigm. While the former is associated with the discourse and practices of the Bretton Woods institutions, the IMF, World Bank and GATT/WTO, the latter is associated with the discourse and practices of UN agencies. He writes: 'there exists a major divergence between the Bretton Woods paradigm, where globalisation is a factor favouring integration and progress, and the UN paradigm, where it is a multiplier of inequalities. On one side of this basic divide, poverty is considered a residual phenomenon that is waning geographically, while on the other it is seen as a serious problem on the rise. According to the Bretton Woods paradigm, the roots of poverty lie in the economic policy choices of national governments, whereas the UN paradigm emphasises the lack of international cooperation. These differences in perspective ultimately result in highly disparate political projects: the Bretton Woods paradigm favours a complete market liberalisation, while the UN paradigm insists on the need to subordinate the functioning of the world economy to objectives of social equity and sustainability'. He considers the Bretton Woods paradigm to be the dominant paradigm, but argues that the UN paradigm 'offers the most coherent alternate narrative on world poverty'. While the adoption of the Millennium Development Goals was clearly influenced by the UN paradigm, the adoption of the Sustainable Development Goals, discussed in the next chapter, made some concessions to those who favour the Bretton Woods paradigm, for example by emphasising the importance of economic growth, and industry, innovation and infrastructure, in the achievement of sustainable development. This chapter begins with an introduction to the UN's agenda for development and then goes on to examine its assessment of the progress made in the achievement of the Millennium Development Goals.

THE AGENDA FOR DEVELOPMENT

The Agenda for Development adopted by the UN General Assembly (1997) describes development as 'a multidimensional undertaking to achieve a higher quality of life for all people. Economic development, social development and environmental protection are interdependent and mutually reinforcing components of sustainable development'. It emphasises that 'sustained economic growth is essential to the economic and social development of all countries, in particular developing countries. Through such growth, which should be broadly based so as to benefit all people, countries will be able to improve the standards of living of their people through the eradication of poverty, hunger, disease and illiteracy, the provision of adequate shelter and secure employment for all, and the preservation of the integrity of the environment'. At the same time, 'democracy, respect for all human rights and fundamental freedoms, including the right to development, transparent and accountable governance and administration in all sectors of society, and effective participation by civil society are also an essential part of the necessary foundations for the realization of social and people centred sustainable development'. Thus development is qualified as sustainable development and the definition of sustainable development can be found in the report of the World Commission on Environment and Development chaired by Gro Harlem Brundtland (appointed in 1983 'to propose long- term environmental strategies for achieving long term development by the year 2000 and beyond'[8]) entitled *Our Common Future* and published in 1987. It is development that 'meets the needs of the present without compromising the ability of future generations to meet their own needs'.

Soon after the publication of this report, the United Nations Conference on Environment and Development (UNCED) also known as

---

[8] The Commission's mandate was to (1) re-examine the critical issues of environment and development and to formulate innovative, concrete, and realistic action proposals to deal with them; (2) to strengthen international co-operation on environment and development and to assess and propose any new forms of cooperation that can break out of existing patterns and influence policies and events in the direction of needed change; and (3) to raise the level of understanding and commitment to action on the part of individuals, voluntary organizations, businesses, institutes, and governments.

the Rio Summit and the Earth Summit was held in Rio de Janeiro in June 1992. Both governments and non-governmental organisations (NGOs)/ civil society participated in this conference. It led to the Rio Declaration on Environment and Development; Agenda 21; Forest principles. The Rio Declaration sought to strike a balance between the need to promote economic growth and development, especially in developing countries, and the protection of the environment, by making environmental protection 'an integral part of the development process' (principle 4). Principle 5 made the eradication of poverty an indispensable requirement for sustainable development, and principle 6 called for the prioritization of the needs of developing countries, particularly the least developed countries and those most environmentally vulnerable. The Rio Declaration proclaimed 27 general principles which included national responsibilities and international co-operation on environmental protection. Agenda 21 aimed to provide a programme of action for sustainable development (UN 1992a). In addition, two important and legally binding agreements were opened for signature: Convention on Biological Diversity and Framework Convention on Climate Change (FCCC).

PEACE AND DEVELOPMENT

The Agenda for Development (UN 1997, 3) argues that 'peace and development are closely interrelated and mutually supportive', although 'development should also be pursued in its own right'. Furthermore, 'development is indispensable to the achievement and maintenance of peace and security both within and among nations. Without development there can be neither peace nor security'. This is an important point to make as in many developing countries this is indeed the case although there are also other factors that cause conflict. The relationship between development on the one hand, and peace and security, on the other, is also illustrated by the conditions that peace and security create for development to take place. 'Development cannot be attained in the absence of peace and security or in the absence of respect for all human rights and fundamental freedoms. Under conditions of war, and during periods of short-term emergencies and humanitarian needs, development efforts are often neglected, diminished or abandoned'. Excessive military expenditures are also bad for development. 'Excessive military expenditures, arms trade, investment for arms production, acquisition and stockpiling have a negative impact on development prospects'. The UN underlines the need for increasing resources for social and economic development, as well as the UN's operational developmental activities, and notes that the overall decline in ODA is a serious cause for concern. It also argues that for 'peace and stability to endure, national action and effective international cooperation are required to promote a better life for all in larger freedom, a critical element of which is the eradication of poverty'.

The Agenda for Development notes that 'poverty continues to affect far too many people in the world. Hunger and malnutrition, ill-health, lack of access to safe drinking water, low access to education and other public services and resources, exclusion, lack of participation and violence are some of the many aspects that characterize poverty'. Needless to say, 'though poverty occurs in all countries, its extent and manifestation are particularly severe in developing countries'. The goal of eradicating poverty in the world is 'an ethical, social, political and economic imperative', and can only be achieved through a multidimensional and integrated approach. Equitable social development is a necessary foundation for development and an important factor for the eradication of poverty. The commitments agreed at the World Summit for Social Development (1995) should be fully implemented. It is the primary responsibility of states to attain social development. But the international community, the United Nations system, the multilateral financial institutions, all regional organisations and local authorities and civil society actors also need to contribute to social development and the reduction of inequalities among people and narrow the gap between developed and developing countries. UNDP, which is the UN's main agency for coordinating global and local efforts to promote development (Peet and Hartwick, 2010, 95), argues that poverty, neglect and marginalization can lead to extremism. A report on their website, entitled 'Journey to extremism' (accessed on 14.9.17) attempts to give an insight into what drove recruits to join some of Africa's deadliest groups (UNDP, 2017). A similar argument is put forward by Fink and Bhulai (2016, 48-49) in their article entitled 'Development and countering violent extremism'. They write that 'Poverty appears to play an important role in creating a hospitable environment for extremist groups to operate and recruit'. But they also acknowledge that 'there are a number of recognised conditions conducive to – or factors that create – an enabling environment for violent extremist groups to drum up support and recruits'. These include prolonged unresolved conflicts, lack of the rule of law and violations of human rights, ethnic, national and religious discrimination, political exclusion, socio-economic marginalisation, and lack of good governance.

THE ADOPTION OF THE MILLENNIUM DEVELOPMENT GOALS

The UN Millennium Declaration was adopted by world leaders at the UN Millennium Summit held in New York, in September 2000. It made a commitment to promoting the right to development for everyone and eradicating poverty, and identified the key objectives which the UN and its member states would pursue, and which led to the establishment of the Millennium Development Goals (MDGs). The eight MDGs are as follows: Eradicate extreme poverty and hunger; Achieve universal primary education; Promote gender equality and empower women; Reduce child mortality; Improve maternal mortality; Combat HIV/AIDS, malaria and other diseases; Ensure environmental sustainability; and Develop a global partnership for development. Helen Clark (2013, 10), Administrator of the UNDP, remarks that 'Since their adoption in 2000, the Millennium Development Goals (MDGs) have provided a unifying vision for policymakers, development experts and civil society'. She adds that 'Their clarity, conciseness and measurability brought diverse actors together around a common cause and inspired many to take action against poverty in all its dimensions'.

In the foreword to the Millennium Development Goals Report 2015, the UN Secretary-General, Ban Ki-Moon writes that 'the global mobilization behind the Millennium Development Goals has produced the most successful anti-poverty movement in history. The MDGs helped to lift more than one billion people out of extreme poverty, to make inroads against hunger, to enable more girls to attend school than ever before and to protect our planet' (UN, 2015b). The results achieved may be summarised as follows:

Goal 1: Eradicate Extreme Poverty and Hunger

'Extreme poverty has declined significantly over the last two decades. In 1990, nearly half of the population in the developing world lived on less than $1.25 a day; that proportion dropped to 14 per cent in 2015. Globally, the number of people living in extreme poverty has declined by more than half, falling from 1.9 billion in 1990 to 836 million in 2015. Most progress has occurred since 2000'. Moreover, the working middle class is growing and 'now makes up half the workforce in the developing regions'.

Goal 2: Achieve Universal Primary Education

The primary school net enrolment rate in the developing regions has reached 91 per cent in 2015, up from 83 per cent in 2000. The number of out-of-school children of primary school age worldwide has fallen by almost half, to an estimated 57 million in 2015, down from 100 million in 2000. Sub-Saharan Africa has had the best record of improvement in primary education.

Goal 3: Promote Gender Equality and Empower Women

Many more girls are now in school compared to 15 years ago. The developing regions as a whole have achieved the target to eliminate gender disparity in primary, secondary and tertiary education. Women have gained ground in parliamentary representation in nearly 90 per cent of the 174 countries with data over the past 20 years.

Goal 4: Reduce Child Mortality

The global under five mortality rate has declined by more than half, dropping from 90 to 43 deaths per 1,000 live births between 1990 and 2015.

Goal 5: Improve Maternal Health

Since 1990 the maternal mortality rate has declined by 45 per cent worldwide, and most of the reduction has occurred since 2000.

In Southern Asia, the maternal mortality rate declined by 64 per cent between 1990 and 2013, and in Sub-Saharan Africa it fell by 49 per cent.

More than 71 per cent of births were assisted by skilled health personnel globally in 2014, an increase from 59 per cent in 1990.

Goal 6: Combat HIV/AIDS, Malaria and Other Diseases

New HIV infections fell by approximately 40 per cent between 2000 and 2013, from an estimated 3.5 million cases to 2.1 million.

By June 2014, 13.6 million people living with HIV were receiving antiretroviral therapy (ART) globally. It is estimated that ART averted 7.6 million deaths from AIDS between 1995 and 2013.

The global malaria incidence rate has fallen by an estimated 37 per cent and the mortality rate by 58 per cent.

Goal 7: Ensure Environmental Sustainability

Ozone depleting substances have been virtually eliminated since 1990, and the ozone layer is expected to recover by the middle of this century. Other achievements include the following:

- Terrestrial and marine protected areas have increased substantially since 1990
- 1.9 billion people have gained access to piped drinking water on premises since 1990
- Globally, 147 countries have met the drinking water target, 95 countries have met the sanitation target, and 77 countries have met both. Target 7.C was to halve by 2015 the proportion of the population without sustainable access to safe drinking water and basic sanitation
- The proportion of urban population living in slums in the developing regions fell from approximately 39.4 per cent in 2000 to 29.7 per cent in 2014

Goal 8: Develop a global partnership for development

Official development assistance from developed countries increased by 66 per cent in real terms between 2000 and 2014, reaching $135.2 billion (United Nations 2015 b).

THE UN'S ASSESSMENT OF THE PROGRESS MADE IN THE ACHIEVEMENT OF THE MDGS

Goal 1: Eradicate Extreme Poverty and Hunger

The MDG target (1.A) of reducing by half (from 1990 levels) the proportion of people living in extreme poverty (i.e., on less than $1.25 a day) was achieved 5 years ahead of the 2015 deadline. By 2011, all developing regions except sub-Saharan Africa had met this target. The world's most populous countries, India and China, played a central role in the global reduction of poverty. In sub-Saharan Africa, more than 40 per cent of the population continued to live in extreme poverty in 2015. Sub-Saharan Africa and South Asia together account for 80 per cent of the global total of extremely poor people, living on less than $1.25 a day.

According to UN estimates, women face a greater risk of living in poverty. Factors that contribute to this include, unequal access to paid work, lower earnings, lack of social protection, and limited access to assets, including land and property. Yet another factor is the lack of or a lower level of education than men. But the MDG report (United Nations, 2015a) admits that it is difficult to differentiate poverty rates within households because data is collected at the household level, rather than at the individual level. As a result differences in poverty rates on the basis of gender are not reflected in this data. The report notes that 'it is clear that greater efforts are needed to produce high quality poverty and gender statistics if we are to monitor progress effectively in eradicating extreme poverty for all people everywhere' (Ibid., 16).

Target 1.B, achieve full and productive employment and decent work for all, including women and young people, was an ambitious target and has not been met. The MDG report notes that 'as the global economy has entered a new period combining slower growth, widening inequalities and turbulence, employment is not expanding fast enough to keep up with the growing labour force'. Employment opportunities have declined in both the developed and developing world but unemployment is higher in the developing world, for example in Eastern and Southern Asia. There are other problems such as high under employment, informal employment and lower labour productivity, for example, in sub-Saharan Africa. The report also notes that 'youth, especially young women, continue to be disproportionately affected by limited employment opportunities and unemployment'. Globally the rate of youth unemployment is almost three times higher than the rate of adult unemployment, but the situation is most acute in Northern Africa and Western Asia. Finally, the report notes that although some progress has been made, almost half of the world's employed people are still working in vulnerable conditions. There is obviously a lot that remains to be done, especially in the developing world. The report notes that 'much work needs to be done to raise productivity, promote sustainable structural transformation and expand social protection systems for the poorest and most vulnerable workers and their families'.

Target 1.C is halve, between 1990 and 2015, the proportion of people who suffer from hunger. The MDG report notes that 'current estimates suggest that about 795 million people are undernourished globally. This means that nearly one in nine individuals do not have enough to eat. The vast majority of them (780 million people) live in the developing regions'. But overall, the target is close to being met. The long term trend that has been observed is that rapid progress during the 1990s was followed by periods of slower progress. There are many factors that have impacted on the prevalence of hunger and global food insecurity. They include volatile commodity prices, higher food and energy prices, dependence on food imports, unemployment and economic recessions, extreme weather and natural disasters, political instability and civil strife, the last three often leading to humanitarian crises. Conversely, rapid economic growth in some regions has made it easier to meet this target.

Another area in which some progress has been made is the proportion of children under five who are underweight. Underweight children are at greater risk of dying from common infections. South Asia has the highest underweight prevalence, with approximately one in three children still affected in 2015. But the region has experienced 'the largest absolute decrease since 1990, a 22 percentage point drop'. In sub-Saharan Africa 'the underweight rate has fallen by only one third since 1990. However, due to the region's growing population, the number of underweight children has actually risen'.

Wars and conflicts that lead to the massive displacement of people do not help the UN to meet its targets. According to the MDG report, in 2014, an average of 42,000 people each day were forced to abandon their homes and seek protection due to conflicts, such as those in Iraq, Nigeria, Pakistan, South Sudan, the Democratic Republic of the Congo, the Syrian

Arab Republic, and Ukraine. They included internally displaced people as well as refugees and asylum seekers. Many of them were under the responsibility of the UNHCR. Nine out of 10 refugees under the UNHCR mandate were located in the developing world in 2014, and half of them were children. The proportion of children within the refugee population has been growing as a result of the conflicts in Afghanistan, Somalia and Syria: the top three source countries of refugees at the end of 2014. The report of the High Level Panel of Eminent Persons on the post-2015 development agenda (UN, 2013) points out that the MDGs did not 'focus enough on reaching the very poorest and most excluded people'. They were also 'silent on the devastating effects of conflict and violence on development'.

Goal 2: Achieve Universal Primary Education

Good progress has been made in the achievement of this goal and related targets. The first target, target 2.A is to 'ensure that, by 2015, children everywhere, girls and boys alike, will be able to complete a full course of primary schooling'. The MDG report notes that 'the primary school net enrolment rate in the developing regions has reached an estimated 91 per cent in 2015, up from 83 per cent in 2000'. In sub-Saharan Africa, the number of children enrolled in primary school more than doubled from 62 million to 149 million, between 1990 and 2012. Also, the literacy rate among youth aged 15 to 24 has increased globally, from 83 per cent to 91 per cent, between 1990 and 2015.

But the primary school enrolment rate, on its own, is not enough as in many developing countries some children do not attend school and do not complete their schooling. The MDG report presents a graph on the number of out of school children of primary school age in the world and in selected regions (i.e., south Asia and sub-Saharan Africa). It shows that some progress has been made as the 'number of out of school children has been cut almost in half since 2000'. However, it is estimated that in South Asia, 57 per cent of the out of school children will never go to school, while in sub-Saharan Africa the proportion is 50 per cent. More girls, than boys, will never go to school, while boys are likely to drop out of school. In countries affected by conflict, the number of out of school children increased from 30 per cent in 1999 to 36 per cent in 2012. The affected regions include Northern Africa and Southern Asia. But in more recent years, the ongoing conflict in Syria has had a devastating impact on children's education.

The MDG report also makes the point that household wealth remains an important determinant of a child's likelihood of attending school. As a result there are large disparities in primary school enrolment and 'the poorest and the most disadvantaged children bear the heaviest burden'. This also applies to completing primary education. There is also a rural-urban divide, with more children in rural areas out of school than in urban areas. Disability is another impediment to accessing education. Nevertheless, a trend noted by the MDG report is that more children are completing primary school in lower-income countries (up from 70% in the early 1990s to over 80% in 2015).

The literacy rate worldwide has improved. 'Since the 1990s global progress in youth and adult literacy has been slow but steady, and the gap between women and men has narrowed'. This is the impact of increasing attendance in primary and secondary school among younger generations. Northern Africa and Southern Asia have shown the greatest improvement in youth literacy, especially among young women.

The MDG report ends this section with the comment that 'the unfinished work on education must rank high on the post-2015 development agenda' and must draw on the lessons learned from the MDGs, and be targeted more effectively. 'Interventions will have to be tailored to the needs of specific groups of children – particularly girls, children belonging to minorities and nomadic communities, children engaged in child labour and children living with disabilities, in conflict situations or in urban slums'. It also emphasises the importance of investing in the quality of education and ensuring a sustainable source of funding for education.

Goal 3: Promote Gender Equality and Empower Women

The first target, target 3.A, related to the achievement of this goal is 'Eliminate gender disparity in primary and secondary education, preferably by 2005, and in all levels of education no later than 2015'. Some progress has been made as about two-thirds of countries in the developing world have achieved gender parity in primary education. However, disparities persist at higher levels.

The MDG report argues that 'the education of women and girls has a positive multiplier effect on progress across all development areas'. This is a very significant point to make and there is greater awareness about this today than there was in the past. 'Driven by national and international efforts and the MDG campaign, many more girls are now in school compared with 15 years ago. Gender disparity has narrowed substantially at all levels of education since 2000'.

The MDG report also notes that 'women's access to paid employment continues to expand, but remains low in some regions'. Women have always been at a disadvantage in the labour market and that is still the case. The problem is that despite the progress they have made in education, 'women face a more difficult transition to paid work and receive lower earnings than men'. Globally women earn 24 per cent less than men, with the largest disparities found in Southern Asia and sub-Saharan Africa.

Another area in which some progress has been made is the political representation of women, as indicated by the proportion of seats held by women in single or lower houses of parliament. However, parity remains a distant goal.

A lot of progress has been made in the last twenty years as indicated by the data published by the UN on the achievement of the third MDG. But many gaps remain as the MDGs did not address the fundamental causes of inequality between men and women. The report states that 'to achieve universal realization of gender equality and empowerment of women, it is critical to address the key areas of gender inequality, including gender based discrimination in law and practice; violence against women and girls; women's and men's unequal opportunities in the labour market; the unequal division of unpaid care and domestic work; women's limited control over assets and property; and women's unequal participation in private and public decision-making'. On this basis, gender perspectives need to be integrated fully into all the goals of the post-2015 development agenda.

Goal 4: Reduce Child Mortality

The main target related to this goal is reduce by two-thirds, between 1990 and 2015, the under-five mortality rate. The MDG report states that substantial progress has been made in this area, for example, measles immunization has saved millions of children's lives, but more children can be saved from death due to preventable causes, such as pneumonia, diarrhea, and malaria. Sub-Saharan Africa has the world's highest child mortality rate. But some progress has been made and the under-five mortality rate has fallen from 179 deaths per 1,000 live births in 1990 to 86 in 2015. 'Yet the region still faces an urgent need to accelerate progress as the population is growing and this means that the number of under-five deaths will increase unless progress in reducing the under-five mortality rate is enough to outpace population growth. Southern Asia is another region that has a high under-five mortality rate at 50 deaths per 1,000 live births in 2015, and a large number of total deaths, at 1.8 million.

The MDG report makes a few other points about child mortality that are worth noting. Focusing on newborns is critical in further accelerating progress in child survival as the first day, week and month of life /after birth are the most critical for the survival of children. Many neonatal deaths could be avoided by interventions that are simple, cost-effective and have a high impact.

There is also a correlation between child mortality rates and family income, place of birth, i.e., rural or urban, and mother's level of education. 'Household survey data suggest that children from poorer households remain disproportionately vulnerable compared with the wealthiest households. On average, under-five mortality rates are almost twice as high for children in the poorest households as for children in the richest'. Mortality rates for children in rural areas are higher than for children born in urban areas, and children born to mothers with secondary or higher education have much better chances of survival. These findings call for strategies that target the most vulnerable children from the poorest households and from rural areas, and that support women's education and empowerment.

The report concludes that reducing under-five mortality requires political will, sound strategies, and adequate resources. The progress made in the achievement of this goal by a significant number of countries, even very poor/low-income countries, for example Bangladesh, Cambodia, Eritrea, Ethiopia, Liberia, Malawi, Nepal and Niger, shows that it can be done. Child survival must remain at the heart of the post-2015 global development agenda. (It should be noted, however, that there isn't a SDG on child mortality. But this could potentially be covered by SDG 3 - Good health and well–being).

Goal 5: Improve Maternal Health

The related targets are 5.A, Reduce by three-quarters, between 1990 and 2015, the maternal mortality ratio; and 5.B, Achieve by 2015 universal access to reproductive health. Good progress has been made in meeting these targets. Since 1990, the maternal mortality ratio has been cut nearly in half, and most of the reduction has occurred since 2000. According to the MDG report, Southern Asia and Eastern Asia have made the greatest progress in reducing maternal mortality. But despite this progress, too many women die during pregnancy or from childbirth related complications. According to the MDG report, 'in 2013, most of these deaths were in the developing regions, where the maternal mortality ratio is about 14 times higher than in the developed regions'. Sub-Saharan Africa and southern Asia together accounted for 86 per cent of maternal deaths globally in 2013.

Haemorrhaging was responsible for a high percentage, and the greatest number, of these deaths. Other causes included infections, high blood pressure during pregnancy, and complications from delivery and unsafe abortions. 'Proven healthcare interventions can prevent or manage these complications, including antenatal care during pregnancy, skilled care during childbirth and care and support in the weeks after childbirth'. Adolescent childbearing is another cause of maternal mortality. One way of preventing adolescent childbearing is by ensuring that all girls go to school and receive an education. As discussed above, the educational level of a woman will also have an impact on her own health as well as the health of her children. It will also contribute to the reduction of poverty, gender equality and the empowerment of women.

There is a relationship between maternal mortality rates and access to reproductive health care. For example, Southern Asia and the regions in Africa have a high maternal mortality ratio (i.e., number of maternal deaths per 1,000 live births) and low access to reproductive health. In other words, the problem is structural. As the MDG report notes, 'profound inequalities in access to and use of reproductive health services persist within and across regions', and this includes the rural-urban divide. Another problem the MDG report highlights is the lack of data on maternal health and causes of death, especially in developing regions. The capacity of countries to collect this data needs to be strengthened so that evidence based policies can be adopted, and resources more efficiently targeted for improvements in maternal health and universal access to sexual and reproductive health care, as well as monitoring progress made and measuring these improvements.

Goal 6: Combat HIV/AIDS, Malaria and Other Diseases

The targets related to the achievement of this goal are, target 6.A, halt and begin to reverse the spread of HIV/AIDS by 2015; target 6.B, achieve by 2010, universal access to treatment for HIV/AIDS for all those who need it; and target 6.C, halt and begin to reverse the incidence of malaria and other major diseases by 2015. Some progress has been made in the achievement of all three targets. The MDG report states that new HIV infections fell by approximately 40 per cent between 2000 and 2013, from an estimated 3.5 million new cases to 2.1 million. By June 2014, 13.6 million people living with HIV were receiving antiretroviral therapy globally, an increase from just 800,000 in 2003. The expansion of anti-malaria interventions prevented over 6.2 million deaths, between 2000 and 2015, primarily of children under five years of age in sub-Saharan Africa. Between 2000 and 2015, the global malaria incidence rate has fallen by an estimated 37 per cent, and the global malaria mortality rate has decreased by 58 per cent. As a result the global MDG malaria target has been achieved.

However, knowledge of HIV and HIV prevention remains low among young people, especially in sub-Saharan Africa. It remains the region most severely affected by the HIV epidemic, with 1.5 million new infections in 2013. Almost half of them occurred in three countries, Nigeria, South Africa and Uganda. However, South Africa, which is the country with the largest number of people living with HIV, recorded the largest decline in the absolute number of new infections, with 98,000 fewer new infections in 2013 than in 2010.

Some progress has clearly been made but the MDG report warns that 'an estimated 36 per cent of the 31.5 million people living with HIV in developing regions were receiving ART in 2013, with coverage varying significantly across regions. For example, sub-Saharan Africa had both the largest share of people living with HIV and the largest increase in the number of people receiving ART. Yet despite this progress the region is also home to 78 per cent of the people living with HIV in developing regions who are not receiving ART.'

The tuberculosis (TB) incidence rate has also been falling in all regions since 2000. But the rate of decline is slow, although all regions were expected to achieve the MDG target of halting the spread and reversing the incidence of TB by 2015. The MDG report notes that intensive efforts, over many years, to implement the DOTS strategy and its successor, the Stop TB strategy had produced good results. 'Between 2000 and 2013, an estimated 37 million lives were saved by TB prevention, diagnoses and treatment interventions'.

The MDG report concludes that 'Health is a precondition, an indicator and an outcome of sustainable development. As part of the 2015 development agenda, robust efforts are needed to sustain gains made to date and integrate additional health issues into a broad health and development agenda'. The focus has to remain on the countries in the developing regions, and within those countries on the poorest populations. For example, the Ebola crisis showed how vulnerable countries are that lack (robust) basic health services, the capacity for early detection and comprehensive reporting, and a rapid response system for public health outbreaks. Even where MDG targets have been met there can be reversals of the gains made. Thus the report warns that 'Sustained political commitment, predictable financing and strategic investments in health systems, disease surveillance and new tools are necessary to reduce resurgences and the malaria disease burden in the years ahead'. This also applies to other diseases.

Goal 7: Ensure Environmental Sustainability

There are four targets that were set to help achieve goal seven. They are as follows: target 7.A, integrate the principles of sustainable development into country policies and programmes, and reverse the loss of environmental resources; target 7.B, reduce biodiversity loss, achieving by 2010, a significant reduction in the rate of loss; target 7.C, halve, by 2015, the proportion of the population without sustainable access to safe drinking water and basic sanitation; target 7.D, by 2020 achieve a significant improvement in the lives of at least 100 million slum dwellers.

One area in which substantial progress has been made is in the elimination of ozone depleting substances. The Montreal Protocol (1987) on substances that deplete the ozone layer has been universally ratified. This will allow the ozone layer to recover by the middle of this century, it is estimated. But more remains to be done, such as phasing out the last of the ozone depleting chemicals, hydro chlorofluorocarbons, avoiding the use of alternatives such as hydrofluorocarbons, and promoting the sound management of substances still in use, such as in refrigerators, air conditioners and firefighting equipment. On the other hand, the biggest failure has been the failure to reduce global greenhouse gas emissions which continue to rise and are now more than 50 per cent higher than their 1990 level. The MDG report explains the likely consequences of this trend: 'A continual rise in greenhouse gas emissions is projected to further warm the planet and cause long-lasting changes in the climate system, threatening severe and irreversible consequences for people and ecosystems. Impacts on natural and human systems are projected to span the globe, with varying effects region to region. They include altered ecosystems and habitats; detrimental impacts on agriculture, potentially leading to food shortages; and more and longer lasting weather extremes and natural disasters, along with numerous risks to society'. There was some evidence of extreme weather events in 2017, for example, the floods in South Asia (mainly Nepal and Bangladesh) and hurricanes in the Caribbean.

The global community has to deal with this critical challenge and is trying to do so by promoting international agreements. The United Nations Framework Convention on Climate Change (UNFCCC) conference that was held in Paris in December 2015 led to an agreement open for signature and subject to ratification, acceptance or approval by states and regional economic integration organisations that are parties to the Convention. This, it was hoped, would provide a framework for strengthening international action to mitigate climate change. The Paris agreement states that in enhancing the implementation of the Convention, including its objective, 'aims to strengthen the global response to the threat of climate change, in the context of sustainable development and efforts to eradicate poverty'.[9]

---

[9] "Convention" means the United Nations Framework Convention on Climate Change, adopted in New York on 9 May 1992. The ultimate objective of this convention and any related legal instruments that the Conference of the Parties may adopt is to achieve, in accordance with the relevant provisions of the Convention, stabilization of greenhouse gas concentrations in the atmosphere at a level that would prevent dangerous anthropogenic interference with the climate system. Such a level should be achieved within a time-frame sufficient to allow ecosystems to adapt naturally to climate change, to ensure that food

While the burning of fossil fuels is the largest contributor to climate change, deforestation is the second largest contributor. The MDG report states that deforestation has slowed down from 8.3 million hectares annually in the 1990s to an estimated 5.2 million hectares each year from 2000 to 2010. But in spite of this improvement, deforestation remains alarmingly high in many countries. Forests are carbon sinks and are a source of clean air. Apart from that, they are a source of livelihoods for around 1.6 billion people, provide a home for millions of animals and plants/ species, and are a catchment for three-quarters of the world's fresh water. Some regions have experienced higher rates of deforestation than others, such as South America and Africa. On the other hand, some countries, like China, have embarked on large-scale afforestation programmes.

Other problems that need to be dealt with include the overexploitation of marine fisheries which has implications for global food security, livelihoods and economies, as well as marine ecosystems. Efforts to achieve a significant reduction in the rate of biodiversity loss (target 7.B) is likely to help address this problem. Many regions are leading the way in protecting land and marine areas. For example, Latin America and the Caribbean, Oceania and Western Asia. As the MDG report notes, 'terrestrial and marine protected areas help to prevent loss of biodiversity, maintain food security and water supplies, strengthen climate resilience, and improve human health and well- being'. From the point of view of the post-2015 development agenda and its goals and targets, this is a critical area that will need to be monitored, in terms of the progress that is made in different regions.

---

production is not threatened and to enable economic development to proceed in a sustainable manner (Article 2, United Nations Framework Convention on Climate Change, UN, 1992). The Paris Agreement (2015) will achieve its aim to strengthen the global response to the threat of climate change by: (a) Holding the increase in the global average temperature to well below 2°C above pre-industrial levels and pursuing efforts to limit the temperature increase to 1.5°C above pre-industrial levels, recognizing that this would significantly reduce the risks and impacts of climate change; (b) Increasing the ability to adapt to the adverse impacts of climate change and foster climate resilience and low greenhouse gas emissions development, in a manner that does not threaten food production; and (c) Making finance flows consistent with a pathway towards low greenhouse gas emissions and climate-resilient development (Article 2, Paris Agreement, UN, 2015).

Water scarcity is yet another problem affecting more than forty per cent of the world's population, and is projected to rise. The MDG report states that 'water scarcity already affects every continent and hinders the sustainability of natural resources as well as economic and social development'. But target 7.C has been met five years ahead of schedule. Between 1990 and 2015, the proportion of the global population using an improved drinking water source increased from 76 per cent to 91 per cent. While Sub-Saharan Africa lagged behind other regions, it nonetheless achieved a 20 percentage point increase in the use of improved sources of drinking water. On the other hand, the target for improved sanitation has not been achieved. According to the MDG report, 147 countries have met the drinking water target, 95 countries have met the sanitation target and 77 countries have met both. The MDG report notes that 'people living in rural areas and those from poor and marginalized groups are less likely to have access to improved water and sanitation facilities and less likely to enjoy piped water on premises. Progressive elimination of inequalities in access and service levels will continue to be an important focus of the post-2015 agenda'.

Finally, target 7.D was met as the proportion of urban population living in slums in the developing regions fell from approximately 39 per cent in 2000 to 30 per cent in 2014. But the 'absolute numbers of urban residents living in slums continue to grow, partly due to accelerating urbanization, population growth and the lack of appropriate land and housing policies'. Countries that are affected or have been affected by conflict in recent years, such as Iraq, have also seen an increase in the proportion of their population living in slums. The number of slum dwellers worldwide has risen from 689 million in 1990 to over 880 million in 2015.

Emphasizing the importance of this MDG, the MDG report states that 'Environmental sustainability is a core pillar of the post-2015 agenda and a prerequisite for lasting socio-economic development and poverty reduction'. It also emphasises that a lot more has to be done given the acute environmental challenges the world is facing, such as climate change, food and water insecurity, and natural disasters. This leads on to an assessment of the achievement of the last MDG, namely, Goal 8: Develop a global partnership for development.

Goal 8: Develop a Global Partnership for Development

The targets are as follows: 8.A: Develop further an open, rule based, predictable, non-discriminatory trading and financial system; target 8.B and 8.C: Address the special needs of the least developed countries, landlocked developing countries and small island developing states; target 8.D: Deal comprehensively with the debt of developing countries. Given the structure of the world system and the gap between the developed and developing regions, this is one of the most important goals from the point of view of achieving the rest of the goals. Without global co-operation many countries, especially in the developing world, would find it difficult to achieve the MDGs and their successor goals. The MDG report informs us that official development assistance (ODA) from developed countries increased by 66 per cent in real terms between 2000 and 2014. The top five donor countries by volume were the US, the UK, Germany, France and Japan. Some donor countries such as the UK, Denmark, Luxembourg, Norway, and Sweden continued to exceed the UN's ODA target of 0.7 per cent of GNI. The report also notes that 84 per cent of imports from LDCs were admitted by developed countries duty free in 2014, along with 79 per cent of imports from other developing countries. While agricultural products from LDCs receive the greatest trade preferences, imports of oil and arms are excluded from the preferential treatment given to developing countries' imports. But there are some trade barriers that are unfavourable to developing countries, for example, 'the largest LDC exporters of apparel are located in Asia and do not benefit from duty-free access to the US market'. This is unfortunate given the level of poverty in some of these countries.

On target 8.D, the MDG report notes that the debt burden of developing countries fell dramatically over the first decade of the new millennium as a result of better debt management, expansion of trade and substantial trade relief for the poorest countries, but has since stabilized and is expected to rise. The report also suggests that attractive borrowing conditions in international capital markets could ease the debt burden of developing countries. The Heavily Indebted Poor Countries Initiative (HIPC) has also helped many developing countries. The countries that have fulfilled all the conditions for receiving debt relief are receiving full debt relief under the Multilateral Debt Relief Initiative.

Finally, considerable progress has been made in achieving targets 8.E on access to affordable essential drugs in developing countries, and 8.F on access to new technologies, especially in the field of information and communication. The MDG report notes that the surveys that have been undertaken suggest that there is access to affordable essential drugs in many developing countries. The present author of this chapter can corroborate these research findings in relation to India. However, the Indian health care system is not satisfactory as only the wealthy can afford hospital treatment at good hospitals, and those with medical insurance. For the masses there are government hospitals but they are under -funded and do not offer good quality health care. Similarly, Matshidiso Moeti (2016), Regional Director for Africa, World Health Organization, writes that 'The most significant obstacle to progress on the health-related MDGs in Africa were the inadequate resources available and the often unpredictable, non-sustainable nature of external donor resources that were sometimes not aligned to country priorities. The situation was frequently compounded by weak health systems that did not permit the desired coverage with the necessary interventions'. One of the lessons learnt is that progress on health will require countries and partners to take effective action to ensure sustainable financing for health and for strengthening health systems.

Similarly, as the MDG report notes, 'mobile-cellular and internet penetration rates have grown strongly, but the digital divide between the rich and the poor is growing'. This issue is discussed in chapter 5. As a result of technological progress, information and communication technologies (ICTs) have made it easier to communicate with people on a daily basis, as well as access information, and conduct business. The MDG report notes that 'the proportion of the population covered by a 2G mobile-cellular network grew from 58 per cent in 2001 to 95 per cent in 2015. The number of mobile-cellular subscriptions has grown almost tenfold in the last 15 years, from 738 million in 2000 to over 7 billion in 2015'. Mobile phones are affordable in many developing countries, like India and most people use them. Another achievement is that 'internet penetration has grown from just over 6 per cent of the world's population in 2000 to 43 per cent in 2015'. But it is mainly the middle classes who access the internet, have email accounts, and send and receive emails. In spite of all the progress that has been made, unfortunately, the digital divide is still a reality.

The MDG report notes that 'The digital divide is particularly pronounced with respect to internet use and quality of access. For instance just over one third of the population in developing countries uses the internet, compared to 82 per cent in developed countries. The contrast is even more dramatic in sub-Saharan Africa, where less than 21 per cent of the population uses the internet, and in LDCs, where the figure is less than 10 per cent'. There are many structural reasons for the digital divide and they include the lack of infrastructure/ capacities required for providing affordable, high speed internet access throughout the country, availability of ICT skills, and location/ geography of the country, for example, small island developing states are particularly disadvantaged. It is therefore essential to address the digital divide, as chapter 5 in this book discusses: 'Only then will the transformative power of ICTs and the data revolution be harnessed to deliver sustainable development for all'.

At the same time, the post-2015 development agenda needs to be adequately funded. ODA is critically important for countries that are unable to raise all the resources they need domestically, and could attract other financial flows as well. In other words, international co-operation is essential for achieving the new sustainable development goals. And it isn't just ODA, trade is equally important for the economic and social development of countries in developing regions. They need to be integrated into the multilateral trading system but as chapter 7 discusses, the multilateral trading system itself seems to be in crisis and this does not augur well for the developing countries, especially the least developed countries. In an excellent article entitled 'Why trade matters', Mukhisa Kituyi (2016, 69), Secretary-General, United Nations Conference on Trade and Development (UNCTAD), writes that trade can contribute to higher levels of investment, which can enhance production, help upgrade technology and boost productivity. This catalyses the structural transformation of economies, creates jobs and develops skills in direct support of the SDGs, especially SDG8 (promoting decent work and economic growth), SDG9 (building resilient infrastructure, promoting inclusive and sustainable industrialisation and fostering innovation), and SDG10 (reducing inequality within and among countries).

CONCLUSION

The progress made in the achievement of the MDGs showed that where there is a will there is a way; but there is still a long way to go. Richard Jolly (2016, 16) comments that setting goals 'can help provide focus and often commitment'. He considers the adoption of global goals by member states, collectively, at the UN 'a major advance over the nationalist focus of international rivalries in the centuries before the UN was created'. In a similar vein and expressing similar opinions and sentiments, Greenstock and Samarasinghe (2016, 10) write: 'For all their flaws, the Millennium Development Goals (MDGs) were arguably the most successful anti-poverty initiative in history'. Over a period of fifteen years, the goals served as a 'development blueprint, generating programmes and funding that have helped to lift over a billion people out of extreme poverty, fight hunger and boost health and education.' But they also note that the extent to which the UN deserves credit for these achievements is debated. As Mahmoud Mohieldin (2016, 13), Senior Vice President for the 2030 Development Agenda, United Nations Relations, and Partnerships, World Bank, argues, the world we live in today is more prosperous and 'the gravity of the global economy is shifting'. In 2000, 41 per cent of the global population lived in low-income countries, since then the percentage has gone down to 12. Developing countries now account for a much larger share of global GDP, up from 22 per cent in 2000 to 41 per cent in 2014. This in itself is a big achievement. In addition, the proportion of the world's population living in extreme poverty has fallen by more than half, from 28 percent in 2000 to about 9.6 per cent (or approximately one in ten people) in 2015. Chandvi and Lewis (2013, 23) of the World Bank also argue that economic growth has driven much of the success of the MDGs, but caution that growth on its own is not sufficient, it needs to be equitable. The twin goals of ending extreme poverty and boosting shared prosperity should go hand in hand. This is a moral imperative.

One of the criticisms of the MDGs was that they did not focus enough on reaching the very poorest and most excluded people. This was the verdict of the UN High Level Panel on the Post-2015 Development Agenda (UN, 2013). Elaborating on this criticism, Natalie Samarasinghe, Executive Director of UNA-UK (2014, 81) writes that the 'MDG focus on broad targets has served to mask inequalities within and between countries and communities'. The framework that had been adopted had incentivised decision-makers and donors to pursue the easiest gains, instead of focusing on those hardest to reach. Thus in some countries, goals had been met nationally with little or no change for the poorest. Having learnt this lesson, the 2030 Agenda for Sustainable Development pledges that 'no one will be left behind' by the new set of goals.

Another criticism of the MDGs by the UN High Level Panel, cited above, was that they were silent on the devastating effects of conflict and violence on development. In an excellent article on 'Conflict and poverty: a vicious cycle', Abiodun Williams (2013, 18-19), President of the Hague Institute for Global Justice, argues that violent conflict is 'the major impediment to development progress in many countries'. He admits that although the causal linkages between conflict and development are complex and contested, there is widespread agreement that the outbreak, or even the risk, of conflict inhibits development and that poverty in turn exacerbates the risk of conflict. Thus 'fragile states' caught in vicious cycles of conflict and underdevelopment have struggled to achieve the MDGs and there is a significant gap between them and other middle income countries that are not affected by persistent insecurity.

The MDGs were also criticised by the Panel for not giving sufficient importance to the development of good governance and institutions that guarantee the rule of law, free speech and open and accountable government. The Panel also recognised, as indeed have other writers, for example, Chandvi and Lewis cited earlier, that there is a need for inclusive growth to provide jobs. But the Panel felt that the most serious criticism of the MDGs is that they 'fell short by not integrating the economic, social, and environmental aspects of sustainable development as envisaged in the Millennium Declaration, and by not addressing the need to promote sustainable patterns of consumption and production. The result was that environment and development were never properly brought together. People were working hard – but often separately – on interlinked problems'. The post-2015 development agenda, discussed in the next chapter, attempts to address some of these concerns and criticisms.

REFERENCES

Browne, S. and T. G. Weiss (eds.). 2014. *Post-2015 UN Development, Making change happen?* Abingdon, Oxon and New York: Routledge.

Chandvi, Jaime S. and Jeffrey D. Lewis. 2013. "Economic growth must be equitable." In *Global Development Goals, Leaving no one behind*, edited by Natalie Samarasinghe, 23-24. London: UNA-UK.

Clarke, Helen. 2013. "Accelerating progress." In *Global Development Goals, Leaving no one behind*, edited by Natalie Samarasinghe, 10-11. London: UNA-UK.

Dutt, Sagarika. 2015. "Global development goals." Review of *Global Development Goals, Partnerships for Progress*, edited by Natalie Samarasinghe. *New Zealand International Review*, November/ December 2015, 40 (6): 27-28.

Emmerij, R. Jolly and T. G. Weiss. 2001. *Ahead of the curve?* Bloomington: Indiana University Press.

Fink, Naureen Chowdhury and Rafia Bhulai. 2016. "Development and countering violent terrorism." In *Sustainable Development Goals, The*

People's Agenda, edited by Natalie Samarasinghe, 48-51. London: UNA-UK.

Greenstock, Jeremy, and Natalie Samarasinghe. 2016. "A new era for development." In *Sustainable Development Goals, The People's Agenda*, edited by Natalie Samarasinghe, 10-11. London: UNA-UK.

Jackson, Peter. 2007. "A prehistory of the Millennium Development Goals: Four Decades of Struggle for development in the United Nations." *UN Chronicle* XLIV, No.42007.

Jolly, Richard, L. Emmerij and T. G. Weiss. 2009. *UN ideas that changed the world*. Bloomington: Indiana University Press.

Jolly, Richard. 2016. "Breaking the cycle of poverty." In *Sustainable Development Goals, The People's Agenda*, edited by Natalie Samarasinghe, 15-17. London: UNA-UK.

Kituyi, Mukhisa. 2016. "Why trade matters." In *Sustainable Development Goals, The People's Agenda*, edited by Natalie Samarasinghe, 69-71. London: UNA-UK.

Moeti, Matshidiso. 2016. "Investing in health." In *Sustainable Development Goals, The People's Agenda*, edited by Natalie Samarasinghe, 28-31. London: UNA-UK.

Mohieldin, Mahmoud. 2016. "Development re-imagined." In *Sustainable Development Goals, The People's Agenda*, edited by Natalie Samarasinghe, 12-14. London: UNA-UK.

Murphy, Craig, N. 2006. *The United Nations Development Programme, A better way?* Cambridge: Cambridge University Press.

Peet, Richard, and Elaine Hartwick. 2010. *Theories of Development, contentions, argument, alternatives*. New Delhi: Rawat Publications.

Sachs, J. D. 2015. *The Age of Sustainable Development*. New York and Chichester, West Sussex: Columbia University Press.

Samarasinghe, N. 2014. "Leave no one behind." In *Global Development Goals, Partnerships for Progress,* edited by Natalie Samarasinghe, 81-82, London; UNA-UK.

Thérien, Jean-Philippe. 2005. "Beyond the North-South Divide: The two tales of world poverty." In *The Global Governance Reader*, edited by Rorden Wilkinson. 218-238. Abingdon and New York: Routledge.

UNA-UK. 2013. *Global Development Goals, Leaving no one behind*, London: UNA-UK.

UNA-UK. 2014. *Global Development Goals, Partnerships for Progress*, London: UNA-UK.

United Nations. 1987. *Our Common Future*, Report of the World Commission on Environment and Development, available online.

United Nations. 1992a. *The Global Partnership for Environment and Development*. Geneva: UNCED.

United Nations. 1992b. *United Nations Framework Convention on Climate Change*. Available online.

United Nations. 1997. *An Agenda for Development*. New York: United Nations.

United Nations. 2013. *A New Global Partnership: Eradicate Poverty and Transform Economies Through Sustainable Development*. New York: United Nations Publications.

United Nations. 2014. The road to dignity by 2030: ending poverty, transforming all lives and protecting the planet, *Synthesis report of the Secretary-General on the post-2015 sustainable development agenda*, UN General Assembly resolution A/69/700.

United Nations. 2015a. *The Millennium Development Goals Report 2015*. New York: United Nations.

United Nations. 2015b. *The Millennium Development Goals Report 2015*, Summary. New York: United Nations.

United Nations. 2015c. *Outcome of the third international conference on financing for development, Report of the Secretary-General*, General Assembly Resolution, A/70/320.

United Nations. 2015d. *Transforming our World: The 2030 Agenda for Sustainable Development*, General Assembly Resolution A/RES/70/1.

United Nations. 2015e. *Paris Agreement*, available online.

UNDP, 2017, 'Journey to extremism', available on the UNDP's website, accessed on 13. 9.17, available at http://undp.org.

Williams, Abiodun. 2013. "Conflict and poverty: a vicious cycle." In *Global Development Goals, Leaving no one behind*, edited by Natalie Samarasinghe, 18-21. London: UNA-UK.

In: Global Governance
Editor: Sagarika Dutt

ISBN: 978-1-53612-969-4
© 2018 Nova Science Publishers, Inc.

Chapter 3

THE UNITED NATIONS AND THE POST-2015 SUSTAINABLE DEVELOPMENT AGENDA

Sagarika Dutt

Senior Lecturer in International Relations and Subject Leader,
Nottingham Trent University, Nottingham, UK

ABSTRACT

The United Nations Conference on Sustainable Development was held in Rio in June 2012. Its outcome document, entitled 'The Future We Want,' begins with an introduction outlining *our common vision*: 'a world that is just, equitable and inclusive.' It also renewed our commitment to sustainable development and to ensuring the promotion of an economically, socially and environmentally sustainable future for our planet and for present and future generations, as well as to making every effort to accelerate the achievement of internationally agreed development goals, including the Millennium Development Goals. A decision was also made to develop a new set of sustainable development goals, based on 'an open and transparent intergovernmental process' that is open to all stakeholders. This led to the establishment of an Open Working Group on Sustainable Development which submitted its final report to the UN in 2014, paving the way for the adoption of the post-2015 sustainable development agenda and the new sustainable development goals by the UN's member states. The national voluntary reviews that have been submitted so far suggest that most of the UN's member states are making an effort to achieve these goals, and also identifying the main issues as well as sharing their experiences with other member states.

INTRODUCTION

The United Nations Conference on Sustainable Development (Rio+20) was held in Rio in June 2012. The importance of this conference is explained in a UN report as follows: 'The cornerstone for the current global process of renewal was established in Rio de Janeiro in June of 2012, with the adoption of the outcome document of the United Nations Conference on Sustainable Development "The Future We Want." The document described the lessons learned from two decades of development experience and provided an extensive assessment of the progress and gaps in the implementation of the sustainable development agenda' (UN, 2014b). It begins with an introduction outlining *'Our Common Vision':* 'a world that is just, equitable and inclusive,' and renewing 'our commitment to sustainable development and to ensuring the promotion of an economically, socially and environmentally sustainable future for our planet and for present and future generations.' It categorically states that 'eradicating poverty is the greatest global challenge facing the world today and an indispensable requirement for sustainable development.' It reaffirms the 'commitment to make every effort to accelerate the achievement of the internationally agreed development goals, including the Millennium Development Goals by 2015' (UN, 2012).

Sachs (2015) writes that the world is off course for achieving sustainable development. The issue has been on the global agenda for more than 40 years, dating back to 1972 and the United Nations Conference on the Human Environment, held in Stockholm. The Rio+20 conference was an opportunity for world leaders to take stock of the situation. 'All of the evidence showed that the diagnosis first made back in 1972 was fundamentally correct.' This meant that 'the challenges of combining economic growth with social inclusion and especially environmental sustainability were still unmet, and indeed were intensifying' (Sachs 2015). This chapter examines the post- 2015 sustainable development agenda and the process of adopting the new Sustainable Development Goals. This is based on a study and analysis of UN documentation as well as the secondary literature. The UN's vision for achieving sustainable development, it is argued, is based on (and supported by) a universal agenda that is supported by all its member states and other stakeholders.

SHAPING THE NEW AGENDA

The Rio+20 conference recognised that 'the 20 years since the United Nations Conference on Environment and Development in 1992 [had] seen uneven progress, including in sustainable development and poverty eradication.' It emphasised the need to make progress in implementing previous commitments and to 'accelerate progress in closing development gaps between developed and developing countries,' and 'to seize and create opportunities to achieve sustainable development through economic growth and diversification, social development and environmental protection.' This will require *an enabling environment at the national and international levels, as well as continued and strengthened international cooperation, particularly in the areas of finance, debt, trade and technology transfer, as mutually agreed, and innovation, entrepreneurship, capacity building, transparency and accountability.'* Wide ranging topics and issues were covered by the conference and are included in the outcome document such as poverty eradication, food security and nutrition and sustainable agriculture, water and sanitation, energy, sustainable tourism, sustainable transport, sustainable cities and human settlements, health and population, productive employment, decent work for all and social protection, oceans and seas, small island developing states, least developed countries, landlocked developing countries, Africa, climate change, forests, biodiversity, desertification, land degradation and drought, education, gender equality and the empowerment of women. [10]

Important decisions were taken regarding the 'importance and utility of a set of sustainable development goals,' for pursuing focused and coherent action on sustainable development, based on Agenda 21 (1992) and the Johannesburg Plan of Implementation, which fully respect all the Rio Principles (1992), take into account different national circumstances, capacities and priorities, and are consistent with international law. It was recommended that they should build on the commitments already made and contribute to the full implementation of the outcomes of all major summits in the economic, social and environmental fields, including Rio+20. These goals 'should address and incorporate in a balanced way all three dimensions of sustainable development and their interlinkages. They should be coherent with and integrated into the United Nations development agenda beyond 2015, thus contributing to the achievement of sustainable development, and serving as a driver for implementation and mainstreaming of sustainable development in the United Nations system as a whole' (UN 2012).

OPEN WORKING GROUP ON THE SUSTAINABLE DEVELOPMENT GOALS

A decision was also made to establish 'an inclusive and transparent intergovernmental process,' that is open to all stakeholders, for the development of the new global sustainable development goals. A 30

---

[10] The document has a section on '*Engaging major groups and other stakeholders*' which states that 'sustainable development requires the meaningful involvement and active participation of regional, national, and subnational legislatures and judiciaries, and all major groups: women, children and youth, indigenous peoples, non-governmental organizations, local authorities, workers and trade unions, business and industry, the scientific and technological community, and farmers, as well as other stakeholders, including local communities, volunteer groups and foundations, migrants and families as well as older persons and persons with disabilities'. It makes a commitment to working more closely with the major groups and other stakeholders and encouraging their active participation, as appropriate, 'in processes that contribute to decision-making, planning and implementation of policies and programmes for sustainable development at all levels' (UN 2012).

member open working group was to be constituted for preparing a proposal and submitting a report to the UN General Assembly, at its 68th session in 2014. Accordingly, an Open Working Group on Sustainable Development Goals was established by a decision of the UN General Assembly in January 2013 consisting of 30 representatives from the UN's member states 'as designated by the five United Nations regional groups' (A/67/L.48/Rev.1). It submitted its final report to the UN General Assembly, at its 68th session in 2014, as planned. There were two main phases in the group's work. In the first phase the group focused on stock-taking, collecting the views of experts, member states and other stakeholders. In the second phase the group prepared its final report. A progress report submitted by the group to the UN General Assembly notes that 'poverty eradication remains the overarching objective of the international community and needs to be central to a proposal on SDGs and the post-2015 UN development agenda.' It also noted that 'There is widespread recognition that poverty eradication can only be made irreversible if the SDGs advance sustainable development in a holistic manner, that is, if they address and incorporate in a balanced manner all three dimensions of sustainable development and their interlinkages.' But at the same time, the targets associated with the SDGs 'need to be differentiated for countries taking into account the different levels of development.' These targets need to be quantifiable in order to measure progress and it will, therefore, be necessary to ensure that all countries have the 'necessary data collection and statistical capacities to support robust indicators of progress.' The importance of a 'substantially strengthened global partnership' was recognised as 'critical to advancing sustainable development,' as some of 'the direst problems we face do not lend themselves to solely national or local solutions.' It was also recognised that the SDGs will not be achieved without adequate resources, and for this reason, many stressed that a proposal on the SDGs 'would need to include provision for means of implementation such as financing, technology, and capacity building.' But, in general, the argument that was put forward was that 'dynamic and resilient economies and a healthy and resilient environment underpin poverty eradication as well as sustained and sustainable social and economic progress.'

The final report of the Open Working Group contained its proposals on the sustainable development goals. It is clear from the report that the group was carrying out its mandate in accordance with the outcome document of the United Nations Conference on Sustainable Development, entitled 'The Future We Want.' It reiterated the promise made in this document 'to strive for a world that is just, equitable and inclusive' and the commitment made 'to work together to promote sustained and inclusive economic growth, social development and environmental protection and thereby to benefit all, in particular the children of the world, youth and future generations of the world, without distinction of any kind such as age, sex, disability, culture, race, ethnicity, origin, migratory status, religion, economic or other status.' The report stressed that people are at the centre of sustainable development, and that 'poverty eradication is the greatest global challenge facing the world today and an indispensable requirement for sustainable development.' The overarching objectives of and essential requirements for sustainable development, therefore, are: 'Poverty eradication, changing unsustainable and promoting sustainable patterns of consumption and production and protecting and managing the natural resource base of economic and social development.'[11]

But notwithstanding the importance given to the reduction of poverty, authors such as Hulme and Wilkinson (2014, 186-87) argue that following the Rio+20 conference, Latin American countries (and particularly Brazil) focused on leading negotiations for a set of sustainable development goals, as conceived by them, that include poverty eradication – rather than a set of poverty eradication goals that include sustainability. They argue that the leaders of these countries 'see the SDGs as more relevant to their needs and interests, especially as recent growth means that national politics are increasingly about middle-class voters, and poverty is viewed as a residual rather than a structural problem.' These days, many African countries too

---

[11] It should be noted, however, that this intergovernmental process ran parallel to a UN Secretary-General led process on the post-2015 development agenda, which involved a number of consultations to assess the options for a successor framework to the MDGs.

are experiencing economic growth and are less dependent on aid. Sachs (2015), who was tasked with the creation of the Sustainable Development Solution Network, by the UN Secretary-General, argues that *the call for the new Sustainable Development Goals is a potentially historic decision,* a powerful way to move to a new global agenda that engages the world community, including not only governments but also businesses, scientists, leaders of civil society, NGOs, and, of course, students everywhere. Unlike the MDGs, which apply largely to poor countries and reference the rich countries mainly as donors, the SDGs will be universally applicable. The United States, just like Mali, needs to learn to live sustainably! The rich countries like the poor have to promote more social inclusion, gender equality, and of course energy systems that are low carbon and resilient.' In fact, that is precisely what has happened, as developed countries have begun to engage with the 17 new SDGs.

THE REPORT OF THE HIGH-LEVEL PANEL OF EMINENT PERSONS ON THE POST-2015 DEVELOPMENT AGENDA

In 2012, a high-level panel of eminent persons was tasked with making recommendations to the UN Secretary-General on the development agenda beyond 2015. The members of this panel 'consulted extensively, in every region and across many sectors, including listening to the voices and priorities of people living in poverty themselves.' In May 2013 they submitted a report to the UN Secretary-General, Ban-Ki-Moon, outlining five transformational shifts, applicable to both developed and developing countries alike, including *a new Global Partnership* as the basis for a single, universal post-2015 agenda that will deliver this vision for the sake of humanity. These are as follows: Leave no one behind; Put sustainable development at the core; Transform economies for jobs and inclusive growth; Build peace and effective, open and accountable institutions for all; and Forge a new global partnership. The report offered a set of illustrative goals and targets to show how these transformative changes could be expressed in precise and measurable terms. They included ending poverty; empowering girls and women and achieving gender equality; ensuring food security and good nutrition; creating jobs, sustainable livelihoods and equitable growth; managing natural resource assets sustainably; ensuring good governance and effective institutions, and so on. This report was one of the inputs into the process of developing the post-2015 sustainable development agenda.

THE UN SECRETARY-GENERAL'S SYNTHESIS REPORT ON THE POST 2015 SUSTAINABLE DEVELOPMENT AGENDA

The UN Secretary-General produced a report in December 2014 synthesizing the full range of inputs available on the post-2015 sustainable development agenda, as an input to intergovernmental negotiations, as requested by resolution 68/6 of the UN General Assembly. The report refers to the 'valuable inputs from a wide range of stakeholders' and says that the 'international community has come a long way in its deliberations on the sustainable development agenda.' A common understanding has emerged that there must be *a universal agenda.* There are global challenges that all nations have to make a concerted effort to deal with, and despite national differences, there are common themes that cut across national borders, for example, even in the richest countries there can be destitution and exclusion. The report says that 'all voices have called for a people-centred and planet-sensitive agenda to ensure human dignity, equality, environmental stewardship, healthy economies, freedom from want and fear and a renewed global partnership for sustainable development.' It argues that tackling climate change and fostering sustainable development agendas are two mutually reinforcing sides of the same coin. All parties want action to address climate change, to accelerate the reduction of greenhouse gas emissions and to keep the rise in global average temperature below 2 degrees Celsius. At the same time, this must be done 'on the basis of equity for present and future generations and in accordance with common but differentiated responsibilities and respective capabilities.'

Table 1. Sustainable development goals

Goal 1: End poverty in all its forms everywhere

Goal 2: End hunger, achieve food security and improved nutrition and promote sustainable agriculture

Goal 3: Ensure healthy lives and promote well-being for all at all ages

Goal 4: Ensure inclusive and equitable quality education and promote lifelong learning opportunities for all

Goal 5: Achieve gender equality and empower all women and girls

Goal 6: Ensure availability and sustainable management of water and sanitation for all

Goal 7: Ensure access to affordable, reliable, sustainable and modern energy for all

Goal 8: Promote sustained, inclusive and sustainable economic growth, full and productive employment and decent work for all

Goal 9: Build resilient infrastructure, promote inclusive and sustainable industrialization and faster innovation

Goal 10: Reduce inequality within and among countries

Goal 11: Make cities and human settlements inclusive, safe, resilient and sustainable

Goal 12: Ensure sustainable consumption and production patterns

Goal 13: Take urgent action to combat climate change and its impacts*

Goal 14: Conserve and sustainably use the oceans, seas and marine resources for sustainable development

Goal 15: Protect, restore and promote sustainable use of terrestrial ecosystems, sustainably manage forests, combat desertification, and halt and reverse land degradation and halt biodiversity loss

Goal 16: Promote peaceful and inclusive societies for sustainable development, provide access to justice for all and build effective, accountable and inclusive institutions at all levels

Goal 17: Strengthen the means of implementation and revitalise the Global Partnership for Sustainable Development.
Acknowledging that the United Nations Framework Convention on Climate Change is the primary international, intergovernmental forum for negotiating the global response to climate change.

Based on the experience of two decades of development practice and from the inputs gathered 'through an open and inclusive process,' the report claims that it 'charts a roadmap to achieve dignity in the next 15 years.' It proposes one universal and transformative agenda for sustainable development, underpinned by rights, and with people and the planet at the centre. It acknowledges the report of the Open Working Group on Sustainable Development Goals that proposed 17 specific goals and 169 associated targets, which have been described as action-oriented, global in nature and universally applicable, taking into account different national realities, capacities and levels of development. The Group sought to combine 'aspirational global targets, with country-specific targets to be set nationally.' These goals are set out in Table 1. They were officially adopted at the Sustainable Development Goals Summit held in New York in September 2015 (General Assembly resolution A/RES/70/1). Helen Clarke (2014, 11) comments that the report of the Open Working Group on Sustainable Development Goals 'represents a welcome recognition of the need to address the drivers of long-term development. If the cycle of major humanitarian crises is to be broken, more peaceful, cohesive, and resilient nations that can sustain development progress need to be built. Significant deficits in governance, major inequalities and exclusions, and unmitigated exposure to natural disasters are setting countries back time and time again. But these deficits can be tackled.' She adds that with UNDP's assistance, many countries are expanding access to justice; establishing more effective institutions; conducting fair and transparent elections; promoting open dialogue with civil society; strengthening parliaments and meeting their human rights obligations. UNDP considers these efforts 'as an investment in development, peace, stability and prosperity.'

Six Essential Elements

The Secretary-General's synthesis report set out six essential elements for delivering on the sustainable development goals. These are: Dignity; People; Prosperity; Planet; Justice; and Partnership. The first element refers to the firm resolve to end poverty and fight inequalities. 'The defining challenge of our time is to close the gap between our determination to ensure a life of dignity for all, and the reality of persisting poverty and deepening inequality.' The second refers to healthy lives and access to health services, the right to an education, and the inclusion of women and children. The third refers to shared prosperity: 'We need inclusive growth, built on decent jobs, sustainable livelihoods and rising real incomes for all.' The fourth focuses on the protection of our ecosystems: 'We must protect our oceans, seas, rivers and atmosphere as our global heritage and achieve climate justice.' It identifies fossil fuels usage and deforestation as the two main sources of human induced climate change. We must, therefore, adopt a meaningful universal climate agreement by the end of 2015. The fifth element, justice, is about safe and peaceful societies and strong institutions, the enablers and outcomes of development. Laws and institutions must protect human rights and fundamental freedoms. Press freedom and access to information, freedom of expression, assembly and association are enablers of sustainable development. The rule of law must be strengthened at the national and international level to secure justice for all. There is a need to rebuild and reintegrate societies after crises and conflicts. This includes supporting internally displaced persons and contributing to resilience of people and communities, as well as developing cohesive societies and strong institutions. Finally, the sixth element, partnership, emphasises the need for a revitalised global partnership for mobilizing the means and creating the environment to implement the post-2015 sustainable development agenda. These six elements need to be integrated in delivering the new sustainable development agenda.

Financing the New Agenda

The Secretary-General's synthesis report on the post-2015 sustainable development agenda has a lot to say about mobilizing the means to implement the agenda. It argues that sustainable development 'is a complex challenge,' and 'All financing streams need to be optimized towards sustainable development and coordinated for the greatest impact.'

The financing streams are domestic public, domestic private, international public, international private and blended finance. The outcome document of the Rio+20 conference had stated that 'each country has primary responsibility for its own economic and social development and that the role of national policies, domestic resources and development strategies cannot be overemphasized.' But it also emphasised that developing countries need additional resources for sustainable development. 'We recognise the need for significant mobilisation of resources from a variety of sources and the effective use of financing, in order to promote sustainable development.' The active participation of the private sector can contribute to the achievement of sustainable development, including through the important tool of private-public partnerships. Moreover, national regulatory and policy frameworks can enable business and industry to advance sustainable development initiatives, taking into account the principles promoted by the UN Global Compact and corporate social responsibility. Private resources, including foreign direct investment, can lead to long-term investments in critical sectors, especially in developing countries. These include sustainable energy, infrastructure and transport, as well as information and communication technologies.

Official development assistance (ODA) and other international public funds can also help developing countries meet their targets. While all developed countries should meet the target of spending 0.7 per cent of gross national income (GNI) on ODA to developing countries, the proportion of ODA going to the least developed countries should not decline, but should continue to increase, 'to be better targeted, more efficient and more transparent and to leverage additional resources.' SDG 17.2 addresses this issue although it does not make it mandatory for developed countries to achieve the target of 0.7 per cent of GNI for ODA to developing countries. But foreign aid alone will not be sufficient. According to the Addis Ababa Action Agenda adopted by the third International Conference on Financing for Development held in Addis Ababa from 13-16 July 2015, 'the financing needed to achieve the 2030 agenda for sustainable development is extremely large, of the order of trillions of dollars annually.' It is a challenge, but not one that is insurmountable. 'Global public and private investment would be sufficient to address them, but only if financial resources are invested in and aligned with sustainable development. That requires public finance, policies, and regulatory frameworks, unlocking the transformative potential of people and the private sector and incentivizing changes in consumption, production and investment patterns to support sustainable development' (UN 2015b). The Addis Ababa Action Agenda is an integral part of the 2030 Agenda for Sustainable Development. The UN and its member states recognise that 'the full implementation of the Addis Ababa Action Agenda is critical for the realization of the Sustainable Development Goals and targets'.

There are other aspects that have been addressed by the Addis Ababa Action Agenda, for example, international development cooperation, international trade as an engine for development, and debt sustainability. But the language used in the Secretary-General's synthesis report, cited earlier, is much stronger. On the subject of international trade it states that 'we must move, seriously and expeditiously, to correct the inequities that have long plagued the international system to the disadvantage of developing countries. We need a more equitable multilateral trading system, a conclusion of the Doha round and better access to technology, medicines and long-term investments for developing countries. We need a more fair representation of emerging and developing countries in international financial and economic decision-making, better regulation and more stability in the international financial and monetary systems and sustainable debt solution. We must continue to remedy the policy incoherence between current modes of international governance in matters of trade, finance and investment on the one hand, and our norms and standards for labour, the environment, human rights, equality and sustainability on the other.'

The other two means considered to be important for implementing the sustainable development agenda are technology, science and innovation and capacity-building for sustainable development. The Secretary-General's synthesis report points out that large amounts of public resources are allocated to military budgets, while a lot less is spent on research and development for public goods. It also argues that 'Public funding often subsidizes private sector research, at times leading to the public being priced out of the benefits through disadvantageous licensing and patents. This also leads to frequent subsidies for innovations that are not aligned with promoting sustainable consumption and production patterns.' We need to invest in innovation and the development of (clean) technologies that will help us to implement the sustainable development agenda. Developing countries, and especially the least developed countries, need to be given the support they need so that they can benefit from these new technologies and ultimately develop their own technological solutions. There is evidence to suggest that multi-stakeholder, solution-driven initiatives can lead to technological advances, and these should, therefore, be promoted. A Technology Facilitation Mechanism has been launched by the UN in accordance with the Addis Ababa Action Agenda in order to support the SDGs. It is based on multi-stakeholder collaboration and is composed of a UN interagency task team on science, technology and innovation for the SDGs, a collaborative multi-stakeholder forum on science, technology and innovation for the SDGs and an online platform that will facilitate access to information, knowledge and experience, as well as best practices and lessons learned, on science, technology and innovation facilitation initiatives and policies.

The importance of capacity-building has been highlighted by both the Secretary-General's synthesis report and SDG 17.9 which urges enhanced 'international support for implementing effective and targeted capacity-building in developing countries to support national plans to implement all the Sustainable Development Goals, including through North-South, South-South and triangular cooperation.' As the Secretary-General's synthesis report says, in order to achieve the SDGs, all countries will need to integrate them into national planning, policy, budgets, law and institutions. Institutional and human capacities will, in many cases, need to be strengthened for effective implementation and monitoring. SDG 17.18 and 17.19 on 'Data, monitoring and accountability' make the same point: 'By 2020, enhance capacity-building support to developing countries, including for least developed countries, and small island developing States, to increase significantly the availability of high-quality, timely and reliable data disaggregated by income, gender, age, race, ethnicity, migratory status, disability, geographic location and other characteristics relevant in national contexts' and 'By 2030, build on existing initiatives to develop measurements of progress on sustainable development that complement gross domestic product, and support statistical capacity-building in developing countries.' The UN claims that it is working to revitalize and improve its role in capacity development.

TRANSFORMING OUR WORLD: THE 2030 AGENDA FOR SUSTAINABLE DEVELOPMENT

The 2030 agenda for sustainable development was the result of over two years of intergovernmental negotiations and intensive public consultation and engagement with civil society and other stakeholders around the world, including the poorest and most vulnerable people. It begins with a preamble that states that it is 'a plan of action for people, planet and prosperity.' It 'also seeks to strengthen universal peace in larger freedom.' The 17 SDGs and 169 targets seek to build on the MDGs and 'complete what they did not achieve.' The Secretary-General's synthesis report had earlier emphasised that 'We must invest in the unfinished work of the Millennium Development Goals and use them as a springboard into the future we want, a future free from poverty and built on human rights, equality and sustainability. This is our duty, and it must be the legacy we strive to leave for our children.' The 2030 Agenda recognises that 'eradicating poverty in all its forms and dimensions, including extreme poverty, is the greatest global challenge and an indispensable requirement for sustainable development.' It is also an agenda for protecting the planet from degradation, 'including through sustainable consumption and production, sustainably managing its natural resources and taking urgent action on climate change, so that it can support the needs of the present and future generations.' The agenda recognises that peace is an essential element for achieving sustainable development, and is determined to 'foster peaceful, just and inclusive societies which are free from fear and violence.' Prosperity for all human beings is also seen as necessary for achieving sustainable development. The new agenda has been accepted by all countries and is applicable to all, 'taking into account different national realities, capacities and levels of development and respecting national policies and priorities.' The implementation of this agenda requires a revitalised global partnership for sustainable development, based on a spirit of strengthened global solidarity, focused in particular on the needs of the poorest and the most vulnerable. It is an ambitious agenda that seeks to transform our world. In many ways it represents the unfolding of a global agenda that has its roots in the purposes and principles of the UN Charter, the Universal Declaration of Human Rights, the Millennium Declaration and the 2005 World Summit Outcome, as well as the outcomes of all major UN conferences and summits which 'have laid a solid foundation for sustainable development and have helped to shape the new Agenda.' The new SDGs are universal goals and are integrated and indivisible and balance the three dimensions of sustainable development: the economic, social and environmental.

Of course, the adoption of goals has to be accompanied by a follow-up and review process. The 2030 Agenda makes a commitment 'to engaging in systematic follow-up and review of the implementation of this Agenda over the next 15 years.' The follow-up and review process will help countries and the international community to 'track progress in implementing this Agenda in order to ensure that no one is left behind.' Regular and inclusive reviews of progress will be conducted at the subnational, national, regional and global levels. Country led national reviews will be the foundation for reviews at the regional and global levels. The global review will be primarily based on national official data sources. It will therefore be necessary to strengthen the capacity of national statistical offices and data systems, in developing countries, and particularly in the least developed countries, to ensure that high-quality, timely, reliable and disaggregated data is collected.

The SDGs and related targets will be followed up and reviewed using a set of global indicators. The 2030 Agenda states that the global indicator framework is 'to be developed by the Inter-Agency and Expert Group on Sustainable Development Goal Indicators, [and] agreed by the Statistical Commission by March 2016 and adopted thereafter by the [ECOSOC] and the General Assembly, in line with existing mandates.' These global indicators will be complemented by indicators at the regional and national levels which will be developed by member states. Work also has to be undertaken for the development of the baselines for those targets where national and global baseline data does not yet exist.

At the global level, the High-Level Political Forum (HLPF) on Sustainable Development is the UN's central platform for the follow-up and review of the 2030 Agenda for Sustainable Development and the SDGs. This forum replaces the Commission on Sustainable Development, which had met annually since 1993. It is expected to 'provide political leadership, guidance and recommendations on the 2030 Agenda's implementation and follow-up; keep track of progress of the SDGs; spur coherent policies informed by evidence, science and country experiences; as well as address new and emerging issues.'[12] Follow-up and review at the High-Level Political Forum will be informed by an annual progress report on the SDGs to be prepared by the Secretary-General in cooperation with the UN system, based on the global indicator framework and data produced by national statistical systems and information collected at the regional level. The High-Level Political Forum will also be informed by the Global Sustainable Development Report, which shall strengthen the science-policy interface and could provide a strong evidence-based instrument to support policymakers in promoting poverty eradication and sustainable development (UN 2015c).

CONCLUSION

The United Nations was established to 'maintain international peace and security'; 'develop friendly relations among nations'; 'achieve

---

[12]   Sustainable Development Knowledge Platform available at: https://sustainable development.un.org/hlpf/2016

international co-operation in solving international problems of an economic, social, cultural, or humanitarian character, and in promoting and encouraging respect for human rights'; and 'to be a centre for harmonizing the actions of nations in the attainment of these common ends.' Poverty, hunger, disease and environmental degradation are some of the international problems that the UN, its funds, programmes and specialised agencies are trying to solve. The UN's conceptualisation of development has helped it to maintain a focus and develop a powerful narrative, beginning with UN support for the self-determination of nations under colonial rule which led to the independence of many countries around the world in the 1960s and 1970s, and the UN development decades. The UN resolution (A/RES/1710 (XVI)) designating the 1960s as the first UN development decade noted that 'economic and social development of the economically less developed countries is not only of primary interest to those countries but is also basic to the attainment of international peace and security and to a faster and mutually beneficial increase in world prosperity.' The MDGs were, therefore, primarily aimed at eradicating extreme poverty in the developing world. As Jackson (2007) argues, 'the MDGs were not part of a new agenda, but an attempt to refocus years of debate, efforts and struggle to advance the economic and social development of the world's poorest nations.' But since environmental degradation is an equally pressing issue development has had to be qualified as sustainable development. The Agenda for Development, adopted by the UN General Assembly in 1997, says that development is 'a multidimensional undertaking to achieve a higher quality of life for all people. Economic development, social development and environmental protection are interdependent and mutually reinforcing components of sustainable development.'

The UN's assessment of the progress made in the achievement of the MDGs shows that the adoption of specific goals and targets is a good idea, and if there is a political will to achieve these goals a lot of progress can be made. But clearly, the success of the MDGs has made the international community even more ambitious, and has led to the adoption of a universal agenda and a set of 17 new Sustainable Development Goals. As the

Secretary-General's synthesis report on the post-2015 sustainable development agenda notes, achieving these goals will be a 'complex challenge.' The sheer number of goals will require more careful planning and the adoption of policies, at all levels, to facilitate the implementation of the new agenda. Both the 2030 Agenda and the Addis Ababa Action Plan have given some thought to the means to implement the agenda, including financing. But as each country has primary responsibility for its own economic and social development, its national policies, development strategies and resources, the developing countries, especially, the least developed countries, will require a lot of support, including support from the UN system. (The UN has already promised support for capacity-building. But developing indicators for measuring progress at the national level could be an equally challenging task.) The first HLPF held in July 2016 in New York was encouraging. Its theme was 'Ensuring that no one is left behind.' Secretary-General Ban Ki-moon launched the first SDG report which will serve as a benchmark for the 15 year implementation period of the 2030 Agenda. He stated that it 'provides an accurate evaluation of where the world stands on the 17 goals, using data currently available to highlight the most significant gaps and challenges.' It was also an opportunity for 22 countries to submit their Voluntary National Reviews. As the Secretary-General emphasised, 'progress in achieving the SDGs will be greatly enhanced by making sure that lessons are shared and best practices are replicated.'[13]

At the 2017 High-Level Political Forum on Sustainable Development (HLPF) 43 countries presented voluntary national reviews (VNRs). The overarching theme for all the sessions of the forum was 'Eradicating Poverty and promoting prosperity in a changing world.' The ECOSOC President's report notes that 'Overwhelmingly, the national preparations were considered extensive and impactful, a welcome tool to keep momentum on the implementation efforts, in part due to strong commitment from the highest levels of Government.' The VNRs noted the importance of bringing all stakeholders together in a joint, multi-

---

[13] 'UN chief launches first report to track Sustainable Development Goals', available at https://sustainabledevelopment.un.org/hlpf/2016

stakeholder, whole of society approach to implementing the SDGs. While there are different approaches on how to do this, it was important to create ownership at all levels, including the level of individual citizens, 'to create and sustain momentum for the implementation and monitoring of the agenda.' The report notes that 'policy making for the SDGs could become more effective, for instance through active political commitment and engagement of traditional and community leaders, opinion leader, the media and political leaders to address the social, economic and environmental challenges faced by the countries.' But it also notes that 'the role of international (state and non-state) partners would be critical to complement national budgets with financial support, especially in countries facing national budget constraints. In many developing countries, continued and strengthened support from the UN system could contribute to the preparation of the VNRs, as well as implementation of the Agenda.' Finally, 'it was widely recognised that data is vital for achieving the SDGs, building trust and accountability, but also constitutes a key challenge. Localization of targets and indicators, as well as capacity development and investments in data collection, disaggregation, analysis and dissemination needs to be prioritised.' The importance of data for development has been highlighted by Claire Melamed, Director of Poverty and Inequality, Overseas Development Institute who says that 'one of the unexpected but very welcome consequences of the negotiation of new global goals has been the focus on the data that is needed to achieve and monitor them. This is the moment for people who care…to bring resources, energy and expertise to bear on making the invisible visible, and putting data to work to improve people's lives' (Melamed 2016, 58). Mahmoud Mohieldin, Senior Vice President for the 2030 Development Agenda, United Nations Relations, and Partnerships, World Bank, makes the same point. He argues that the 2030 Agenda 'requires a more holistic and universal approach that recognises the interrelatedness of the goals and targets, the importance of data in monitoring progress and in targeting interventions for maximum impact,' as well as resource mobilisation on an unprecedented scale, including domestic resource mobilisation and private-sector resources, in addition to ODA (Mohieldin 2016, 14).

Finally, as far as the UN's role in achieving the SDGs is concerned, there are different views. At the 2017 HLPF, it was noted that many countries had asked the UN to help with national implementation, demonstrating the confidence they had in the UN. However, Stephen Browne and T. G. Weiss (2016) are more critical and ask 'Will the UN be able to deliver on the ambitious global development agenda set for the next 15 years, or does the world need a new breed of organisations to promote international cooperation ?' They point out that the UN needs to be fitter-for-purpose if it is to be a useful partner in the post-2015 era. They also point out that there have been serious debates but only half-hearted efforts at reform, including the 2006 'Delivering as One' initiative. In their opinion, one of Secretary-General Ban Ki-moon's legacies 'will have been to preside over the continuing decline of the UN's development system.' But at the 2017 HLPF member states expressed support for the Secretary-General's initiative on UN reform to make the UN fit for purpose. Richard Jolly (2016) is more optimistic about the UN's role and argues that first of all, the UN initiated a decision making process that led to the adoption of the SDGs. 'This was probably the most all-embracing decision-making process ever undertaken by the UN.' Secondly, while the member states have primary responsibility for the implementation of this agenda, the UN has a role to play in periodic reviews and reporting – nationally, regionally and internationally. This was confirmed by the discussions at the 2017 HLPF which highlighted the critical role of the HLPF as the global platform for follow-up and review. It offered an opportunity for considering challenges and structural barriers that require coordinated action at the global level. The HLPF also served as a platform for collaboration, partnerships, peer learning and exchange of experiences and lessons learnt. In short, the 'facilitative momentum of the HLPF enhanced national efforts towards SDG implementation.' But as Nina Hall and Ngaire Woods (2016) point out, the UN 'needs better leadership than ever before.' In every part of the world, people are at risk from challenges that no government can resolve on its own. This is where the UN must step in. It is the responsibility of the UN Secretary-General to ensure that the UN is fit for purpose by appointing qualified personnel to key UN positions and brokering new resources for the UN, in order to strengthen the capacity of the UN to serve all its members.

REFERENCES

Browne, S. and T. G. Weiss (eds). 2014. *Post-2015 UN Development, Making change happen?* Abingdon, Oxon and New York: Routledge.

Browne, S. and T. G. Weiss. 2016. "A UN fit for purpose?" In *Sustainable Development Goals, The People's Agenda*, edited by Natalie Samarasinghe, 152-154. London: UINA-UK.

Clarke, Helen. 2013. "Accelerating progress" In *Global Development Goals, Leaving no one behind* edited by Natalie Samarasinghe, 10-11. London: UNA-UK.

Emmerij, R. Jolly and T. G. Weiss. 2001. *Ahead of the curve?* Bloomington: Indiana University Press.

Hall, Nina and Ngaire Woods. 2016. "Leading the change." In *Sustainable Development Goals, The People's Agenda*, edited by Natalie Samarasinghe, 156-158. London: UNA-UK.

Hume, David and Rorden Wilkinson. 2014. "The UN and the post-2015 development agenda." In *Post-2015 UN Development, Making change happen?* edited by Stephen Browne and Thomas G. Weiss,181-194. Abingdon, Oxon and New York: Routledge.

Jackson, Peter. 2007. "A prehistory of the Millennium Development Goals: Four Decades of Struggle for development in the United Nations." *UN Chronicle* XLIV, No.42007.

Jolly, Richard, L. Emmerij and T. G. Weiss. 2009. *UN ideas that changed the world.* Bloomington: Indiana University Press.

Jolly, Richard. 2016. "Breaking the cycle of poverty." In *Sustainable Development Goals, The People's Agenda*, edited by Natalie Samarasinghe, 15-17. London: UNA-UK.

Melamed, Claire. 2016. "Data for development." In *Sustainable Development Goals, The People's Agenda*, edited by Natalie Samarasinghe, 56-58. London: UNA-UK.

Mohieldin, Mahmoud. 2016. "Development re-imagined." In *Sustainable Development Goals, The People's Agenda*, edited by Natalie Samarasinghe, 12-14. London: UNA-UK.

Murphy, Craig N. 2006. *The United Nations Development Programme, A better way?*, Cambridge: Cambridge University Press.

Peet, Richard, and Elaine Hartwick. 2010. *Theories of Development, contentions, argument, alternatives*. New Delhi: Rawat Publications.

Sachs, J. D. 2015. *The Age of Sustainable Development*. New York and Chichester, West Sussex: Columbia University Press.

Thérien, Jean-Philippe. 2005. "Beyond the North-South Divide: The two tales of world poverty." In *The Global Governance Reader*, edited by Rorden Wilkinson. 218-238. Abingdon and New York: Routledge.

UNA-UK. 2013. *Global Development Goals, Leaving no one behind*. London: UNA-UK.

UNA-UK. 2014. *Global Development Goals, Partnerships for Progress*. London: UNA-UK.

UNA-UK. 2015. *Climate 2020*, London: UNA-UK.

UNA-UK. 2016. *Sustainable Development Goals, The people's agenda*. London: UNA-UK.

United Nations. 1987. *Our Common Future*, Report of the World Commission on Environment and Development, available online.

United Nations. 1997. *An Agenda for Development*. New York: United Nations.

United Nations. 2012. *The Future We Want*, Outcome of the United Nations Conference on Sustainable Development (Rio +20), Rio de Janeiro, Brazil, 20-22 June 2012.

United Nations. 2013a. *A New Global Partnership: Eradicate Poverty and Transform Economies Through Sustainable Development*. New York: United Nations Publications.

United Nations. 2013b. *Progress report of the Open Working Group of the General Assembly on Sustainable Development Goals*.

United Nations. 2014a. *Report of the Open Working Group of the General Assembly on Sustainable Development Goals*. General Assembly resolution A/68/970.

United Nations. 2014b. The road to dignity by 2030: ending poverty, transforming all lives and protecting the planet, *Synthesis report of the Secretary-General on the post-2015 sustainable development agenda*, UN General Assembly resolution A/69/700.

United Nations. 2015a. *The Millennium Development Goals Report 2015*. New York: United Nations.

United Nations. 2015b. Outcome of the third international conference on financing for development, *Report of the Secretary-General*, General Assembly Resolution, A/70/320.

United Nations. 2015c. Transforming our World: The 2030 Agenda for Sustainable Development, *General Assembly Resolution A/RES/70/1*.

United Nations. 2016a. *Global Sustainable Development Report 2016*, New York: Department of Economic and Social Affairs, United Nations.

United Nations. 2016b. Ministerial declaration of the high-level segment of the 2016 session of the Economic and Social Council on the annual theme "Implementing the post-2015 development agenda: moving from commitments to results" and Ministerial declaration of the 2016 high-level political forum on sustainable development convened under the auspices of the Economic and Social Council, on the theme "Ensuring that no one is left behind", Resolution E/HLS/2016/1.

United Nations. 2017. *President of the Economic and Social Council's summary of High-Level Political Forum on Sustainable Development*, available online.

In: Global Governance
Editor: Sagarika Dutt

ISBN: 978-1-53612-969-4
© 2018 Nova Science Publishers, Inc.

Chapter 4

MAINTAINING SOVEREIGN IDENTITY AMONG STATES FACING EXISTENTIAL THREATS: EXAMPLES FROM THE PACIFIC REGION

Roy Smith

Principal Lecturer in International Relations
and Subject Leader for Global Studies
at the Nottingham Trent University, Nottingham, UK

ABSTRACT

This chapter considers challenges and opportunities in relation to three low-lying atoll states of the Pacific region; the Republic of the Marshall Islands (RMI), Kiribati and Tuvalu. These territories all experience climate change and sea-level rise. RMI has a close relationship with the United States due to a Compact of Free Association agreement. Kiribati and Tuvalu have no such agreement, although they both have ties with Australia, New Zealand and other Pacific Islands territories, notably Fiji. Kiribati is already developing a relocation strategy of 'migration with dignity'. In contrast, Tuvalu looks on migration and resettlement as a policy of last resort and continues to focus on pressing for international agreements to reduce the greenhouse gas emissions that are contributing towards climate change.

INTRODUCTION

This chapter considers both challenges and opportunities in relation to three low-lying atoll states of the Pacific region; the Republic of the Marshall Islands (RMI), Kiribati and Tuvalu. These territories are all subject to the negative consequences of climate change and related rise in sea-level. However, they have differing positions on how to respond to these challenges. RMI, although a sovereign state, has a close relationship with the United States as a result of a Compact of Free Association agreement. This is relevant as it allows Marshall Islanders a potentially easier route for migration and resettlement to the US should this become necessary. Kiribati and Tuvalu have no such agreement, although they both have ties with Australia, New Zealand and the other Pacific Islands territories, notably Fiji, through their membership of the Pacific Islands Forum. Kiribati is already developing a relocation strategy of 'migration with dignity'. In contrast, Tuvalu looks on migration and resettlement as a policy of last resort and continues to focus on pressing for international agreements to reduce the greenhouse gas emissions that are contributing towards climate change.

Mainstream media reporting of the above territories tends to refer to them as 'vulnerable', 'threatened' or even 'disappearing'. Whilst there can be little contention with the first two epithets, apart from among the small and dwindling number of entrenched climate change deniers, it is the suggestion of disappearance that is of particular interest here. The insinuation of the use of this term is that should mass migration occur then these territories would cease to exist as viable sovereign entities. Presumably this line of reasoning indicates that should these islands become completely inundated and no longer habitable then the exclusive economic zones (EEZs), currently the sovereign territory of these states, would revert to international waters with no sovereign control. This chapter challenges this view and suggests an alternative vision whereby, even allowing for mass migration, these territories could retain sovereignty over their existing EEZs and, crucially, any income derived from these marine resources. If a 'blue economy' could be maintained then this would present a much more optimistic outlook for the citizens of these states. Notwithstanding the upheaval and sense of loss that would inevitably be felt by those that were forced to relocate it is still possible to focus on the opportunities that such a move could present.

THE REPUBLIC OF THE MARSHALL ISLANDS

RMI has a land area of less than two hundred square kilometres, but this is spread across in excess of two million square kilometres of the Pacific Ocean. As with Kiribati and Tuvalu there is a massive distinction to be made between the land area of these states and their maritime EEZs. The land area of RMI is made up of two island groups, Ratak and Ralik. Both comprise of scattered islands and islets with only a small number of these being inhabited. The highest point of RMI is Likiep Atoll at just over 10 metres, although the majority of the population live in areas only 1-3 metres above sea level. As of July 2017 the total population was estimated at a little over 54,000 with two thirds of this number living on the capital island of Majuro and the secondary urban centre of Ebeye. There are conflicting estimates on how many Marshallese are now living abroad but as many as 25,000 islanders are now thought to be living in the US, predominantly in Hawaii, Guam, California and Arkansas. Emigration from RMI can be attributed to both push and pull factors.

The terms of the Compact of Free Association between RMI and the US allow for access to US-based education, health care and more employment opportunities than are available in the island territories. The increasing impact of storm surges, coastal erosion and decreasing supplies of potable water are also significant environmental issues which make life in RMI less attractive for those with the option of relocating. Over time it has been younger generations that have tended to move away from the islands to gain higher education, with relatively few of these islanders then returning to take up graduate level employment. The consequence of this has been a demographic pattern skewed towards children being brought up by grandparents, with many of these children then emigrating when they become teenagers. The economic consequence of this is RMI is losing those that are most economically productive and also has a disproportionate number of elderly people who no longer contribute economically, although they may well contribute to Marshallese society in many other ways. Health services are also under pressure with RMI having one of the world's highest rates of obesity, diabetes and related amputations (Parry 2010). In part the increase in non-communicable disease is related to both changes in lifestyle and also environmental factors. Rising sea levels and increasingly long periods of drought have led to salt intrusion into groundwater supplies, meaning that taro pits and other traditional forms of agriculture have declined. This, in turn, had resulted in an increased consumption of imported foodstuffs that are often processed with a high content of fat, sugar and salt.

RMI was one of the first Pacific island states to formally address the issue of relocation in terms of what this might mean for the sovereignty of a nation. In May 2011 RMI and the US co-sponsored a conference held at Columbia University's Center for Climate Change Law in New York entitled 'Threatened Island Nations: Legal Implications of Rising Seas and a Changing Climate' (Gerrard and Wannier 2013). The starting point for discussion was the generally accepted, yet still contentious, definition of what constitutes the characteristics of statehood. Based on the 1933 Montevideo Convention on the Rights and Duties of States there are four key attributes that are required for a political entity to be considered as a state and, thereby, achieve sovereignty. First it must occupy identifiable physical territory with defined borders separating it from other states. Simply put, one should be able to point to it on a map of the world. This territory is expected to have a resident population and an established government. Finally it must be able to enter into relations with other states. In order to fulfil this last criteria other states must recognize the existence and legitimacy of said sovereign territory, although Article Three of the Convention suggests that the lack of such recognition does not rule out unilateral declarations of independence and statehood, 'The political existence of the state is independent of recognition by the other states' (http://avalon.law.yale.edu/20th_century/intam03.asp#art3). For Marshall Islanders the threat of rising sea level and related factors making their homeland potentially uninhabitable does raise issues with regard to ongoing sovereignty. Some residual land area is likely to remain in parts of RMI when the main urban areas become uninhabitable. Current patterns of inundation usually involve 'wash over' whereby storm surges and king tides result in seawater temporarily covering the thin strips of land between the ocean and the lagoon (Davenport 2015). Although some of the lowest-lying islets now appear to be permanently submerged the majority of RMI's land area survives these incidents, but with increasing damage to the infrastructure and quality of life for residents. Under such circumstances mass relocation is likely to occur while there is still a visible, but no longer habitable, land area.

The issue of land area remaining without inhabitants is important in terms of maintaining sovereignty as residual land could still be the basis for ongoing claims to EEZs. Under the terms of the Third UN Convention of the Law of the Sea, held in 1982, territories can claim sovereignty over marine resources extending up to two hundred miles from their coastline. For the scattered island states under consideration here this is hugely significant as losing what might be a relatively small land mass among the outer islands could translate into the loss of a far greater proportion of the state's overall EEZ, and all of the marine and potential seabed resources within that area. One of the proposals considered at the 'Threatened Island Nations' conference was that the international community should acknowledge the risk of decreasing EEZs and issue a comprehensive statement that would recognize existing EEZ boundaries in perpetuity, regardless of loss of land area to rising sea level. Whilst this was welcomed by the island nations' representatives this would both set a precedent in international law and might also be resisted by other nations that are currently involved in disputed maritime claims. For example, in the South China Seas several nations have competing claims over the waters around the Spratly and Paracel Islands (Smith and Bradford 1998). That said, there is no compelling argument that would prevent an acknowledgement of specific EEZs in the Pacific Islands necessarily impacting on any territorial disputes in other parts of the world. Although such recognition of ongoing sovereignty over territory that has become depopulated would be a novel development within international diplomacy, there are strong grounds for arguing that this is something that could be achieved at no discernible cost to other states, but which could mean the survival of Pacific island economies and, therefore, communities.

The issue of responsibility and liability for the 'loss and damage' caused by climate change goes to the heart of current international climate change negotiations (Mogelgaard and McGray 2015). Article 8 of the Intergovernmental Panel on Climate Change's Paris Agreement of 2015 formalised the international community's commitment to addressing the loss and damage initially highlighted by the establishment of the Executive Committee of the Warsaw International Mechanism for Loss and Damage in November 2013. This body includes a Task Force on Displacement and an Expert Group on non-economic losses. Whilst it is a significant breakthrough in climate change negotiations that loss and damage has become an established part of these discussions, there is no specific reference within the related documentation to maintaining recognition of EEZs in the event of mass migration. It is not clear if this is an intended error of omission or simply something that has not been fully thought through and addressed. Given the media coverage of low-lying atoll states it is perhaps surprising that greater attention has not been given to the more optimistic scenario of 'migration with dignity' and the potential to maintain 'domestic' revenue at distance post-relocation. This is something that is rarely discussed, even among those that see large-scale migration as eventually inevitable.

KIRIBATI

The island state most closely associated with a declared strategy of migration with dignity is Kiribati, although this position has been seen as controversial within the Pacific region with not all Pacific leaders adopting this stance. Kiribati shares many of RMI's topographical characteristics being equally low-lying and with a very high disparity between land area and overall marine territory. The combined land area of Kiribati is slightly over eight hundred square kilometres, but this is spread over an EEZ in excess of three and a half million square kilometres. This is the only state in the world that has territory in all four hemispheres of the world. When looked at from this perspective rather than the commonly used term of being a small island developing state (SIDS) Kiribati, and several other Pacific island territories, could be more accurately described as large oceanic states. It is by reversing this view of the island states and placing greater emphasis on their marine (and potential sub-marine, sea-bed) resources that the undoubted challenges of adapting to sea-level rise and relocation might be looked at more optimistically. The former president of Kiribati, Anote Tong, has often been outspoken in appearing to accept that mass migration for I-Kiribati would be an inevitable consequence of the prevailing patterns of climate change (Pashley 2016). For some other Pacific island leaders this position was often seen as overly negative and somewhat defeatist. Arguably by accepting the inevitability of mass migration this shifted the discourse of international climate change negotiations away from mitigation to one of adaptation. Critics of Tong's position, however realistic it may be, felt that this shift away from lobbying the major, industrialised powers to radically cut their greenhouse gas emissions would fail to address the underlying reasons for why migration would, eventually, become necessary.

To be fair to the former president he was not suggesting that there should be any lessening in calling the major powers to account for the negative impacts of their industries. On the contrary, he highlighted the need for *both* ongoing lobbying to reduce greenhouse gas emissions in conjunction with a realistic assessment of how rapidly the situation in many Pacific island communities is deteriorating. This position also relates to the above point on acknowledging the loss and damage associated with climate change. To take this issue further the logical consequence of this discussion is to ask if loss and damage has occurred can anyone be deemed responsible and, therefore, liable to provide some form of compensation? This is where Tong's argument takes on an interesting, and potentially very far-reaching, aspect as it raises questions about the politics of international aid and how this might best be applied. The issue of international aid and its positive and, arguably, negative impacts has been the subject of much debate within the field of development studies. This debate becomes even more complex and multi-faceted when considering major power aid programmes to the atoll states. Setting aside any arguments about moral duty and responsibility for addressing the loss and damage caused, regardless of any intention, by the industrialised powers, there remains the question of how might any aid programmes best address the issue of climate change. On one hand this could be through programmes to help communities remain in situ via measures such as the building of sea defences or funding the repair of infrastructure impacted by storm damage. Alternatively, at some stage it seems likely that a tipping point will be reached when donors will need to assess if their funding might be better directed towards supporting relocation measures, as opposed to continuing to try to maintain communities in locations that are becoming increasingly unviable.

The resident population of Kiribati is approximately 100,000. As with RMI there are also a significant number of I-Kiribati individuals and communities living overseas, predominantly in New Zealand and Fiji. Unlike RMI these islanders do not have a Free Association relationship with any other state to ease migration and resettlement. Some temporary employment opportunities are available overseas, such as New Zealand's Recognized Seasonal Employer Scheme, but these are short-term and no basis for permanent relocation. Similarly the main training and employment opportunity for young men in Kiribati is based around work on fishing fleets and overseas merchant shipping. These are welcome sources of income and remittances but when contracts are fulfilled these workers are more likely to return home then settle overseas. To aid employment opportunities overseas the Kiribati government, and related donor agencies, are placing greater emphasis on vocational education and training programmes to equip younger I-Kiribati with internationally-recognized qualifications with a view to them competing in the international job market (Government of Kiribati 2014).

TUVALU

As with RMI and Kiribati, Tuvalu is comprised of numerous islands and atolls spread over a large expanse of ocean. Of the three nations under consideration here Tuvalu is the smallest with an overall population of approximately ten thousand, about half of whom live on the capital atoll of Funafuti. Tuvalu is the island nation that has become most emblematic of the challenges these low-lying territories face. This symbolism was highlighted by various non-governmental activists at the United Nations' Intergovernmental Panel on Climate Change conference in Copenhagen in 2009. Following an impassioned speech by Ian Fry, the Tuvaluan representative to this meeting, several campaigning groups adopted slogans such as 'We are all Tuvalu' and 'Tuvalu is the real deal'. With some direct actions that successfully attracted media attention, reporters presented stories that drew world attention to Tuvaluans in terms of them living on the 'frontline' of climate change. This term has been widely adopted by both journalists and academics (Ferris et. al., 2011). This media coverage and academic attention has certainly raised global awareness of where Tuvalu is and the environmental challenges facing its population. Yet there is also a potential downside to this form of stereotyping and what Chimamanda Adichie has described as the 'danger of a single story' (Adichie 2009). For many outside of Tuvalu these islands and their inhabitants are now *only* associated with the threat of apparently unavoidable relocation. This situation is often portrayed as being simply a matter of time until these islands will become uninhabitable and Tuvaluans will have to seek refuge in another state's territory, or territories if the community cannot be accommodated within a single host nation. Many in Tuvalu resist and reject this assertion, including some of the government's most senior politicians. At an event held in Fiji to mark the opening of the Climate Action Pacific Partnership in July 2017 the Prime Minister of

Tuvalu, Enele Sopoaga, said that 'It's a matter of addressing the cause of climate change and global warming and, of course, sea-level rise. It's much bigger than sending a ship to go and pick up Tuvaluans, it's much bigger than ourselves, so we really need to contextualise it' (Quonadovu, Sikeli 2017).

The context that PM Sopoaga is referring to includes the intergovernmental negotiations on climate change and the economies of the world's largest industrialised nations, who are responsible for the majority of greenhouse gas emissions. In terms of global governance it has to be recognized that there are enormous variations in the power, influence and capabilities of different states to promote their interests in relation to other states. For example, the small island states under consideration here cannot compete militarily or economically with the far larger power bases supporting China or the United States. In part this is why it was important for Tuvalu to gain the support of non-governmental organisations and, in turn, the media in reporting the challenges they are facing. These island states have limited resources and human capital to promote their interests. Whereas the US, China and other large powers can send hundreds of delegates to represent their nation's interests at climate change negotiations the small island states can only send a relatively small number. This disadvantage is compounded when one thinks of how many international governmental meetings take place annually. Smaller nations sometimes have to decide which meetings to prioritise. Should their officials and advisors attend World Trade Organisation meetings, or meetings on biodiversity, fishing, telecommunications, health and development et cetera? This list is far from exhaustive. Moreover, with many small island states being quite heavily aid dependent there are practical budgetary issues to consider as to whether or not such trips are seen to be cost-effective.

For Tuvalu its number one foreign policy issue is tackling climate change. Clearly, other factors are important. Managing good relations with their aid donor partners or trying to ensure that the revenue from their fishing resources is maximised. Yet, from their perspective, if the majority of these islands are going to become inundated and those remaining are increasingly uninhabitable then maintaining some land area and sovereign control over this territory is obviously their primary concern. This creates something of a dilemma for Tuvalu when presenting themselves to the rest of the world. On the one hand, they want to highlight their vulnerability and the threats that they face. On the other hand, they try to stress their resilience and determination not to be relocated away from their homeland. Their delegates to climate change negotiations have been quite critical of Pacific Island leaders from other nations, notably Kiribati, who they appear to view as showing a 'defeatist' attitude in seeming to accept that relocation is inevitable.

PERSPECTIVES

Each of the three distinct political territories considered here face a shared challenge of navigating an uncertain future. To some extent this is a common human condition but these communities are particularly vulnerable to the negative impacts of climate change, sea-level rise and a broad range of related consequences. Yet their perspectives are different as they are operating in quite different international political contexts. As mentioned above the Republic of the Marshall Islands has entered into a Compact of Free Association with the US which provides some sense of potential entry to another state should the need arise. Of course, how any such relocation might be managed would be determined largely by the US who is, by far, the dominant partner in this relationship. The Trump administration's pronouncements on the vetting and restricting of other nationalities' entry into the US does not bode well for the Marshallese, although the fact that many Marshall Islanders have already relocated to the US, undertaken higher education in the US and, disproportionally in terms of overall population, served in the US military may increase their chances of being made welcome.

The Marshall Islanders have an unusual relationship with the US with some of their atolls, most famously Bikini, already having experienced community relocation to make way for the US' nuclear test programme.

Although these tests have now ceased their legacy continues to strain US/Marshallese relations due to ongoing claims for compensation and the inability of the Bikinians to return to their homeland. Yet over decades of dependency on income from the US, and some of the advantages of Free Association status noted above, Marshall Islanders continue to look towards the US as their closest international partner. This perspective may face further challenges as the Trump administration has distanced itself from the landmark Paris climate change agreement with implications for all low-lying areas, not simply those living in the atoll states. However, the same administration is also massively increasing its expenditure on the US military budget and some of this additional expenditure will feed into the Marshallese economy via the US military base on Kwajalein atoll (Perry 2016).

The close relationship between the US and the Marshall Islands has built up over a number of decades. Most of the Marshallese cabinet and related civil servants have been educated in the US higher education system. Whilst maintaining a very distinct sense of cultural uniqueness Marshallese are 'bound' to the US far more than they are to nearer neighbours such as Japan or China. With out-migration to the US already a significant trend and second generation Marshallese having been born and brought up in the US the cultural overlap between the two communities is palpable, although, again, this is a rather one-sided process with US culture impacting on and influencing the Marshallese rather than vice versa. So, in terms of global governance despite Marshallese having good grounds to harbour somewhat negative feelings towards the US, historically due to the nuclear legacy and currently in light of a borderline climate change denying Trump administration, they are so economically dependent that they have little option other than to remain closely allied to the US.

Kiribati also has a nuclear legacy from the tests conducted by both the US and the UK on Christmas and Malden islands. However, this appears to be less of an issue for I-Kiribati when compared to the Marshallese. This is not to under-estimate the impact of these tests but the Kiribati government have not pursued their claims with such vigour or associated them with other aspects of relations with their UK former colonial rulers. For Kiribati the over-riding issue in recent years has been the threat of rising sea levels and the risk of mass migration. Former President Anote Tong has been arguably the highest profile head of state campaigning on the international stage promoting climate change awareness and action. In itself this approach is not so unusual but Tong went further than most leaders when he predicted that his nation faced an existential threat. There remain disputes among climate scientists, and less well-qualified commentators, on how rapidly climate change is occurring and with what consequences. Tong has been quite unequivocal in his statements indicating that although the timeframe may be subject to some dispute and debate it is inevitable that relocation is no longer a matter of if, but when. This perspective is very important as it allows for forward planning and what Tong has described as a policy of 'migration with dignity'. Moreover, this necessarily engages with a sense of global, or at least regional, governance as such a policy would require a high level of cooperation with host nations willing to accept I-Kiribati migrants.

Tong's view of the inevitability of relocation has often been viewed and interpreted as overly pessimistic. However, this is not necessarily the case. He has always stated that relocation would be an option of last resort and every effort should be made to avoid such a scenario if at all possible. From his perspective it would be far better to plan for managed migration rather than wait for more of a disaster response scenario when relocation would still have to happen, but in a more haphazard, ad hoc manner. Tong was also one of the few people to question the narrative of 'disappearing' islands. He raised the possibility of I-Kiribati being able to maintain sovereign control over their existing exclusive economic zone territorial waters, even if there was no longer a resident population. This raises a number of interesting questions relating to international law and what are the recognized characteristics of statehood. The generally accepted minimum criteria for statehood are a defined territory, resident population and recognition by other states. Arguably the exclusive economic zone already recognised under the UN Convention of the Law of the Sea constitutes territory, albeit marine territory. No number is set for minimum population so a residual population on any remaining land area, or potentially even a floating platform of some description, could meet this criteria. The crucial element is recognition by other states. If this could be secured then Kiribati could continue to maintain statehood, albeit with a relocated population, and also any income derived from marine resources, including potentially lucrative sea-bed mining operations.

There is no reason why Tuvalu could not also be thinking in terms of managed migration and presenting a case similar to Kiribati's whereby they could retain sovereign control over their marine resources. Yet Tuvaluans' perspective appears to be far more entrenched in resisting relocation despite all the indications that this will, eventually, become necessary. Many Tuvaluans are deeply religious with a number adopting a quite fatalistic attitude. Some will quote the Bible saying that God had told Noah there would be no second great flood, therefore the sea will not rise as climate scientists predict. Whilst this may seem quite irrational to some outside of the community if it is a strongly held belief then it has to be understood and acknowledged. It may also be the case that Tuvaluans are generally more resistant to accepting things they would prefer to deny. They certainly have a very strong sense of belonging to their homeland, but so to do Marshallese and I-Kiribati.

CHALLENGES

Although each of the communities considered here have differing perspectives they do share some common challenges. For the Marshall Islanders they have to balance their criticism of US policies, especially in relation to the failure of the Trump administration to maintain some of the more environmentally-friendly policies of the previous Obama administration, against the likelihood of having to relocate. Some Marshall Islanders may prefer to choose an alternative destination but the US would be the most straightforward to relocate to in terms of the long-standing relationship built up under the Compact of Free Association. There are also several Marshallese communities already well-established in the US which would make relocation and integration easier than would be the case in countries that do not already have such Diaspora communities. Therefore, the Marshallese challenge is to determine to what extent they wish to fight for survival within their homeland or at what point to recognize that present and future generations do not have a future in situ but need to make the most of the opportunities they can find or create in the US.

Kiribati appears to have already come to terms with one of the greatest challenges they face. The government, if not all of the population, have taken a position of begrudgingly accepting the argument that there will need to be some form of relocation. The challenge now is how to develop the necessary training to enhance the skills of the population to make them employable and welcomed overseas. This is all the more challenging in an era of austerity and cutbacks with employment opportunities reducing in the potential host destinations. What could make a fundamental difference, to all of the states facing so-called 'existential' threats, would be the possibility of a viable national income being sustained post-relocation. This would be a novel development among the community of nation-states but not impossible. There would be a marked difference in attitude towards hosting migrants who are arriving following the loss of their territory and those that arrive with an ongoing revenue stream. This could reverse the widespread conception of refugees and asylum seekers as being problematic to a scenario where there could even be competition among states to act as their host country. Even if such an arrangement were to be accepted by the international diplomatic community there would still be some challenges to address with regard to the practical aspects of managing this income and then deciding how to distribute this wealth throughout the community. Some proportion would have to be paid to the host country with regard to rental for physical space or some form of taxation. This may involve some lengthy and contentious discussions between the migrant community and their 'host'. However, this is a far better problem to have than to be without territory and also without income.

The challenge for Tuvalu is perhaps the most serious as many of the islanders feel that the threat of climate change and sea-level rise has been exaggerated and over-emphasised. Moreover, the dynamic of this

understanding of their situation has been impacted upon by international
non-governmental organisations and related media reporting suggesting
that the demise of Tuvalu as a functioning state is imminent. In some
respect one might imagine that having external actors 'championing'
Tuvalu's cause would be welcomed. The counter-argument to this though
is that if the international community, particularly donor governments,
believe Tuvalu is living on borrowed time then why should anyone invest
aid and other resources to support what might be seen as a lost cause. As
an overseas aid-dependent economy the fear of losing long-term support
from donors must be a significant concern.

OUTLOOK

The longer-term outlook for each of the states referred to here will vary
both in terms of what actually happens to them and, equally importantly,
how they react to such changes. For the Marshall Islands they have the,
arguably dubious, advantage of close political, economic and military ties
to the US mainland. The US continues to see these islands as important
strategic outposts in the central Pacific region. The Obama administration's
'Pacific Pivot' strategy of building up military investment and presence in
the Asia-Pacific region is one aspect of the Obama legacy that appears to
be staying in tact under President Trump. If anything there seems to be
even more military spending in the US budget and a proportion of this
expenditure is being directed towards the Marshall Islands. Of course,
investment in the US bases in this territory will not necessarily make the
islands any more habitable for the majority of Marshallese. Some may
benefit from employment opportunities at US military installations but the
strategic priorities for the US will, understandably, be focussed on the
operation of the bases and far less on the well-being of the wider
population. Over time it is likely that environmental conditions in the more
densely populated islands will deteriorate and food and water insecurity
will rise. With the exception of those directly employed on the bases many
Marshallese, particularly those in the younger generations, will look

towards the US as more appealing in terms of education and employment opportunities and a generally improved standard of living. There is already a pattern of out-migration among younger Marshallese and this is likely to increase.

With the active support of the Kiribati government it follows that out-migration will increase here as well. Again the younger generation are understandably being targeted with revised education strategies that place a greater emphasis on vocational training and the development of transferable skills. Such an approach could be seen to be applicable in any community, but has greater resonance within a community that is increasingly seeing the future of its youthful population being overseas. It should be noted though that however developed these skills become any migration for employment will be determined not so much by I-Kiribati but within the economies and societies they are aiming to migrate to. Australia and New Zealand already operate seasonal worker schemes that attract Pacific islanders from across the region. By definition these are temporary contracts with the expectation that workers will return to their home islands at the end of the contract period. Despite, or possibly because of, significant numbers of Pacific Islanders already resident in Australia and New Zealand both of these states have elements within their respective societies that would argue against further in-migration from the region. Across the world controlling migration has become a matter of political concern and something that has lent itself to the whipping up of racial and cultural tension by some within the popular media. In periods of economic downturn or recession it will also be harder for migrant workers to secure well-paid employment. Moreover, it is one thing for a host country to take in individuals on temporary work visas and quite another to accommodate whole, extended families on a more permanent basis.

The outlook for Tuvalu is perhaps the most difficult to estimate of all of the territories considered here. Whereas Marshallese and I-Kiribati have a sense of where their respective futures might lie, if Tuvaluans are determined to stay on their islands for as long as possible then their future will largely be determined by climatic conditions and their consequences. Therefore, this could take decades of slowly deteriorating living conditions or, more likely, a combination of strong winds and a king tide could lead to a catastrophic inundation which does not subsequently recede. The international network of climate change activists continues to cite Tuvalu as being the 'canary in the coalmine' in terms of their 'front-line' position facing the negative impacts of climate change. As noted above this could be an advantage for Tuvalu as this should continue to put pressure on the major industrialised powers to cut-back on their greenhouse gas emissions. Yet this approach could backfire if the reaction is to think Tuvalu is already beyond saving and that the best thing the international community can do is to assist with the relocation of the islanders - a short-term curative rather than long-term preventative approach.

CONCLUSION

With regard to the issue of global governance these small island developing states in the central Pacific region may appear fairly inconsequential to anyone not living in one of these communities. However, they have achieved international prominence because of the extreme environmental challenges they are facing. What should be remembered is that although they are 'remote' island states the difficulties they are experiencing in terms of maintaining food and water security should be thought of as representing similar patterns on a global scale, although these are often barely noticed by wealthier individuals who have sufficient disposable incomes to meet all of their basic needs. When environmental activists proclaim 'We are all Tuvalu' they are making connections between the immediacy of environmental degradation in a very specific location with the broader, global patterns of resources depletion, pollution and dwindling biodiversity that has an impact on everyone in the world.

As individual 'micro-states' each of the above have very little power or influence in the global political sphere. There are bodies such as the Alliance of Small Island States (AOSIS) which can act as a forum for collective action. Yet, even with over forty members, this body is still not realistically comparable to the US, China, Russia or the European Union. What these island states may be able to achieve, and repeatedly try to, is act as a warning and wake-up call to the rest of the global community of states and their citizens. If the more developed states do not recognize the broader patterns of unsustainable development that most of their economies are based on then they will also soon be on the 'front-line' of climate change. In many respects of course we already are on this front-line, yet some of us are able to maintain a sense of denial by closing ourselves off from the natural world. For too many people the negative impacts of climate change are things that happen to other people in other places.

REFERENCES

Adichie, Chimamanda Ngozi. 2009. *The Danger of a Single Story*, https://www.youtube.com/watch?v=D9Ihs241zeg. Accessed 8th July 2017.

Davenport, Coral. 2015. http://www.nytimes.com/interactive/2015/12/02/world/The-Marshall-Islands-Are-Disappearing.html?_r=0. Accessed 8th July 2017.

Ferris, Elizabeth, Cernea, Michael M. and Daniel Petz. 2011. *On the Frontline of Climate Change and Displacement: Learning from and with Pacific Island Countries*. London: The Brookings Institution and the London School of Economics Project on Internal Displacement.

Gerrard, Michael B. and Gregory E. Wannier. 2013. *Threatened Island Nations: Legal Implications of Rising Seas and a Changing Climate*. Cambridge: Cambridge University Press.

Government of Kiribati. 2014. *'Kiribati students graduate with internationally-recognized qualifications'*, Office of the President of Kiribati, http://www.climate.gov.ki/2014/07/21 Accessed 8th July 2017.

http://avalon.law.yale.edu/20th_century/intam03.asp#art3 Accessed 8th July 2017.

Mogelgaard, Kathleen and Heather McGray. 2015. *When Adaptation is not Enough: Paris agreement recognizes "Loss and Damage."* World Resources Institute Blog. Accessed 8th July 2017.

Parry, Jane. 2010. "Pacific Islanders pay heavy price for abandoning traditional diet." *Bulletin of the World Health Organization*, 88(7): 481-560.

Pashley, Alex. 2016. "Kiribati President: Climate-induced migration is 5 years away", *Climate Change News*. http://www. Climate change news.com. Accessed 8th July 2017.

Perry, Nick. 2016. "The US is spending nearly $1 billion to build a radar instillation that could end up underwater", *UK Business Insider*. Associated Press, http://uk.businessinsider.com/us-radar-global-warming-climate-change-2016-10?r=US&IR=T. Accessed 8th July 2017.

Quonadovu, Sikeli. 2017. "Tuvalu Prime Minister: Relocation not the Answer to Climate Change", *Pacific Islands Report*, 3rd July 2017. http://www.pireport.org/articles/2017/07/03/tuvalu-prime-minister-relocation-not-answer-climate-change. Accessed 8th July 2017.

Smith, Robert W. and Thomas L. Bradford. 1998. "Island Disputes and the Law of the Sea: An examination of sovereignty and delimitation disputes." *Maritime Briefing*, 2(4), International Boundaries Research Unit, University of Durham.

In: Global Governance
Editor: Sagarika Dutt

ISBN: 978-1-53612-969-4
© 2018 Nova Science Publishers, Inc.

Chapter 5

UNESCO'S CONTRIBUTION TO GLOBAL COMMUNICATIONS: RECONCILING THE FREE FLOW OF INFORMATION WITH INCLUSIVE DEVELOPMENT?

Sagarika Dutt

Senior Lecturer in International Relations and Subject Leader,
Nottingham Trent University, Nottingham, UK

ABSTRACT

UNESCO's activities in the field of communications have always been geared to the free flow of information on a global scale. However, third world protests against the dominant flow of news from the industrialised countries and demands for a New World Information and Communication Order, in the 1970s, were construed by the western liberal democracies and western media as an attack on the free flow of information. The issue was resolved by adopting a technical approach that led to the creation of the International Programme for the Development of Communication (IPDC). This research assesses how successful UNESCO has been in maintaining a balance between promoting the free flow of information and helping developing countries build up their own information and communication infrastructure. The organisation acknowledges that 'inequalities persist in the capabilities of Member States to identify, produce, disseminate and use information to build and apply knowledge for human development'.

INTRODUCTION

The terrorist attacks on Charlie Hebdo on 7 January 2015 in Paris were described by the (western) media as a war on freedom and an assault on democracy. It was one of the most high profile terrorist attacks on French soil in recent years and was dubbed 'The French 9/11' by Le Monde. The article published in *The Guardian* the following day said that 'French newspapers have united in condemning the killing of journalists at the satirical magazine Charlie Hebdo as an unacceptable assault on the freedom of expression' (Penketh and Branigan, 2015). This is a reference to Article 19 of the Universal Declaration of Human Rights that says that 'Everyone has the right to freedom of opinion and expression; this right includes freedom to hold opinions without interference and to seek, receive and impart information and ideas through any media and regardless of frontiers'.

The Twitter hashtag #je suis Charlie (I am Charlie), a slogan and logo created by French art director, Joachim Roncin, expressed worldwide solidarity after the attack. It is ironical that these attacks took place in Paris where UNESCO has its headquarters. UNESCO works in the fields of education, natural sciences, social and human sciences, culture, and communication and information. Its strategic objectives for 2014-2021 include promoting freedom of expression, media development and access to information and knowledge. UNESCO's Director-General, Irina Bokova, condemned the attack on Charlie Hebdo, and described it as an attack on the media and freedom of expression. She stated: 'The world community cannot allow extremists to silence the free flow of opinions and ideas. The perpetrators of this attack must be brought to justice and UNESCO is ever more determined to stand for a free and independent press' (UNESCOPRESS 2015). The attacks on Charlie Hebdo have highlighted, yet again, the challenges to the freedom of expression.

This chapter traces the history of UNESCO's involvement in efforts to promote the freedom of expression and the free flow of information on a global scale.[14] It argues that UNESCO was created after the Second World War to promote western liberal values and principles but like the rest of the UN system has had to broaden its agenda to promote development. The recognition of the importance of communications to the development process lies at the heart of UNESCO's work. But unfortunately, it lost the good will of some of its western member states when it became involved in debates that they did not approve of such as those relating to a New World Information and Communication Order (NWICO). Third World protests against the dominant flow of news from the western developed countries and demands for a New World Information and Communication Order, in the 1970s, were construed by the western liberal democracies and the western media as an attack on the free flow of information. This research assesses how successful UNESCO has been in maintaining a balance between promoting the free flow of information and helping developing countries build up their own information and communication infrastructure. The organisation acknowledges that *'inequalities persist in the capabilities of Member States to identify, produce, disseminate and use information to build and apply knowledge for human development'. (Approved Programme and Budget, 2010-2011, 35/C5 Approved, Major Programme V, para. 05003, Paris: UNESCO, 2010, p.168).*

The Global Communication Problematique

Global communication has always been an important part of international relations and the growth of capitalism. This led to the establishment of two of the oldest UN specialised agencies, the UPU and the ITU. The ITU was founded in 1865 in Paris as the International

---

[14] UNESCO makes it very clear that 'As the UN agency with a specific mandate to foster freedom of expression, and its corollaries, press freedom and freedom of information, UNESCO sees these rights as crucial foundations of democracy, development and dialogue, and as preconditions for protecting and promoting all other human rights' ('Press freedom on all platforms', UNESCO website, accessed April 2017).

Telegraph Union and was renamed the International Telecommunications Union in 1934. The UPU (Universal Postal Union) was established in 1874 and has its headquarters in Berne. ITU claims that it is 'committed to connecting all the world's people – wherever they live and whatever their means. Through our work, we protect and support everyone's fundamental right to communicate'. (ITU website). It goes on to say that 'virtually every facet of modern life …depends on information and communication technologies (ICTs)' and that 'ITU is at the very heart of the ICT sector'. However, global communication is as much about content as it is about technology.

While advances in information and communication technologies are welcomed by all states and societies as they have the potential to benefit them, the issues of ownership and control of the means of communication are more problematic as they shape structures of power that exist between and within states. The irony is that while the freedom of expression has always been associated with human progress and democratic societies, 'the rise and expansion of major western communication companies…has reflected the extension of neoliberal policies of liberalisation, deregulation and privatisation of markets and industries' (Wilkins 2001, 20). Wilkins argues that 'these developments have been extremely harmful for the prospects of attaining human security not only in terms of the satisfaction of human needs but also in terms of the meaningful participation of citizens in the political, economic and cultural processes that structure daily life'.

LAYING THE LIBERAL FOUNDATIONS
OF THE ORGANISATION

When UNESCO was founded in 1946, western states had considerable influence in the drafting of its constitution. The Conference of Allied Ministers of Education (CAME), that met for the first time in November 1942, submitted a draft constitution for the consideration of the founding conference, as did the French government. (Dutt 2002; Krill de Capello

1970; Sewell 1975; Laves and Thomson 1958) At the initiative of the US delegation, article 1.2 (a) was incorporated into the constitution which states that the organization will 'collaborate in the work of advancing the mutual knowledge and understanding of peoples, through all means of mass communication and to that end recommend such international agreements as may be necessary to promote the free flow of ideas by word and image' (Dutt 1995, 197). The US argued in favour of a privileged position for freedom of information from state control among the human rights and fundamental freedoms for which the UN was to have general responsibility.[15] The Commission on Human Rights was called upon, by the UN, to examine the concept of freedom of information from a human rights perspective, and to convene a conference on the subject.

But these initiatives also raised the issue of the obligations and responsibilities inherent in freedom of information, and of the content and goals of communication (Wells 1987, 47-8). A division of labour began to emerge between the UN and UNESCO based on the distinction between the 'political' and the 'technical' aspects of the subject. Wells writes that debate within UNESCO on the goals and the responsibilities of information remained muted until the 1970s when the rise of satellite communication led to a greater sense of the relationship between the means and ends of communication, i.e., the 'technical' and the 'political' aspects of the subject (Wells 1987, 57), and UNESCO was drawn into political debates about information and communication policy. She argues that this should not, however, be seen as 'politicisation', but rather as 'de-

---

[15] The first amendment to the United States Constitution makes freedom of expression the constitutive principle of democracy: in the absence of freedom of expression, no society can truly call itself 'free'...The protection of freedom of expression and of freedom of information should therefore be absolute and without exception. The conception defended by Article 10 of the European Convention on Human Rights is rather different. There can be no freedom (and therefore no freedom of expression) without the exercise of a corresponding responsibility. Thus, the Convention justifies certain legitimate and desirable restrictions when certain content can prove damaging. These two possible approaches to the conflict between freedom of expression and other rights explain the difficulties that arise when one tries to implement the second one – the 'European' view that implies a certain form of regulation – to a vector of freedom of expression such as the internet, whose principles derive from the first view (extract from UNESCO 2005, p.43).

technicisation', 'through active resumption by UNESCO of concern with a neglected portion of its constitutional mandate' (Wells 1987, 58).

SOVIET INITIATIVES IN THE FIELD OF COMMUNICATIONS

Although up to the mid-1960s UNESCO played mainly a technical role in the field of communications, the values underlying its activities and the ideological principles guiding its work were based on western liberalism. In other words, geared to promoting the free flow of information and ideas on a global scale. However, from the mid-1960s Soviet ideology in the field of communications began to make inroads into the organisation. In 1972, the 17th UNESCO General Conference adopted a Soviet sponsored 'Declaration of Guiding Principles on the Use of Satellite Broadcasting for the Free Flow of Information, The Spread of Education and Greater Cultural Exchanges'. It also adopted another Soviet sponsored resolution requesting the Director-General 'to prepare and to submit to the General Conference at its 18th session a draft declaration concerning the fundamental principles governing the use of the mass information media with a view to strengthening peace and international understanding and combating war propaganda, racialism and apartheid' (Dutt 1995, 198-200).

However, a group of experts with a mandate to advise the Director-General about the text of the draft declaration reported that it had been difficult to strike an appropriate balance between the concept of freedom of information, and the need for a sense of responsibility to prevent abuses of this freedom. Several changes were made in the draft declaration by the experts. The title of the declaration was changed from 'Draft Declaration on Fundamental Principles Governing the Use of the Mass Media' to 'Draft Declaration on Fundamental Principles on the Role of the Mass Media in Strengthening Peace and International Understanding and in Combating War Propaganda, Racism and Apartheid'. The purpose of this change was to show that the Declaration would not be a 'statement of moral duties resting upon the mass media and was not intended to set out principles that would...be imposed upon the mass media by legislation' (Dutt 1995, 200).

There was a debate on this draft declaration in the Programme Commission during which divergent and conflicting views were expressed. The conflict was mainly of a East-West and North-South nature. While some delegates expressed the view that countries should have the right to take measures to protect themselves against mass media that did not act responsibly, others felt that government intervention was not the way to encourage mass media to respect ethical standards and act responsibly. Delegates of developing countries addressed the North-South divide in the field of information and communication and stressed the need for a multidirectional flow of information. They felt that the cultural integrity of their countries required freedom from undue influence of large foreign media organisations, serving private interests and often monopolistic in character. They also expressed the view that the principle of free flow of information was not being practiced when countries lacked the production capacity to participate in such a flow on an equal basis (Dutt 1995, 200-201).

THREE DIFFERENT IDEOLOGICAL POSITIONS

Thus during the cold war years, three different ideological positions on the issue were held by the member states of the UN/UNESCO. The western position centred on the free flow of information and ideas between peoples. The freedom of information from state control, it was posited, would lead to mutual knowledge, and understanding between peoples, and to peace. This sits well with the minds of men thesis on which UNESCO is based. The preamble to UNESCO's constitution begins with the famous words 'since wars begin in the minds of men, it is in the minds of men that the defenses of peace must be constructed.' The statement has its origins in British prime minister, Clement Attlee's inaugural address to UNESCO's founding conference in which he stressed the necessity of creating an organization for educational and cultural co-operation with the statement that 'wars begin in the minds of men'. The system of supranational co-operation in different fields was incomplete without intellectual co-operation. It was argued that since the Second World War had its origins in the perversion of human values, re-construction and the establishment of a new order of peace would have to be founded on the basis of intellectual understanding. Attlee's statement was developed further by Archibald MacLeish, and thus became the basic idea on which UNESCO is based (Dutt 2002, 8; Krill de Capello 1970; Wells 1987, 26).

The Soviet bloc position was diametrically opposite to the western position, although the Soviets objected to the western definitions of the debate in terms of free versus state-controlled presses. The Soviets held that the state has an ethical duty under the UN Charter and UNESCO constitution to ensure the conditions necessary for peace, including restricting the dissemination of certain types of material such as war propaganda. They were also not in favour of the domination of global information flows by the western media (Wells 1987, 32-34; Dutt 1995, 198). The third world position was that 'given existing global communications structures, traditional rights and freedoms in this sphere have served mainly to advance the interests of a few well-endowed countries and groups, but are virtually meaningless for the larger part of the world's population' (Wells 1987, 37). This was the basis on which the demand for a New World Information and Communication Order was made, as discussed later in this chapter.

These ideological divisions were reflected in the work of the 18th General Conference, held in 1974, which authorized the Director-General 'to prepare, with a view to strengthening international understanding and world peace, guidelines for national codes of ethics designed to promote the sense of responsibility which should accompany the full exercise of freedom of information, including those principles of democratization in the use of the media of mass communication that ensure this, and to encourage their application by national media councils' (Dutt 1995, 201). However, the idea of a code of ethics has never appealed to the western states which felt that it was inimical to the concept of 'freedom of information'. During the discussion in the Programme Commission several speakers expressed their reservations. Some delegates were of the opinion that international standards in this field would be unacceptable to the professional organizations. It was also pointed out that the constitutions of many countries would not permit intervention in a field which fell within the purview of professional organizations themselves. However, the Assistant Director-General for Communication indicated that what was planned were guidelines which would not impose rules of conduct on individual countries (Dutt 1995, 201-202).

In 1976 a new draft declaration on the 'Fundamental principles governing the use of the Mass Media in strengthening peace and international understanding and in combating war propaganda, racialism and apartheid', was debated in the Programme Commission III of the 19th General Conference. Different opinions were expressed on the issue of government control of the media. Some members cautioned that complete freedom of the press and the absence of censorship were essential guarantees of individual rights, a protection against the inroads of government and an early warning device for the authorities, allowing them to adapt their policies to the wishes of the broad public in time. Others argued that the draft should not be interpreted as promoting state control of all media, but only of those already under state jurisdiction. A third group of speakers, who were in favour of some regulation of the media, argued that the freedom of communication and the free flow of information should be protected, but coupled with the notion of responsibility. They felt that freedom could not mean the right of the stronger to impose their values on the weaker (Dutt 1995, 203). The draft was referred to the Drafting and Negotiations Group. But it was unable to reach a consensus. Eventually, after extremely wide-ranging consultations the 20th session of the General Conference succeeded in adopting by consensus a 'Declaration on Fundamental Principles concerning the Contribution of the Mass Media to Strengthening Peace and International Understanding, to the Promotion of Human Rights and to Countering Racialism, Apartheid and Incitement to war'. The 21st General Conference followed this up by adopting a resolution on the application of this declaration (Dutt 1995, 203-206).

Nordenstreng comments that the Mass Media Declaration was the product of the Non-Aligned Movement (NAM) and the Soviet-led East sharing the same strategic interests against the corporate-dominated West. But he also describes it as 'a monument to political compromise' (Nordenstreng 2012, 33-38). The irony is that taken at face value, all aspects of this Declaration, except apartheid, are relevant even today as the world is still dealing with these issues.

THE DEMAND FOR A NEW WORLD INFORMATION AND COMMUNICATION ORDER (NWICO)

The demand for a NWICO by the developing countries was a reaction to the dominance of the western media that had led to **an imbalance in the flow of information** with most of the news flowing from developed to developing countries.[16] This quantitative assessment created a sense of injustice, especially as it was accompanied by other more qualitative observations. For instance, that the most powerful countries did not only 'shout down' a number of developing countries but that they also painted a distorted, not to say disparaging, picture of them. However, the western countries held the view that the imbalance in the flow of information was essentially the result of the inadequacy of human, technical and material resources in the developing countries. The problem was thus considered to be structural in the technical sense and one that could be solved by technical and financial means. The approach that western states preferred to take in dealing with the problems and aspirations of the developing countries in the field of information and communication was therefore technical rather than normative. The concept of an NWICO was not acceptable to them as it addressed not only the quantitative but also the

---

[16] However, as members of the MacBride Commission noted, 'Communication is not just news. It is a determining factor of all social processes and a fundamental component of the way societies are organized'. Singh writes that 'While seeking to correct the information imbalance (in terms of news and other information content flows) between the North and the South, what also emerged from NWICO were ideas emphasizing self-reliance in individual developing nations and collective reliance across them' (Singh 2011, 117).

qualitative aspects of information, which means content (Dutt 1995, 206-207).

In 1976 the General Conference at its 19th session decided to undertake a review 'of the totality of the problem of communication in modern society'. Following this decision, in December 1977, the Director-General established a 16 member **International Commission for the Study of Communication Problems**, under the chairmanship of Sean MacBride, former Minister for Foreign Affairs of Ireland and holder of the Nobel and Lenin Peace Prizes. The Commission did not have an easy task to perform. MacBride writes that in the 1970s international debates on communications issues 'had stridently reached points of confrontation in many areas. Third world protests against the dominant flow of news from the industrialized countries were often construed as attacks on the free flow of information. Defenders of journalistic freedom were labelled intruders on national sovereignty. Varying concepts of news values and the roles, rights and responsibilities of journalists were widely contended, as was the potential contribution of the mass media to the solution of major world problems'. Given this divisive atmosphere which surrounded the start of the Commission's work, MacBride's concern from the beginning was how to achieve a balanced, non-partisan, and objective analysis of the problem and how to meet the challenge of reaching the broadest consensus possible on the major issues before them (Dutt 1995, 207).

The Commission submitted its interim report at the 20th session of the General Conference which was discussed in the Programme Commission. **Divergent and irreconcilable views** were expressed by the delegates on controversial issues such as codes of behaviour for journalists and content of information. At the 17th plenary meeting of the General Conference, the US delegate commented that though they found much to admire in the descriptive portions of the report, they found the closing pages, which contained certain prescriptions, 'less balanced' and 'less well-grounded'. Nevertheless, the 20th General Conference adopted a resolution inviting the Director-General to request the members of the Commission 'to address themselves, in the course of preparing their final report, to the analysis and proposal of concrete and practical measures leading to the establishment of a more just and effective world information order' (UNESCO 1978, 100; Dutt 1995, 206-211).

THE REPORT OF THE INTERNATIONAL COMMISSION FOR THE STUDY OF COMMUNICATION PROBLEMS

The final report of the Commission was published under the title **'Many Voices, One World'**. The subtitle is a bit more provocative, from a western point of view, 'Towards a new, more just and more efficient world information and communication order'. The report is divided into five parts, each consisting of several chapters, addressing different aspects of that part of the report. The main parts are: Communication and Society; Communication Today; Problems and Issues of Common Concern; The Institutional and Professional Framework; Communication Tomorrow. It identified communication's main functions, such as 'the collection, storage, processing and dissemination of news, data, pictures, facts and messages, opinions and comments required in order to understand and react knowledgeably to personal, environmental, national and international conditions, as well as to be in a position to take appropriate decisions'. Other functions are 'the transmission of knowledge so as to foster intellectual development, the formation of character and the acquisition of skills and capacities at all stages of life'; the promotion of debate and discussion of public issues; the dissemination of cultural and artistic products; and entertainment (International Commission for the Study of Communication Problems 1980, 14). The report recognises that communication is a political instrument and argues that 'Communication, taken as a whole, is incomprehensible without reference to its political dimension' (Ibid., 18).

The crucial relationships are between **communication and power**, and **communication and freedom**. As regards the latter, the report argues categorically that 'the presence or absence of freedom of expression is one of the most reliable indications of freedom in all its aspects in any nation' (Ibid., 19). But it also addresses the issue of responsibility: 'All too frequently, the two concepts, freedom and responsibility, are seen and posited as being at variance with one another, whereas in fact they are both key factors of civilization' (Ibid., 22). There are also varying ideas on the relationship between communication and power (Ibid., 23). While some regard information as a vital instrument for keeping a check on authority, others believe that it should be at the service of the state. 'One thing is certain: communication has taken on such an overwhelming importance that even in societies with privately owned media systems, the State imposes some degree of regulation' (Ibid., 20). But the report also acknowledges that while 'in theory everybody enjoyed the right to the freedom of expression, but not everyone could exercise it equally' (Ibid., 20). The 'financial requisites of technical progress' have also led to the concentration of the power to communicate in the hands of a few (and that includes the state). 'As a result of this concentration, the number of message-transmitters, at least relatively speaking, has been reduced. At the same time, the strength of the surviving transmitters has been reinforced' (Ibid., 20). The report goes on to argue that it isn't 'only at the national level that these inequalities make their impact; on an international scale, they have created the present imbalance in the sphere of communication between rich and poor countries' (Ibid.).

Part I, chapter three, is on **the international dimension**. It argues that while almost eighty nations had been liberated from colonial domination in the second half of the twentieth century, 'political independence is…restricted, and even undermined, by economic dependence, and especially by the nature of relationships and the international division of labour between developed and developing countries' (Ibid., 34). Independence is meaningless without the communication resources needed to safeguard it. 'Unfortunately, in today's world, communication has all too frequently become an exchange between unequal partners' (Ibid.). The report argues that the commitment to the principle of the free flow of information should not lead to a one way flow, and that the principle should be restated as 'free and balanced flow' (Ibid., 36). It also highlights **communication's role in international relations and in solving problems which threaten mankind's survival** – 'problems which cannot be solved without consultations and cooperation between countries: the arms race, famine, poverty, illiteracy, racialism, unemployment, economic injustice, population growth, destruction of the environment, discrimination against women' (Ibid., 34-5). The irony is that even after all these years, the international community is still addressing these problems. The report notes that 'the mass media have a vital role to play in alerting international public opinion to these – and other – problems, in making them better understood, in generating the will to solve them, and equipping ordinary people, if necessary, to put pressure on authorities to implement appropriate solutions' (Ibid.).

CONCLUSIONS AND RECOMMENDATIONS

The final part of the report contains its **Conclusions and Recommendations**. These conclusions, it is claimed, are 'founded on the firm conviction that communication is a basic individual right as well as a collective one required by all communities and nations. Freedom of information – and more specifically the right to seek, receive and impart information - is a fundamental human right; indeed, a prerequisite for many others' (Ibid., 253). The report also argues that communication can achieve its potential only if the prevailing political, economic and social conditions allow it to do so. 'It is in this context that the democratization of communication at national and international levels, as well as the larger role of communication in democratizing society, acquired utmost importance' (Ibid., 253). The report emphasizes that as a result, 'it is essential to develop comprehensive national communication policies linked to overall social, cultural and economic development objectives' (Ibid., 254). Furthermore, national governments and the international community should recognise the urgency of according communications higher priority in planning and funding.

The report then goes on to say that the considerations which are developed in the main body of the report are intended to provide a framework for the development of a new information and communication order. Furthermore, crucial decisions need to be taken at both the national and international levels, regarding the development of communication. 'Since communication is interwoven with every aspect of life, it is clearly of the utmost importance that the existing "communication gap" be rapidly narrowed and eventually eliminated' (Ibid., 254). The report recommends the formulation by all nations, and particularly developing countries, of comprehensive communication policies linked to overall social, cultural, economic, and political goals. It also recommends that 'the communication component in all development projects should receive adequate financing' (Ibid., 256). The report makes it very clear that while developing countries had the primary responsibility to reduce their dependence in the field of communications, it was also the responsibility of the international community to take appropriate steps 'to replace dependence, dominance and inequality by more fruitful and more open relations of interdependence and complementarity, based on mutual interest and the equal dignity of nations and peoples' (Ibid., 268).

McKenna (2012, 96) comments that the MacBride report 'may be seen as generally positive towards the Right to Communicate, although clearly, as with many other elements of the report, compromise was a key feature, reflecting the varying positions taken by the commission's membership [on] specific matters'. In Singh's opinion 'the MacBride Commission Report remains an enduring legacy of the NWICO era. The intellectual heart of the Report is the forceful consistency with which it makes the case for communication for a viable society. It questions the instrumental wisdom of merely providing infrastructures or access, and it broadens communication to beyond messages and information. It connects communication to people's everyday lives in terms of both material prosperity and human dignity' (Singh 2012, 156).

The recommendations are grouped under the following headings or themes: **Strengthening independence and self-reliance**, which includes, communication policies, strengthening capacities and particular challenges and basic needs; **Social consequences and new tasks**, which includes integrating communication into development, facing the technological challenge, strengthening cultural identity, reducing the commercialization of communication, and access to technical information; **Professional integrity and standards**, which includes responsibility of journalists, towards improved international reporting, and protection of journalists; **Democratization of communication** which includes human rights, removal of obstacles, diversity and choice, and integration and participation; **Fostering international co-operation,** which includes partners for development, strengthening collective self-reliance, international mechanisms, and towards international understanding. The final sections of the report emphasise that the mass media can make a substantial contribution towards achieving the international goal of strengthening peace, international security and cooperation, and the lessening of international tensions. It recommends that 'national communication policies should be consistent with adopted international communication principles and should seek to create a climate of mutual understanding and peaceful co-existence among nations' (Ibid., 271). Mansell and Nordenstreng (2007, 17) write that the themes 'emphasise the essential link between media and communication policies and social, cultural, and economic development objectives. They also stress the importance of participation by all factions of society in the definition of these objectives.' The MacBride report was republished in 2004 by Rowman and Littlefield which shows that its insights are still relevant. Mansell and Nordenstreng argue that its 'emphases resonate with the current emphasis on the importance of fostering media literacies, of strengthening capacities for local content production, and of widening access to the communication infrastructure'.

UNESCO'S RESOLUTION ON THE FINAL REPORT OF THE INTERNATIONAL COMMISSION FOR THE STUDY OF COMMUNICATION PROBLEMS

At the 21st session of the General Conference, held in 1980 in Belgrade, the Director-General presented a report on the findings of the International Commission for the Study of Communication Problems.

There was a lengthy debate on this report, as well as on the Final Report of the International Commission, in the Programme Commission of the General Conference. While most of the delegates agreed with the Director-General that the Commission had fulfilled its mandate commendably, a number of them also criticized the report and found deficiencies and faults in it. The criticisms were based on quite divergent viewpoints. At the conclusion of the debate, Mr. MacBride said that he was aware of some deficiencies in the Commission's report, but pointed out that the Commission's work had been the first stage in a long journey ahead. It was generally felt that the Commission's report was an important contribution to the study of world communication and information problems, however, it was only one step, although an important one, towards the solution of these problems (Dutt 1995, 208-9).

On the basis of the ideas and lines of convergence that had emerged from the debate and the draft resolutions submitted by the Group of Nine, the Group of 77 and the Socialist Group, a drafting group set up by the Chairman of the Programme Commission prepared a draft resolution and recommended that the General Conference adopt this resolution. The 21st General Conference adopted the resolution at its 37th plenary meeting by consensus. However, the resolution did not endorse any of the conclusions and recommendations of the Commission's report but merely referred them to the member states for study and reflection, and invited them to circulate it widely. It also invited them to communicate their comments and observations on them to the Director-General so that he could make use of them in the preparation of the Second Medium-Term Plan (1984-89). Interested international and regional intergovernmental, non-governmental and professional organizations were also invited to take note of these recommendations and convey their comments and observations to the Director-General (UNESCO, 1980, Resolution 4/19, 68-71; Dutt 1995, 209-210).

From a western perspective section six of the resolution was the most controversial part of the resolution. It set out a number of guidelines for establishing a new world information and communication order. For example, the removal of the internal and external obstacles to a free flow and wider and better balanced dissemination of information and ideas; improving the capacity of developing countries to achieve improvement of their own situations; promoting the plurality of sources and channels of information. The 'sincere will' of the developed countries to help the developing countries attain their objectives was also part of these guidelines. However, the delegates of the western countries such as the Federal Republic of Germany, the UK and Canada stated that they had serious reservations concerning this section of the resolution, and the attempt to define elements of the new world information and communication order (Dutt 1995, 210; UNESCO, 1980, Resolution 4/19, 71).

Meanwhile, the US Congress approved section 109 of the Department of State Authorization Act for fiscal year 1982-83 (Public Law 97-241) which prohibited US contributions to UNESCO if it implemented any policy or procedure that licensed journalists or their publications or restricted the free flow of information within or among countries, or imposed mandatory codes of journalistic practice or ethics. It also required the Secretary of State to report to the Congress on this matter no later than the 1st of February of each year (Dutt 1995, 211).

The western media reacted sharply to the controversies that were raging on at UNESCO on information and communication related issues. A large number of western journalists attended the 20th session of the General Conference and studies reveal that American press coverage of UNESCO during these years was highly partisan, expressed exaggerated fears about the control of information and opinion and often painted a distorted picture of the initiatives being taken by UNESCO in the field of information and communication. In May 1981, representatives of about 60 print and broadcast organizations from 24 countries including the US met in Talloires in the French Alps where they adopted the *Declaration of Talloires*. In this declaration, they affirmed their commitment to the free flow of information, to the universal human right to be fully informed, to free access to all sources of information, and to international efforts aimed at correcting imbalances. The Declaration also stated opposition to censorship and other arbitrary control of information and opinion, to a code of journalistic ethics (other than a voluntary code), to the licensing of journalists by national and international bodies, and to UNESCO's and other intergovernmental bodies' attempts to regulate news content and formulate rules for the press. UNESCO's Director-General, Mr. M'Bow defended UNESCO at this meeting, and made it very clear that the organisation was not trying to weaken press freedoms (Dutt 1995, 214; Roger Coate 1988; Peter Hajnal 1983; Palmer 2012, 50).

THE INTERNATIONAL PROGRAMME FOR THE DEVELOPMENT OF COMMUNICATION

It should be mentioned, however, that western countries were not completely unsympathetic to the needs and aspirations of the developing states in the field of information and communication, and were in favour of UNESCO and the developed countries providing practical and technical assistance to them in their efforts to build up their own information and communication infrastructures and make their own contribution to the free flow of information in the world. This led to the creation of the **International Programme for the Development of Communication (IPDC)**. However, while the main objective of the IPDC was to promote operational activities in the field of information and communication, neither the DEVCOM Conference (held in Paris in April 1980 for promoting cooperation in communication development) nor UNESCO put their faith solely on operational and technical activities for eliminating the existing disparities in communication among different countries. In the preambular part of the DEVCOM Recommendation, it is recalled that 'the existing disparity in communication among different countries will not be eliminated by the mere material development of infrastructures and professional resources and by the transfer of know-how and technologies but that the solution depends also on the elimination of all political, ideological, psychological, economic and technical obstacles which run counter to the development of independent national communication systems and to a freer, wider and more balanced circulation of information'

(Dutt 1995, 212-213). Finally, it must be said that while the western states had shown a great deal of enthusiasm regarding the creation of the IPDC, their financial contributions to the IPDC Special Account were very meagre. There is evidence to suggest that the western states were anxious to ensure that any financial contributions made by them were not 'misspent', which is spent on programmes that they did not approve of (Dutt 1995, 213; Singh 2011, 119; Palmer 2012, 50).

EFFORTS TO 'DEPOLITICIZE' INFORMATION AND COMMUNICATIONS

Following the withdrawal of the US and the UK from UNESCO in 1984 and 1985 respectively, the organization was anxious to dispel all misunderstandings and emphasize its commitment to the free flow of information and the freedom of expression.[17] The idea of a new communication strategy was first mooted by the Executive Board at its 129th session in May 1989. This was followed by a sustained dialogue within the Executive Board and among member states which led to a new programme which called upon UNESCO to work for the development of free, independent and pluralistic media in both the private and public sectors. UNESCO and its member states were urged to facilitate and guarantee for journalists the freedom to report and to have the fullest possible access to information, and to ensure that public and private media

---

[17] For a discussion of the UK and US withdrawals from UNESCO see Dutt 1995. They returned to UNESCO in 1997 and 2003, respectively. But in recent years the US has withheld funding from UNESCO. The US has not provided any funding to the organisation since 2011 when the Palestinian Authority was granted full membership in the organisation. The US had been UNESCO's largest contributor, providing 22% of the organisation's overall budget. The US withheld 'approximately $80 million in FY2012 funding to UNESCO', according to a CRS report for Congress ('US pulls UNESCO funding after Palestine is granted full membership', *The Guardian*, 31 October 2011; 'US withdraws UNESCO funding after it accepts Palestinian membership', *The Telegraph*, 31 October 2011; Josh Levs, 'US cuts UNESCO funding after Palestinian membership vote', CNN, 1 November 2011; 'US loses UNESCO voting rights after stopping funds over Palestine decision', *The Guardian*, 8 November 2011; 'The UNESCO cuts: What's next on the US chopping block', FP, 3 November 2011; CRS report for Congress, 18 March 2013).

in the developing countries are provided with the conditions necessary to consolidate their independence (Dutt 1995, 214-215).

Several regional seminars were organised by UNESCO, often in co-operation with other organisations, on the media. At a seminar organized in Namibia (29 April – 3 May 1991), and entitled 'Promoting an Independent and Pluralistic African Press', participants adopted the 'Windhoek Declaration', which is an important milestone in the struggle for free, independent and pluralistic media in that part of the world. The appointment of a new Director-General, Dr. Frederico Mayor in 1987, paved the way for the depoliticization of the organisation, as did the end of cold war. He was awarded the 45th anniversary prize of the International Federation of Newspaper Publishers (FIEJ) for his 'outstanding contribution to advancing the cause of freedom of expression' in March 1993 (Dutt 1995, 215). By the late 1990s, UNESCO had stopped referring to a New World Information and Communication Order. But efforts to address the issues it raised continued (Masmoudi 2012, 28; Modoux 2012, 143-145).

THE MEDIUM TERM STRATEGY (2002-2007)

UNESCO may have been successful in burying the old NWICO debates but it was aware that not enough had been done to promote equity. As a result the objectives of its Major Programme V – Communication and Information, for the biennium 2002-2003, were: (a) To promote equitable access to information and knowledge, especially in the public domain (b) To promote freedom of expression and strengthen communication capacities (UNESCO 2002, 31C/5). The Medium Term Strategy for 2002-2007 argues that for many people, globalisation means marginalisation, but with its competences in education, the sciences, culture and communication, UNESCO can assist in the quest to 'bring about globalization with a human face'. 'Indeed, knowledge has become a principal force of social transformation. The leaders of virtually all countries have professed their desire to transform their countries into learning economies and knowledge societies'. A prime example is Prime Minister Narendra Modi of India whose government has adopted the Digital India programme ('Digital India scheme gets cabinet nod', *The Statesman* (Kolkata), 21 August 2014, p.2). Knowledge-based and led development has the potential to alleviate many of the problems confronting human societies. But for the free flow of information to be meaningful, access to knowledge alone will not be enough, 'other needs must also be addressed, such as building human capacities and technical skills and developing content necessary to translate knowledge and information into assets of empowerment and production' (UNESCO 2002, 3).

The medium term strategy also emphasised that **bridging the digital divide** between developing and developed countries and within countries is a prime strategic challenge for UNESCO. 'This will entail activities to strengthen capacities and skills, to create content, to enlarge access, to foster scientific research and to share knowledge and information through networking and the communication media and information systems'[18]. In an article published in UNESCO *Sources* Longworth (2000) argues that 'knowledge is the new asset', it is the key to human and economic development. Those communities and countries able to access and optimise knowledge and information -via new communication technologies – are already far better off than those who cannot. She adds that only about 2 per cent of the world's population has stepped 'into the information loop' and that 88 per cent of these people live in the industrialized countries. Similar views are expressed by Paul Kennedy in

[18] But Wade cautions that 'efforts to bridge the digital divide may have the effect of locking developing countries into a new form of dependency on the West. The technologies and "regimes" (international standards governing ICTs) are designed by developed country entities for developed country conditions. As the developing countries participate in ICTs, they become more vulnerable to the increasing complexity of the hardware and software and to the quasi-monopolistic power of providers of key ICT services'. Wade, R. H. 2002. "Bridging the Digital Divide: New Route to Development or New Form of Dependency?" *Global Governance* 8: 443-466. Pieterse has similar concerns. He argues that the digital divide is a 'deeply misleading discourse: the divide is not digital but socioeconomic, but representing the divide in technical terms suggests technical solutions'. Pieterse, J. N. 2010. Chapter 10, 'Digital Capitalism and Development:The Unbearable Lightness of ICT4D' in *Development Theory*, Los Angeles, London, New Delhi: Sage, p.167.

another article (Kennedy 2000). The concerns raised by UNESCO's World Communication and Information Report 1999-2000 are echoed by many writers. Monique Perrot-Lanaud (2000) writes that the benefits of ICTs are far from being evenly distributed and if present tendencies continue, vast segments of the population will be excluded from the information society. UNESCO's activities in the first decade of the 21st century were thus to be guided by the resolution of the ECOSOC (July 2000) on the role of information technology in the context of a knowledge-based global economy and by the UN Millennium Declaration (September 2000). These texts called for the creation of an international strategic partnership to bridge the digital divide and establish a knowledge society that is open and non-exclusive (UNESCO 2002a, 45).

WORLD SUMMIT ON THE INFORMATION SOCIETY

On 21 December 2001 the United Nations General Assembly adopted resolution 56/183 endorsing the holding of the World Summit on the Information Society (WSIS) to promote the 'urgently needed access of all countries to information, knowledge and communication technologies for development', in two phases. The first phase was to take place in Geneva (10-12 December 2003) and the second phase in Tunis (16-18 November 2005). The International Telecommunications Union (ITU) had taken the initiative of putting it on the agenda of the UN, following a proposal by the government of Tunisia. Resolution 73 of the ITU Plenipotentiary Conference, Minneapolis, 1998, noted 'the emergence of the concept of the information society in which telecommunications play a central role' and recognised 'that ITU is the organization best able to seek appropriate ways to provide for development of the telecommunication sector geared to economic, social and cultural development' and instructed the ITU Council 'to consider and decide on the Union's contribution to the holding of a world summit on the information society, with a view to…drawing up a strategic plan of action for concerted development of the information society by defining an agenda covering the objectives to be achieved and the resources to be mobilized'. The UN resolution recognised 'the urgent need to harness the potential of knowledge and technology for promoting the goals of the United Nations Millennium Declaration'. It invited governments to participate actively in the preparatory process of the summit and to be represented in the summit at the highest possible level. It also encouraged 'effective contributions from and the active participation of' all relevant UN bodies, and encouraged other inter-governmental organisations, including international and regional institutions, non-governmental organisations, civil society and the private sector to contribute to and actively participate in the intergovernmental preparatory process of the Summit and the Summit itself. It was clearly meant to be as inclusive as possible.

More than 11,000 participants from 175 countries attended the Summit held in Geneva in 2003 and related events. The Geneva Declaration of Principles expressed a common desire and commitment 'to build a people-centred, inclusive and development oriented Information Society where everyone can create, access, utilize and share information and knowledge, enabling individuals, communities and peoples to achieve their full potential in promoting their sustainable development and improving their quality of life, premised on the purposes and principles of the Charter of the United Nations and respecting fully and upholding the Universal Declaration of Human Rights'. It emphasized that 'Our challenge is to harness the potential of information and communication technology to promote the development goals of the Millennium Declaration' (WSIS website).

The information society that the WSIS participants are trying to build is a multi-stakeholder society in which the UN and other inter-governmental, international and regional organisations, governments, the private sector, nongovernmental organisations and civil society all have a role to play. ICTs are a powerful instrument that can increase productivity, generate economic growth, improve employability and the quality of life for all. It can also promote dialogue among people, nations and civilizations. The Geneva Declaration outlines the key principles for building an inclusive information society. These include improving access to information and communication infrastructures and technologies as well as to information and knowledge; building capacity; increasing confidence and security in the use of ICTs; developing and widening ICT applications; fostering respect for cultural diversity; recognizing the role of the media; addressing the ethical dimensions of the information society; and encouraging international and regional cooperation. These key principles have given rise to eleven action lines which together constitute the Geneva plan of action. The Tunis Summit held in November 2005 also made a commitment to working together towards the implementation of the Geneva and Tunis decisions and the **Digital Solidarity Agenda** (as agreed in para.27 of the Geneva plan of action) which aims at putting in place the conditions for mobilizing human, financial and technological resources for inclusion of all men and women in the emerging Information Society. It also recognized that greater international cooperation and assistance was required to bridge the digital divide.

UNESCO AND WSIS

UNESCO is responsible for facilitating six of the action lines adopted by WSIS: access to information and knowledge; ICT applications/e-learning; E-science; cultural diversity and identity, linguistic diversity, and local content; media; ethical dimensions of the information society. Under the first action line UNESCO's achievements include the creation of a World Digital library and training programmes for information professionals. Other notable achievements include the creation of portals providing access to information and data on various scientific topics, support for e-learning initiatives in all the regions of the world, and media development projects in more than seventy developing countries as well as the adoption of a set of media development indicators (MDI) recognised as a standard setting tool to analyse the media development of a country. The MDI has been translated into six languages and is being piloted in several countries (UNESCO 2009). At the conceptual level UNESCO's main contribution is the concept of knowledge societies, by which UNESCO means 'societies in which people have the capabilities not just to acquire information but also to transform it into knowledge and understanding, which empowers them to enhance their livelihoods and contribute to the social and economic development of their societies' (Souter 2010, 11) and which is based on four key principles that are central to UNESCO's work in the field of information and communication: freedom of expression; quality education for all; universal access to information and knowledge; and respect for cultural and linguistic diversity (Souter 2010; UNESCO 2009). While an analysis of knowledge societies is somewhat beyond the scope of this paper it is worth noting the general thrust of UNESCO's World Report entitled 'Towards knowledge societies'.

TOWARDS KNOWLEDGE SOCIETIES

UNESCO's world report entitled 'Towards knowledge societies' begins with a brief reference to the age of enlightenment and the values it promoted and which form the foundations of western liberal societies. The diffusion of knowledge through books, the printing press and education for all (through schools and universities) were meant to lead to inclusive knowledge societies. This is also UNESCO's mission. However, the emergence of new technologies and the internet (as a public network) makes it necessary to make a distinction between the information society and knowledge societies. 'The idea of the information society is based on technological breakthroughs. The concept of knowledge societies encompasses much broader social, ethical and political dimensions' (UNESCO 2005, 17). While we now have the technical means to access and share knowledge on the basis of equality and universality (enlightenment values), knowledge should not be defined narrowly. 'Various forms of knowledge and culture always enter into the building of any society, including those strongly influenced by scientific progress and modern technology. It would be inadmissible to envisage the information and communication revolution leading – through a narrow, fatalistic technological determinism – to a single possible form of society' (Ibid.).

In knowledge societies, knowledge is a public good and this requires an approach to development especially in the global south that is inclusive, participatory and based on the concept of human freedoms. 'By giving knowledge an unprecedented accessibility and by engaging in capacity building for everyone, the technological revolution might help to redefine the end goal of human development' (UNESCO 2005, 20). As Amartya Sen (2010) argues, elementary freedoms, such as lifelong education for all are both the end and the tools of development. This approach can lead to new models of development that do not sacrifice human beings at the altar of economic growth. 'Knowledge is a potent tool in the fight against poverty' (Ibid.). The successes achieved by some East and Southeast Asian countries in the reduction of poverty are largely explained by the massive investments they made in education, and research and development over several decades.

Access to information, which is a key characteristic of the global information society, therefore needs to be accompanied by access to education in order to analyse the available information with critical judgement and thinking, and to incorporate it in a knowledge base. 'Information will never be anything but a mass of indistinct data…instead of controlling it many people will realize that it is controlling them' (UNESCO 2005, 19). The processing of information requires tools of many kinds. In knowledge societies everyone must be able to develop cognitive and critical thinking skills to distinguish between 'useful' and 'useless' information as well as analyse what they consider to be useful information. Moreover, useful knowledge is not simply knowledge that can be immediately turned into profit in a knowledge economy. Human progress requires knowledge of different kinds. Humanist and scientific knowledge each obey different information-use strategies.

It has always been recognised that knowledge is a useful tool. Thus in a knowledge economy it is used to produce (more) wealth and is replacing manual labour. Scientific and technological progress has led to the emergence of knowledge economies which are a stage in the development of capitalism. 'Knowledge can confer power on some and exclude others…this political aspect of knowledge is becoming a more important source of conflict as the economy has become more knowledge intensive' (Porter 1999, 137-138). Knowledge structures, argues Susan Strange (1988, 121), determine the political economy of knowledge; 'what knowledge is discovered, how it is stored, and who communicates it by what means to whom and on what terms' are questions that determine who benefits from the knowledge that is 'produced' in any society. On a more philosophical level Foucault (1980, 131) writes that 'each society has its regime of truth, its "general politics" of truth: that is, the types of discourse which it accepts and makes function as true'.

The digital divide helps widen 'an even more alarming divide' – the knowledge divide. It is partly rooted in knowledge structures and the unequal value put on different types of knowledge in the knowledge economy. The knowledge divide is particularly glaring between the countries of the North and those of the South but it is also a problem within a given society. Closing the digital divide will not be enough to close the knowledge divide as the acquisition of knowledge does not depend simply on technology (it also depends on training, cognitive skills and regulatory frameworks geared towards access to contents). UNESCO also warns against the excessive 'commoditization' of knowledge. 'In an economy where the focus is [on] scientific and technical knowledge, what role might certain forms of local and indigenous know-how and knowledge play?' These forms of knowledge have been de-valued and may simply vanish even though they are 'a priceless heritage and a precious tool for sustainable development'. Furthermore, fostering cultural and linguistic diversity also means nurturing the creativity of emerging knowledge societies and arming them to cope with the ever-increasing pace of change that characterizes today's world (UNESCO 2005, 22).

UNESCO's Medium Term Strategy for 2008-2013 and Its Approved Programme and Budget for 2010-11

Towards the end of the first decade of the 21st century UNESCO adopted its Medium Term strategy for 2008-2013. It had five overarching objectives on (1) attaining quality education for all and lifelong learning (2) mobilizing science knowledge and policy for sustainable development (3) addressing emerging social and ethical challenges (4) fostering cultural diversity, intercultural dialogue and a cultural of peace (5) Building inclusive knowledge societies through information and communication. Consistent with previous objectives, strategic programme objectives 12, 13 and 14 that come under overarching objective five above, were on Enhancing universal access to information and knowledge, Fostering pluralistic, free and independent media and infostructures, and Support through UNESCO's domains to countries in post-conflict situations and post disaster situations. In the introduction to the Medium Term Strategy, the Director-General, Irina Bukova, states that it is based on UNESCO's mission statement: *"As a specialized agency of the United Nations, UNESCO contributes to the building of peace, the eradication of poverty, sustainable development and intercultural dialogue through education, the sciences, culture, communication and information."*

UNESCO's Approved Programme and Budget for 2010-11 committed US$ 33,158,000 for Major Programme V: Communication and Information out of a total budget of US$ 653,000,000. It is based on biennial sectoral priority one: promoting freedom of expression and information and biennial sectoral priority two: building capacities for universal access to information and knowledge. It states that 'the Communication and Information Programme is based on the analysis that despite significant advances in providing access to information and knowledge in a people-centred, inclusive and development oriented manner, as called for by the World Summit on the Information Society, inequalities persist in the capabilities of Member States to identify, produce, disseminate and use information to build and apply knowledge for human development. The strategy therefore focuses on further operationalizing UNESCO's concept of inclusive, equitable, open and participatory knowledge societies – based on the four principles of freedom of expression, universal access, quality education and cultural diversity –through both normative and capacity-building activities.' The document makes it very clear that the needs of Africa, the least developed countries (LDCs), small-island developing states (SIDs), and the most vulnerable segments of society, including indigenous people will receive greater emphasis as will the theme of gender equality and youth. The Programme built on the results achieved during the implementation of the Programme and Budget for 2008-09. IPDC will continue to play an important role in UNESCO's strategy to develop free, pluralistic and independent media in the developing countries with particular emphasis on Africa, the LDCs, SIDS and countries in conflict and post-conflict situations.

THE FIRST WSIS+10 REVIEW EVENT AND UNESCO

The first high-level and multi-stakeholder WSIS review event was held on 25-27 February 2013 in Paris. It was hosted by UNESCO, in cooperation with ITU, UNCTAD and UNDP, and was entitled 'Towards Knowledge Societies for Peace and Sustainable Development'. According to UNESCO sources, 1,450 participants from 130 countries attended the event, and an additional 800 participated remotely. The participants included the representatives of governments, inter-governmental and international organizations, private sector businesses and the media. **The Final Statement** of the event entitled 'Information and Knowledge for all: An expanded vision and a renewed commitment' was drafted by a multi-stakeholder drafting group, and adopted by the event's participants (UNESCO, News and In Focus, 2013).

It argued that during the decade following the first World Summit on the Information Society held in Geneva in 2003, considerable progress had been made towards a people-centred, inclusive and development oriented Information Society. The multi-stakeholder approach and implementation at the international level had proved to be a considerable asset in taking forward the WSIS themes and Action Lines. But major challenges still lay ahead for 'counteracting the wide disparities in development and enabling all groups and all countries to benefit from universal access to information and knowledge'. This was reiterated by the WSIS+10 High Level Event held in Geneva the following year. Thus one of the recommendations of the final statement of the review event was 'make efforts to address the challenges in the availability, affordability, quality of access and use of broadband, in order to reduce the digital divide and possible risks of exclusion from the information society' (WSIS 2013; WSIS 2014).

The final statement also emphasised that the participants at this review event were convinced that the development of information and communication technologies (ICTs) contributes to peace and sustainable development. Some of its recommendations were aimed at realising this potential, for example, 'harness the potential of ICTs to help in achieving the internationally agreed development goals, including the Millennium Development Goals'. But others lay more emphasis on UNESCO's key interests, for example, the 'key to empowering people for sustainable development and peace is education – education that reaches out to all members of society, education that provides genuine lifelong learning opportunities for all'.

The WSIS+10 High Level Event produced a list of challenges during implementation of Action Lines and new challenges that have emerged. One of them was 'the need for ensuring proper integration of the WSIS and the Post-2015 development Agenda'. Others are as follows: the need to protect and reinforce all human rights, and to recognize their importance to realizing economic and social development; the need to fully integrate gender equality perspectives in WSIS related strategies; the need for more engagement of youth and enhancement of their participation in the WSIS process; the need for continued extension of access for people with disabilities and vulnerable people to ICTs, especially in developing countries; connecting the entire population of the world to the internet; north-south co-operation, complemented by south-south co-operation to facilitate the transition to a digital economy and reduction of poverty; the need to continue to promote investment and foster entrepreneurship and innovation in ICTs at the national, regional, and international levels as appropriate (WSIS 2014, 16-19). Of course, UNESCO is making a contribution to meeting these challenges. In his report entitled 'Building inclusive knowledge societies, A review of UNESCO's action in implementing the WSIS outcomes', David Souter (2014, 15) informs us that UNESCO has 'pursued WSIS objectives through its own programmes...[and] through programmes undertaken collaboratively with other stakeholders'. He also notes that the pace of change in ICT technology and markets has been rapid. The number of mobile telephone subscriptions has grown from around 1.5 billion in 2005 to over 6.5 billion in 2013. The number of people connected to the internet has grown from just over 1 billion in 2005 to over 2.7 billion in 2013. And there has been progress in other areas as well.

UNESCO's MEDIUM TERM STRATEGY FOR 2014-2021 AND ITS APPROVED PROGRAMME AND BUDGET FOR 2014-2017

In her introduction to the Medium Term Strategy for 2014-2021, the Director-General, Irina Bokova states that 'UNESCO has a unique role to play in strengthening the foundations of lasting peace and equitable and sustainable development' (UNESCO 2014a, 5). Its efforts to advance co-operation in education, the sciences, culture, communication and information is important 'at a time when societies across the world face the rising pressures of change and the international community faces new challenges' (Ibid.). She stresses that the adoption of the Medium Term Strategy is 'our chance to sharpen UNESCO's role and enhance its impact and delivery. This is our opportunity to set a new course for a revitalized, relevant and resilient UNESCO' (Ibid.). Following the 2010 independent, external evaluation of UNESCO and UNESCO's reform, the organization will concentrate on increasing UNESCO's focus; positioning UNESCO closer to the field; strengthening UNESCO's participation in the United Nations system; and developing and strengthening UNESCO's partnerships. These are the guiding principles of the MTS. But she also emphasizes that the MTS 'must reflect the common concerns of all Member States' (Ibid.).

The importance of strengthening UNESCO's participation in the UN system has increased over the years, especially since the UN adopted the policy of all UN agencies 'increasingly collaborating and delivering as one' (Ibid., 6), and is reflected in its mission statement: 'as a specialized agency of the United Nations, UNESCO – pursuant to its Constitution – contributes to the building of peace, the eradication of poverty, and sustainable development and intercultural dialogue through education, the sciences, culture, communication and information' (Ibid., 13). The Director-General claims that 'UNESCO is contributing towards United Nations system-wide cooperation at country, regional, and global levels, aiming at a strong and effective United Nations system' (Ibid., 6).

Strategic objective 9 of the MTS is 'promoting freedom of expression, media development and access to information and knowledge'. It reiterates that 'UNESCO will continue to play a leading role globally in the promotion of freedom of expression, press freedom, media development, and universal access to information and knowledge, for building inclusive knowledge societies' (Ibid., 26). UNESCO has always stood for liberal values (notwithstanding the criticisms of some of its western critics) and its medium term strategies and programmes tend to reflect these values. Thus, the creation of knowledge based societies is linked to enhanced democratic governance. Similarly, UNESCO supports media pluralism as it considers it to be a key pillar in strengthening democratic governance and facilitating the free flow of information.

The main beneficiaries of UNESCO's work programmes are the developing countries, including post-conflict and post-disaster countries and countries in transition. The MTS states that 'UNESCO will continue to support efforts by its Member States - especially in Africa, LDCs and SIDS - in building a vibrant media landscape' (Ibid., 26).

But the organisation recognises that there are unresolved issues and that these include the freedom of expression, ethical dimensions of the information society, multilingualism in cyberspace, and transforming digital divides into digital inclusions. It makes a commitment to support various stakeholders, including member states 'to strengthen efforts to find common ground on these issues' (Ibid., 27).

UNESCO's Approved Programme and Budget for 2014-17 commits US$ 32,714,600 for Major Programme V: Communication and

Information, out of a total budget of US\$ 653,000,000. This shows that both its total budget and its budget for Communication and Information has remained the same since 2010-11. It is also worth noting that out of the five major programmes, Communication and Information has the smallest budget and Education has the largest (US\$ 117,964,600). UNESCO claims that this programme 'has been conceived to ensure that UNESCO maintains and intensifies its prominence and impact as the United Nations specialized agency for building inclusive knowledge societies based on four pillars: freedom of expression; universal access to information and knowledge; respect for cultural and linguistic diversity; and quality education for all'. The programme gives priority and special focus to gender equality, Africa, Least Developed Countries (LDCs), Small Island Developing States (SIDS) and youth. While 16.3% of the budget is spent on Africa, 11.0% is spent on Asia and the Pacific, and 9.8% is spent on Latin America and the Caribbean. However, 54.6% of the budget for this programme is spent at UNESCO's headquarters in Paris. UNESCO's critics have always said that this is unacceptable.

The main lines of action are as follows: (1) Promoting an enabling environment for freedom of expression, press freedom and journalistic safety, facilitating pluralism and participation in media, and supporting sustainable and independent media institutions; (2) Enabling universal access and preservation of information and knowledge. UNESCO claims that it will support the development of an environment that encourages free and independent media, particularly in countries in transition and post-conflict situations. UNESCO is also keen to show that its programmes produce results and that it is a result driven organisation. The approved programme and budget lists six expected results of this programme, including performance indicators and benchmarks. For example, the first expected result is the strengthening of the environment for freedom of expression, press freedom, journalistic safety and self-regulation, through favourable policies and practices. A number of benchmarks are specified, for example, 'policies and norms conducive to freedom of expression, freedom of information, and press freedom strengthened in at least 16 countries, including support for media during elections in at least 6 countries.' Yet another benchmark is 'at least 5 post-conflict countries and countries in transition strengthened their investigative journalist capacity'. There are additional expected results for UNESCO's global priorities, namely Africa, and gender equality, for example, UNESCO-supported community radios transformed into spaces promoting intercultural and intergenerational dialogue. On gender equality an expected result is the development and implementation of gender-sensitive journalism and gender-sensitive media policies and indicators.

WSIS AND SUSTAINABLE DEVELOPMENT

The WSIS Forum held in 2015 in Geneva linked the WSIS Action Lines with the new Sustainable Development Goals adopted by the UN, 'to continue strengthening the impact of Information and Communication Technologies (ICTs) for sustainable development'. The outcome document explains that 'Each UN Action Line Facilitator has analyzed the connections and relations of their respective Action Line with the proposed SDGs and their targets' (ITU 2015, 16). In his message to the Forum, the UN Secretary-General, Ban Ki Moon said that 'people today are better connected than ever. Mobile phones are more affordable, especially in developing countries…I count on this Forum to help bridge the digital divide so that people everywhere can reap the benefits of connectivity' (ITU 2015, 1). The WSIS-SDG matrix maps WSIS Action Lines, for example, C1: The role of governments and all stakeholders in the promotion of ICTs for development, on to the new Sustainable Development Goals, such as End poverty in all its forms everywhere, and Achieve universal health coverage. Thus ICTs allow the private sector to create jobs that contribute to poverty reduction. ICTs can also be used for the creation of various data banks on diseases and assist decision makers in health planning (Ibid., 18).

UNESCO had a contribution to make to WSIS Action Line C9: Media and its links with the Sustainable Developments Goals. It hosted one of the interactive facilitation meetings, C9: Media: Free, Independent and

Pluralistic Media at the heart of the post-2015 development agenda. It was noted that the actions embodied in WSIS C9: Media and promoting free, plural and independent media contribute to sustainable development, particularly in terms of supporting democratic and good governance, monitoring national development and priority setting, and also bringing about peace and stability, as well as inclusive and equal civil participation, including that of marginalized groups such as women and girls (Ibid., 136). It was also noted that the converged media across all traditional and digital platforms have the potential to provide universal and inclusive access to information, including by women and girls.

CONCLUSION

Thus it is very clear that the freedom of expression (and its corollaries press freedom and freedom of information) is one of the main principles on which UNESCO's work is based. UNESCO has always committed itself to assisting member states 'in establishing an enabling environment for freedom of expression and freedom of information.' In addition it wants to assist member states in the application of internationally recognised legal and regulatory standards for freedom of expression, freedom of information and free and independent media (UNESCO, 2010). At the same time, it has made a contribution to bridging the digital divide, as one of the stakeholders participating in the WSIS process. It has done so by focusing on operationalizing its concept of inclusive, equitable, open and participatory knowledge societies – based on the four principles of freedom of expression, universal access, quality education and cultural diversity – through both normative and capacity building activities.

But it also remains true to its original mandate and will continue to 'collaborate in the work of advancing the mutual knowledge and understanding of peoples, through all means of mass communication'. It recognizes that the media is a critically important factor in conflict resolution and peace processes. Thus emphasis has been placed on enabling media 'to provide unbiased information, avoid stereotypes and counteract incitement to hatred and violence, especially within the framework of the *Power of Peace Network (PPN)* aimed at harnessing the power of new technologies to increase mutual understanding' (UNESCO, 2010). UNESCO's assistance to developing countries has aimed at strengthening the institutional capacities of media training and journalism education institutions, and fostering equal opportunities for both men and women in media training and journalism education, as well as fostering media pluralism. An important focus of its programmes has been on enabling media professionals 'to apply the highest ethical and professional standards and enable people to access information and critically assess and use it' (UNESCO, 2010). It has also encouraged the development of media accountability systems based on self-regulation. UNESCO's programme for communication and information for 2014-2017 claims that 'the UNESCO approach to facilitating universal access to information is holistic, human-rights based, gender sensitive, age, ability and culture-specific, goes beyond infrastructure and technological aspects, highlights the critical importance of fostering enabling environments, and builds institutional and human capacities to develop diverse and locally created content, tools and services in different languages for all groups of people including the marginalised'. (UNESCO, 2014 b).

REFERENCES

Albertazzi, D. and P. Cobley (eds.). 2010. *The Media – An Introduction.* Harlow: Pearson Education Ltd.

Coate, R. A. 1988. *Unilateralism, Ideology and U.S. Foreign Policy – The United States In and Out of UNESCO.* London: Lynne Rienner Publishers.

Dany, C. 2013. *Global governance and NGO participation, Shaping the information society in the United Nations.* London and New York: Routledge.

Dutt, S. 1995. *The politicization of the United Nations specialized agencies: A case study of UNESCO.* Lewiston and New York: Mellen University Press.

Dutt, S. 2002. *UNESCO and a just world order.* New York: NOVA Science Publishers Inc.

Foucault, M. 1980. *Power/Knowledge*, Selected Interviews and other writings 1972-1977, edited by Colin Gordon, New York, London etc.: Harvester Wheatsheaf.

Frau-Meigs, D., J. Nicey, M. Palmer, J. Pohle and P. Tupper (eds.). 2012. *From NWICO to WSIS: 30 years of communication geopolitics.* Bristol, UK and Chicago, USA: Intellect.

Hajnal, P. 1981. "Confrontation at Talloires." *Time*, June 1981, p.52.

International Commission for the Study of Communication Problems. 1980. *Many Voices One World.* London: Kogan Page; New York: Unipub; Paris: UNESCO.

ITU. 2011. *WSIS Forum 2011: Outcome document*, Geneva: ITU.

ITU. 2015. *WSIS Forum 2015: Outcome Document*, Geneva: ITU.

ITU. 2016. *Report on the WSIS Stocktaking 2016*, Geneva: ITU.

Kennedy, Paul. 2000. "The electronic gap." *UNESCO Courier*, February 2000.

Longworth, E. 2000. "Adapt or bust." *UNESCO Sources*, December 2000.

Mansell, R. and K. Nordenstreng. 2006. "Great Media and Communication Debates: WSIS and the MacBride Report." *Information Technologies and International Development* 3 (4): 15-36, Summer 2006.

Masmoudi, Mustapha. 2012. "Correlations between NWICO and Information Society: Reflections of a NWICO actor." In *From NWICO to WSIS: 30 years of Communication Geopolitics*, edited by Devina Frau-Meigs, Jérémie Nicey, Michael Palmer, Julia Pohle and Patricia Tupper, 17-28. Bristol and Chicago: Intellect Ltd.

McKenna, Alan. 2012. "The right to communicate – A continuing victim of historic links to NWICO and UNESCO?" In *From NWICO to WSIS: 30 years of Communication Geopolitics*, edited by Devina Frau-Meigs, Jérémie Nicey, Michael Palmer, Julia Pohle and Patricia Tupper, 93-106. Bristol and Chicago: Intellect Ltd.

Modoux, Alain. 2012. "Past witnesses' present comments." In *From NWICO to WSIS: 30 years of Communication Geopolitics*, edited by Devina Frau-Meigs, Jérémie Nicey, Michael Palmer, Julia Pohle and Patricia Tupper, 141-145. Bristol and Chicago: Intellect Ltd.

Nordenstreng, Kaarle. 2012. "The history of NWICO and its lessons." In *From NWICO to WSIS: 30 years of Communication Geopolitics*, edited by Devina Frau-Meigs, Jérémie Nicey, Michael Palmer, Julia Pohle and Patricia Tupper, 29-40. Bristol and Chicago: Intellect Ltd.

Palmer, Michael. 2012. "NWICO: Reuters' Gerald Long versus UNESCO's Seán MacBride." In *From NWICO to WSIS: 30 years of Communication Geopolitics*, edited by Devina Frau-Meigs, Jérémie Nicey, Michael Palmer, Julia Pohle and Patricia Tupper, 41-54. Bristol and Chicago: Intellect Ltd.

Penketh, A. and T. Branigan. 2015. "Media condemn Charlie Hebdo attack as assault on freedom of expression," *The Guardian*, 8 January, 2015.

Perrot-Lanaud, Monique. 2000. "Click goes the revolution." *UNESCO Sources*, March 2000.

Porter, T. 1999. "The late-modern knowledge structure and world politics." In *Approaches to global governance theory*, edited by Martin Hewson and T.J. Sinclair, 137-155. Albany: State University of New York Press.

Sen, Amartya. 2010. *Development as freedom*. New Delhi: Oxford University Press, (seventh impression).

Singh, J.P. 2011. *United Nations Educational, Scientific and Cultural Organization (UNESCO) – Creating norms for a complex world*. Abingdon, Oxon and New York: Routledge.

Singh, J.P. 2012. "Towards knowledge societies in UNESCO and beyond." In *From NWICO to WSIS: 30 years of Communication Geopolitics*, edited by Devina Frau-Meigs, Jérémie Nicey, Michael Palmer, Julia Pohle and Patricia Tupper, 153-162. Bristol and Chicago: Intellect Ltd.

Souter, David. 2010. *Towards inclusive knowledge societies, A review of UNESCO's action in implementing the WSIS outcomes*. Paris: UNESCO.

Souter, David. 2014. *Building inclusive knowledge societies, A review of UNESCO's action in implementing the WSIS outcomes*. Paris: UNESCO.

Stauffacher, D. and W. Kleinwachter (eds). 2005. *The World Summit on the Information Society: Moving from the past into the future*, ICT Task Force Series 8, New York: United Nations.

Strange, S. 1994 (2nd ed.). *States and Markets*. London and New York: Pinter.

UNESCO, 20 C/ Resolution 4/9.1/3, *Records of the General Conference*, 20th session, Volume 1, Resolutions, p.100, Paris: UNESCO, 1978.

UNESCO, 21 C/Resolutions, *Records of the General Conference*, 21st session, Volume 1, Resolutions, Paris: UNESCO, 1980.

UNESCO. 2002a. 31 C/4, *Medium Term Strategy 2002-2007*, Paris: UNESCO.

UNESCO. 2002b. 31C/5, *Approved Programme and Budget, 2002-2003*, Paris: UNESCO.

UNESCO. 2005. *UNESCO World Report, Towards knowledge societies*. Paris: UNESCO.

UNESCO. 2008. 34 C/4, *Medium Term Strategy 2008-2013*, Paris: UNESCO.

UNESCO. 2009. *Fostering information and communication for development, UNESCO's follow-up to the World Summit on the Information Society*, Paris: UNESCO.

UNESCO. 2010. 35 C/5, *Approved Programme and Budget, 2010-2011*, Paris: UNESCO.

UNESCO, *News and In Focus, Communication & Information Sector, '195 UNESCO Member states endorse the Final Statement of the first WSIS+10 Review Event'*, 22.11.2013, available at http://www.unesco.org/new/en/communication-and-information/resources/news-and-complete !

UNESCO. 2014a. 37/C4, *Medium Term Strategy 2014-2021*. Paris: UNESCO.

UNESCO. 2014b. 37C/5, *Approved Programme and Budget 2014-2017*. Paris: UNESCO.

UNESCO website available at http://www.unesco.org.

Wade, R. H. 2002. "Bridging the Digital Divide: New Route to development or New Form of Dependency?" *Global Governance* 8: 443-466.

Wells, Clare. 1987. *The UN, UNESCO and the politics of knowledge.* Basingstoke and London: Macmillan.

Whiteman, Hilary and Laura Smith-Spark, 'Press declares the Charlie Hebdo attack a 'war on freedom', *CNN*, 8 January, 2015, available at: http:/edition.cnn.com/2015/01/08/intl_world/Charlie.

Wilkin, P. 2001. *The Political Economy of Global Communication.* London and Sterling: Pluto Press.

World Summit on the Information Society website available at http://www.itu.int/wsis/documents/.

WSIS, First WSIS+10 Review Event, 'Towards Knowledge Societies for Peace and Sustainable Development, Final Statement, *Information and Knowledge for All: An expanded vision and a renewed commitment'*, Paris 2013.

WSIS, WSIS+10 High-Level Event, *Outcome Documents*, Geneva 2014.

In: Global Governance
Editor: Sagarika Dutt

ISBN: 978-1-53612-969-4
© 2018 Nova Science Publishers, Inc.

Chapter 6

PRINCIPLED MULTILATERALISM AND THE UNITED NATIONS

Spyros Blavoukos[1] and Dimitris Bourantonis[2]

[1] Associate Professor in the Department of International
and European Economic Studies,
Athens University of Economics and Business, Athens, Greece
[2]Professor of International and European Studies in
the Department of International and European Economic Studies,
Athens University of Economics and Business, Athens, Greece

ABSTRACT

The multi-faceted nature of security threats requires and necessitates increased international cooperation. The United Nations (UN) has failed to meet the expectations for a prominent and efficient coordinating role. Our contribution calls for a new UN existential logic based on principled multilateralism applied over the organizational structure and the entire range of UN activities. We look at two important aspects of the UN's functioning, namely the organizational and decision-making *modus operandi* of the UN Security Council (UNSC) and the set of rules that underpin the interactions between the UN and Regional Organizations (ROs). The UN collective security system has been established to manage and orchestrate response to inter-state threats. However, the main security challenges in the last two decades emanate predominantly from intra-state conflicts and non-governmental agents. In this context, regional organizations constitute a potentially key component of regional stability and order and we need to explore ways of integrating them more comprehensively in the UN system of governance. Our main argument is that a new political agenda could emerge gradually in the UN along the lines of a principle-based multilateralism. This agenda could comprise a new set of governing rules for the UN decision-making process and a comprehensive framework for cooperative actions between the UN and regional organizations for the management of intra-state security threats. The new rules should reflect the UN attempt to increase its status as a legitimate multilateral structure of authority. The emerging framework of action could revolve primarily around interactions between the UN and ROs.

INTRODUCTION

The multi-faceted nature of security threats requires and necessitates increased international cooperation. These mostly transboundary threats constitute a major challenge to the core organizational principle of the modern international relations system, namely sovereignty. State boundaries increasingly become irrelevant and their varying degree of porosity simply accentuates the problem; no state can practically insulate itself from the fluid security environment that surrounds it. In this context, the United Nations (UN) emerges as the only legitimate source of global security. Due to its legitimacy and the universality of its membership, the UN is regarded as the most institutionalized arrangement engaged in international security governance (see Diehl and Frederking 2010; Karns and Mingst 2010; Kirchner and Sperling 2007; Rittberger 2001; Thakur 2006; Weiss and Daws 2007; Weiss and Thakur 2010). The end of the Cold War and the rise of an increasingly interdependent and multi-centered world system generated expectations that the UN would emerge as the pivotal actor in global security governance. However, these hopes were short-lived and ephemeral; the UN has turned out to be an inefficient, or at its best, marginally relevant mechanism for coordinating actions needed to manage serious issues and problems of peace and security. Thus, there has emerged a broader debate on the role of the UN and its underlying political reasoning.

Our study contributes to this debate by urging for a new UN existential logic. After highlighting the existing problems encountered by the UN in its operation, we argue that the UN should move more assertively towards a principled multilateralism that will enhance the organization's prospects and foster security more effectively and comprehensively. In the first section, we elaborate on the concept of principled multilateralism and discuss its main features. We understand principled multilateralism as the most legitimate form of multilateral political action that can improve considerably the UN's effectiveness in the field of international peace and security. The ascendance of this concept in the UN political agenda should be complemented with a thorough analysis of how it can be applied over the organizational structure and the entire range of UN activities.

In this work we limit our analysis to two important aspects of the UN's functioning, which we discuss in the second and third sections of the chapter respectively: first, we look at the organizational and decision-making *modus operandi* of the UN Security Council, which is the sole institutional body that can authorize and legitimize the use of force. Second, we examine the set of rules that underpin the interactions between the UN and Regional Organizations (ROs). The UN collective security system has been established to manage and orchestrate response to inter-state threats. However, the main security challenges in the last two decades emanate predominantly from intra-state conflicts and non-governmental agents. In this context, regional organizations constitute a potentially key component of regional stability and order and we need to explore ways of integrating them more comprehensively in the UN system of governance.

Our main argument is that a new political agenda could emerge gradually in the UN along the lines of a principle-based multilateralism. This agenda could comprise a new set of governing rules for the UN decision-making process and a comprehensive framework for cooperative actions between the UN and regional organizations for the management of intra-state security threats. The new rules should reflect the UN attempt to increase its status as a legitimate multilateral structure of authority. The emerging framework of action could revolve primarily around interactions between the UN and ROs. The scope, the depth and the intensity of these interactions are determined by conditions discussed further below.

UN PRINCIPLED MULTILATERALISM

The Cold War period was marked by its rigidity at the center of the international system and the deriving predictability of state action for the majority of international actors. The collapse of the bipolar world after the events of 1989 brought about a new series of international challenges. These challenges advanced the need for security reconceptualization and took multilateralism beyond its earlier nominal and formal dimensions, focusing instead on the quality and substantive dimension of the concept. Multilateralism is not merely about the practice of coordinating states' actions in groups of three or more (Keohane 1990, 731), but also about the kind and nature of institutionalized relations. In other words, '...what is distinctive about multilateralism is not merely that it coordinates national policies in groups of three or more states, which is something that other organizational forms [like bilateralism and minilateralism] also do, but additionally that it does so on the basis of certain principles of ordering relations among states' (Ruggie 1992, 7).

Embracing multilateralism goes well beyond embracing multilateral organizations. It constitutes a generic institutional form, delineating the space and mode of conduct of international relations. The generalized principles specify appropriate courses of action, without regard to the particularistic interests of the parties or the strategic exigencies that may exist in any specific occurrence. A direct corollary is that these principles entail a behavioral indivisibility among the members of the collectivity that practice multilateralism (Ruggie 1992, 11). It is not supposed to be a 'pick and mix option' of the principles to be followed or obeyed occasionally and at will, but rather generates pressure or expectations of cross-time, behavioral isomorphism.

Having acknowledged the institutional nature of multilateralism, the question arises why states prefer such an institutional format for the organization of their interactions. This question raises the broader question of '...whether multilateralism is a means or an end, an instrument or an expression, or both' (Caporaso 1992, 55). Assuming states are conscious, goal oriented actors with exogenous preferences, multilateralism, as an institutional form of international cooperation and coordination, is one functional means –among others – for realizing national interests consistent with the instrumental calculus of each member of the international community (Koremenos et al. 2001; Pierson 2000). By considering multilateralism as a means rather than an end, it is possible to consider alternative organizational options with equal or even superior utility for the constituent members, according to the configuration of state power and interests in particular issue areas. In that respect, multilateralism is a policy option to which states turn only if it best serves their purposes, whatever such purposes may be (Martin 1992, 91-2). In that respect, the embrace of multilateralism may derive from calculations of direct influence and control over multilateral forms of cooperation, in which the legitimizing function of multilateralism may be highly evaluated.

However, in contrast to 'instrumental multilateralism,' the multilateral mode of international interactions may also be an end in itself. According to this approach, states simply prefer doing things multilaterally not because of a hidden agenda to pursue their own interests, but in appreciation of the collective course of action embodied in multilateralism. In that respect multilateralism becomes part of the on-going, taken-for-granted subjective undertakings of international life (Caporaso 1992, 56). It comprises deliberative and communicative aspects and an emphasis on cooperation through mutual understandings and principle- and norm–oriented behavior. Thus, it is possible to identify two different variations of the institution of multilateralism, each associated with a different logic of action (March and Olsen 1998). How each state conceptualizes multilateralism depends on domestic political factors (administration in office, interest groups, civil society, policy-making ethos, and so on) as well as the country's status, current engagement and historical trajectory in the international system. All these features point to the distinctive states' conceptualization of and approach to international relations in general and international organizations more specifically (Katzentsein 1996).

Principled multilateralism within the UN has two dimensions, one quantitative and the other qualitative. When taken together, these two dimensions constitute the most important drivers for UN legitimacy and therefore effective action in the sphere of international security. The first dimension considers the large number of actors engaged in UN multilateralism: 'The more others one acts with, the more multilateral that action is and states boast about the number of partners in their action as proof of its legitimacy' (Finnemore 2005, 195). The second dimension entails a large number of states agreeing to act in the UN setting according to some set of principles and rules. It is this qualitative dimension of UN principled multilateralism that makes it a distinct form of political action in the UN setting: it offers legitimacy not only to the particular international security rules produced by UN bodies, but also to the body that generates the rules (Hurd 1999, 387). Legitimacy presupposes 'a generalized perception or assumption that the actions of an entity are desirable, proper, or appropriate within some socially constructed system of norms, values, beliefs, and definitions' (Suchman 1995, 574).

The embrace of UN principled multilateralism is inexorably linked with the imposition of constraints on all UN constituent members, including the most powerful ones. This kind of multilateralism depends on the existence of a set of multilateral rules of the game that should apply equally to all states, no matter what their geopolitical or geo-economic importance: 'Within the multilateral arrangement [even] great powers cannot do just anything they want... Great powers' restraint and equality under the rules are an important part of what legitimates multilateral arrangements and makes them popular' (Finnemore 2005, 196). Of course, this implies and pre-supposes a self-constraint on the part of the most powerful states that is logically expected to be, and has always been, attractive to weaker states.

However, playing the game by the rules does not mean that multilateral rules do not need to reach some accommodation with the most powerful: 'If rules and multilateralism become no more than tools for the weak to use to coerce and constrain the strong, they will be resisted and ultimately rejected. Conversely, if the rules are viewed as tyrannical by weaker states, they will be illegitimate and resisted' (Finnemore 2005, 198). Thus, the main issue for UN principled multilateralism, as for any other form of multilateral cooperation, is to strike a balance and set rules that accommodate power (so the strong will 'buy in') but are accepted by other members. This is the only way for all the UN stakeholders—its member-states—to abide by the UN's core purposes and contribute the required resources to ensure the compliance of its members, especially those resources related with the use of force. This balance increases significantly the likelihood of cooperation, as well as its effectiveness and legitimacy. These rules govern the most substantive parts of the UN decision-making process (permanent and non-permanent membership of the UN Security Council, veto power, and decision-making rules) as well as the UN's actions, policies, and relations with other security partners (other international/regional organizations and non-state actors).

PRINCIPLED MULTILATERALISM AND THE REFORM OF THE UN DECISION-MAKING PROCESS

Principled multilateralism requires appropriate rules governing the decision making processes within UN institutions, principally the UN Security Council (UNSC) and the UN General Assembly (UNGA). The former is endowed under the UN Charter with primary responsibility for taking a wide range of legally binding measures in order to maintain and restore international peace and security including enforcement measures. The latter, consisting of all UN member states, can discuss any issue that could endanger international peace and security. It adopts recommendations that constitute an important indication of world opinion, although they have no binding effect on member states.

There is an ever-increasing concern with the functioning of, and participation in, these bodies in view of advancing UN multilateralism

(Alger 2007; Bourantonis 2005; Fassbender 2004; Hurd 2002, 35-51; Karns and Mingst 2010, 25-30 and 131-43; Knight 2002, 19-37; Luck 2007; Report of the High-Level Panel 2004, 57-73). The suggested reforms focus mostly on the rules shaping the UNSC's formal and informal structure, revolving around its composition, decision-making rules and, eventually, the roles of the most powerful and weakest states within this structure. In order to implement the multilateral rule-governed system of international security, the UNSC must inevitably reflect a legitimate multilateral structure of authority. Therefore, the argument rightly goes, there is a need to re-structure the UNSC in accordance with key principles, such as *representation*, *inclusiveness*, *transparency* and *accountability* (Woods 1999).

An increase in the UNSC membership would undoubtedly make the body more representative and democratic and therefore more legitimized. However, the principle of representation should be applied with care: a broad expansion of membership would inevitably create a top-heavy and cumbersome body that would have great difficulty in acting swiftly and effectively. In all likelihood, such an expansion would prevent the UNSC from maintaining a balance between representation and effectiveness as happened with the Council of the League of Nations. Several increases in the Council of the League membership made the Council become more representative, but as a consequence also '...lost much of its effectiveness' (Carr 1946, 29). An expanded and therefore a more representative UNSC that nonetheless sustains the prerogatives of the powerful states in decision-making can provide the foundation for effective and meaningful UNSC reform. The most powerful contribute most of the resources that enable the UN to implement and enforce its rules. In that respect, 'if they get to write the rules (or at least have strong influence in their drafting), powerful states are more likely to embrace and respect those rules subsequently' (Finnemore 2005, 198).

However, having a more representative UNSC, with an expansion of its permanent and non-permanent members, as a reflection of power shifts along with a decision-making process with privileges for the most powerful (veto power), is a necessary but insufficient condition to confront challenges to the UNSC in terms both of legitimacy and long-term effectiveness. To do so requires more than that. It requires the participation of those UN members affected by the UNSC decisions but not formally represented in it. Thus, there emerges the need for greater *inclusiveness*. Participation does not entail formal but mainly informal involvement in the UN decision-making process. It is about the right of those not represented in the UNSC to have access to decision-making and eventually an opportunity for substantive input. The growing number of UNSC activities has brought with them a much enhanced impact of its decisions on the UN membership at large. Accordingly a large number of states have significant national interests or specific concerns relating to the issues under discussion in the Council, notably major peacekeeping missions or the imposition of sanctions. There is a growing need for (and demand from) the wider UN membership, which bears a large part of the peace-keeping burden or the costs of sanctions, to have access in discussions at a sufficiently early stage of the UNSC decision-making process for their perspective to be taken into account and potentially, at times, to facilitate the forging of an effective consensus.

This demand also derives from wider concerns about the way the UNSC operates in practice. Much of the substantive work of the UNSC, including the drafting of the resolutions calling for UN actions in the field of security, has moved outside the Council's formal meetings, held in public, to informal consultations. The meetings are structured in such a way that participation by states other than the fifteen UNSC members is restricted despite the discretionary power of the UNSC to engage them in these consultations. It is more than essential to improve the working methods of the UNSC in order to increase the meaningful participation of those states in the UNSC decision-making. By giving them informal access to the UNSC decision-making process, the now excluded states will develop a greater sense of commitment to the Council as they will no longer feel they are merely recipients of, but active participants in shaping and applying its rules, thus taking on responsibility for their effective implementation. Furthermore, the dramatic increase in UNSC activities along with the widening of the spectrum of the UNSC issue agenda create the need for the UNSC to develop systematic contacts with non-governmental organizations (NGOs) that can relay their perspectives to the UNSC members in informal meetings. In a nutshell, the UNSC must open up further for the informal participation of state and non-state actors whose contributions are essential for the Council to manage an expanding and increasingly complex security agenda.

Apart from representation and inclusiveness, two other overlapping principles, *accountability* and *transparency*, could significantly increase the UN members' positive reception of the UNSC rules (Bruhl and Rittberger 2001, 31). The obscurity and lack of transparency inherent in the UNSC's working methods have left most UN members extremely dissatisfied on both fronts. Accountability comprises, among others, the obligation of the UNSC to disclose information about what is actually unfolding behind closed meetings and to provide rationales for its major decisions in a transparent manner. The former can be met by the UNSC President's briefings that could reveal substantive information about the specifics of the issues, problems encountered, and draft resolutions discussed in these meetings. The latter could be met not through the ritual and meaningless practice followed by the UNSC to submit annual reports to the UNGA, but through an obligation of the UNSC to provide monthly analytical reports on its work to the UNGA. These reports, as the most visible source of information about the work of the UNSC, can capture the most important issues discussed at the most crucial stages of the decision-making process and inform the UN members of the substantive grounds on which UNSC decisions were taken. The idea of UNGA holding a monthly meeting for debate on the UNSC report with the participation of the UNSC President would be an important step towards building a more credible system of check and balances into the UN.

PRINCIPLED MULTILATERALISM AND THE ROLE OF REGIONAL ORGANIZATIONS IN THE UN SYSTEM

The international post-Cold War environment found the UN overburdened by crises generated by intrastate/ethnic conflicts, humanitarian crises as well as collapsing states. These crises multiplied demands for peace operations and led to an overstretching of UN resources. This newly emerged security environment has dictated cooperative interactions with regional organizations around the world to uphold peace and foster stability. In this light, ROs have emerged as a critical component of global order, albeit only partly accommodated within the UN system. The scope and depth of UN-ROs interactions remain under-researched as does an empirical investigation of the multitude of interrelations among ROs within the UN setting and the guiding rules and principles that underpin them (Blavoukos and Bourantonis 2017).

All formal organizations strive for their autonomy to be able to pursue their goals free of any political and institutional dependencies (Clark and Wilson 1961; Galaskiewicz 1985, 282). In that sense, inter-organizational cooperation entails not only benefits but also considerable costs, mainly in the form of losing the capacity to follow an independent course of action. The most obvious reason why organizations seek cooperation is resource scarcity, which affects their performance (Levine and White 1961, 587).[19] Resources may have a structuralist essence and refer to material, financial or human means of action but can also be intangible and comprise legitimacy, authority, and even recognition of actorness status. In addition to resource scarcity, organizations engage in some form of cooperation for one additional reason, which is very relevant to our analysis. This reason is associated with the normative underpinnings of inter-organizational cooperation (Schermerhorn 1975). IOs are receptive to cooperation when 'cooperation' *per se* takes on a positive value, in which case the

---

[19] Resource scarcity is present in all six broad contingencies that inform the analysis of inter-organizational relations: necessity, asymmetry, reciprocity, efficiency, stability, and legitimacy (Oliver 1990, 241-6). Necessity captures the exchanges that may occur among IOs in order to meet legal or regulatory requirements; the anticipated repercussions of non-compliance will determine the potential of these mandated relations. Asymmetry refers to inter-organizational relations prompted by the potential of an IO to exercise power or control over another IO or its resources. In contrast, reciprocity emphasizes the pursuit of common or mutually beneficial objectives by two or more IOs. Efficiency has an intra-IO dimension, positing that an inter-organizational relationship may occur in an IO's attempt to improve its input/output ratio. Stability refers to inter-organizational relations that may emerge as a response to a highly turbulent environment in order to reduce uncertainty. Finally, the enhancement of an IO's legitimacy is a significant motivation for organizations to interconnect.

ideological and normative attraction of cooperative engagement in international affairs may tend to pull IOs in the direction of joint inter-organizational activities (Evan 1965, 221).

In the UN setting, it is crystal clear that resource scarcity drives and affects the interactions of the UN with the numerous ROs that operate around the world. The ROs contribute to the UN human and financial resources that increase its capacity to meet the demands and perform the allocated tasks, especially given the significant UN over-stretching nowadays. However, the development of autonomous structures of the ROs to be employed in operations under the UN aegis can also drag resources previously available directly to the UN. Several UN member-states are unwilling to increase their troop contributions, not least because ROs, like the EU and the African Union (AU), have been developing their own peacekeeping structures.[20] This 'crowding out' effect substantially undermines the independence of the UN in terms of peacekeeping operations (Koops 2013, 76) further accentuating the existing problem the UN is facing. Furthermore, the ROs have and offer a better understanding of the political and cultural underpinnings of regional disputes and conflicts, enhancing the problem-solving potential of an intervention (Bennet and Oliver 2002, 236-73; Tacsan 1997). Finally, they also have usually the capacity to mobilise and deploy the necessary resources more rapidly than the UN, thus avoiding the escalation of a conflict.

For member-states, the existence of a multitude of ROs generates important 'forum-shopping' opportunities. ROs offer a more distinct and clearer voice for countries that feel marginalized in the process of forging an international regime and in its management. More broadly, they provide an alternative and perhaps more effective way to have a country's voice heard and its concerns accommodated (Viljoen 2011, 195). Lost in the huge numbers of the UN universalism, member-states may prefer active

---

[20] For example, since the EU has begun deploying autonomously its own forces from 2003 onwards, it has practically stopped contributing troops directly to UN missions (Brosig 2011, 155). The expansion of the EU foreign policy brought about at the UN level the demise of the Standby High Readiness Brigade for United Nations Operations (SHIRBRIG), since the EU member-states have directed their contributions to the EU's own crisis management tools (Koops 2009).

involvement in the formation of a regional order, seeking afterwards its high-jacking and rendering it a means to 'go global.' Member-states may also veil their political aspirations behind the nested status of an RO in the UN, taking the lead in promoting their inter-organizational cooperation. In that respect, for example, the EU-UN cooperation in Africa depends largely on France's military apparatus, with the country in question taking this step to defuse criticisms of neo-colonialism in its political involvement in the continent (Charbonneau 2009, 552).

What the ROs are lacking most and seek to get out of this engagement with the UN is legitimization. This lack severely affects their effectiveness in regional crises by causing doubts about the motivation of their engagement. Other directly involved parties or parties with a stake in the region may challenge the role of ROs and undermine their initiatives. The UN plays a critical role in that respect as the sole agent of collective legitimation in the international arena. The ROs seek UN endorsement of their actions to convey an image of acting with a degree of moral authority and sanctioned purpose (Claude 1966; Franck 1990; Hurd 1999). The ROs take on UN tasks in exchange for legitimacy and an international status of actorness conferred on them by the UN. This is a two-sided coin as the ROs may also bestow legitimacy on the UN. By participating in the UN's decisions and actions, the ROs validate UN responses and increase their likelihood of success. In this sense, the ROs maximize the compliance potential of the UN mandate. In contrast, actions decided and enforced with minimal or no support from the relevant regional entities face severe legitimacy problems, as the experience of UN peacekeeping forces in Lebanon and Iraq has demonstrated (Kingah and Van Langenhove 2012, 210). The 'new regionalism' literature distinguishes between the UN-centered orthodox multilateralism on a global scale and the emergence of regional multilateral arrangements that do not get their mandate and legitimacy from above but rather 'from below and within,' i.e., from the constituent members and regional civil societies (Hettne and Söderbaum 2006). Facing an increasing gap between legality and legitimacy, the UN cannot deliver a legitimate world order on its own; regional integration schemes may entertain local fears of external imposition by a distant global hegemon (Thakur and Van Langenhove 2006). However, ROs do not only add but can also subtract legitimacy from the UN in two ways. First, by entrusting an RO to orchestrate the response of the global and regional community to a crisis, the UN may appear biased and taking sides in regional power games in case the RO in question masks the veiled hegemony of a powerful regional leader. Second, the RO handling of a conflict may have catastrophic outcomes, directing criticism to the UN for the delegation of its tasks to inappropriate partners, as has been the case in many security crises in Africa and elsewhere (Barnett 1995, 429).[21]

Besides resource scarcity, the association of an RO with the UN obviously entails the RO's adherence to the universal UN norms and principles. But the degree of adherence can have an impact on the scope and depth of cooperation. The normative underpinnings of this relationship will affect critically inter-organizational cooperation with extensive normative congruence enhancing the potential of synergistic linkages between the UN and ROs. Besides the functionalist cooperation based on resource exchange, 'principled multilateralism' brings in the foreground the adherence to multilateral engagement also on ideological and normative grounds. Regardless of the capacity to act unilaterally, states and ROs choose to cooperate not only for reasons of increased effectiveness but also because cooperation has its own positive value. For example, the EU refrained from taking a unilateral course of action in the negotiation with Iran over its nuclear program even when the UN Charter and international practice offered such opportunities (Laatikainen 2010). When negotiations broke down, in 2005, the EU could have imposed economic sanctions unilaterally, as other ROs have done in the past –and have escaped with it- without UN authorization. However, the EU took the issue to the UN setting not only to enhance the effectiveness of any collective economic and political response but also to legitimize possible

---

[21] A typical example is the engagement of Nigeria and the Economic Community of West African States (ECOWAS) in Liberia in the early 1990s. Supportive UNSC Resolutions granted legitimacy to the activities of the force in place, only to find out at a later stage that the established monitoring group became so involved in the conflict that any claim to neutrality was eventually lost. This kind of problems brings about the de-legitimization of the UN and its loss of reputation (Smith and Weiss 1997, 598).

enforcement action in concordance with its own normative adherence to multilateralism (Blavoukos and Bourantonis 2014). This incident reveals how ROs can contribute by their course of action to the fostering of a UN-based multilateral global order.

Furthermore, often in practice, ROs add specificity to the norms and principles of the global regime by elaborating the general UN normative frame. In the field of human rights, for example, the African Union (AU) has adjusted and expanded the existing UN-agreed framework of protection to better reflect African conceptualization and understanding of human rights and address particular issues pertinent to the continent. It has done so by adopting standards that constitute a restatement of the universal consensus but also deviate in order to meet the idiosyncratic cultural features and concerns of its members. So far, the regional embodiment and specialization of universality in the African case shows normative compatibility and complementarity. However, even for analytical reasons, it is important to distinguish between supplements or deviations that differ from the global norms but are still consistent with them and the development of contradictory norms that are in conflict with the universal ones (Viljoen 2011). In this case, ROs fully embracing the 'principled multilateralism' of the UN will stop short of expanding, for their own reasons at the regional level, the existing normative frame beyond the area delimited by the UN Charter and deriving decisions.

One such reason may be the pursuit of political and legal autonomy, which can be allegedly jeopardized by too close an interaction. Taking an example from the EU-UN inter-relationship again, the adoption of UNSC Resolution 1373 in 2001 on combatting terrorist funding, which is considered a cornerstone in the UN's counterterrorism effort, was not received uniformly at the EU level. Whereas the European Commission and the Council of Ministers pushed forward the swift implementation of the Resolution (Kaunert and Della Giovanna 2010), the European Court of Justice (ECJ) adopted a more critical stance. In a number of cases, the ECJ highlighted the autonomy of the Community's legal order vis-à-vis the international order, prioritizing its quasi-constitutional rights over the dictates of the Security Council (Nollkaemper 2009, 863). The

Commission and the Council of Ministers have accepted the UN's high degree of influence over the EU's financial sanctions regime on political grounds associated with the 'effective multilateralism' rhetoric of the EU. In contrast, the ECJ has sought to curtail this influence reaffirming the autonomous character of the EU legal order (Léonard and Kaunert 2012, 123-26). This example does not suggest or imply that the EU was not willing to contribute to the international efforts to counter terrorism. Neither does it annul the multilateral essence and credentials of the EU. It rather hints to the potential of ROs –especially influential and powerful ones– to assert their autonomy at the expense of the UN framework of action.

Regardless of the extent of resource scarcity that may drive the UN towards greater cooperation with ROs, any such decision to delegate responsibilities and bestow legitimacy to ROs should be taken with great care. It should take into consideration not only the capability of regional actors to address regional crises but also the level of their commitment and adherence to international norms and principles as envisaged in the UN Charter as well as the acceptability, legitimacy, and accountability of the RO in relation to the parties involved in the crisis (Alagappa 1997, 436-9). Initiatives by ROs may change policy dynamics and render them emerging policy gatekeepers. In the 2011 Libyan crisis, for example, only after the League of Arab States (LAS) had endorsed enforcement action, the UNSC Resolution 1973 that paved the way for military intervention became a feasible political option. The LAS statement persuaded the African members serving at the time at the UNSC (Nigeria, Gabon, and South Africa) to support the Resolution rather than abstain, as the faithful reflection of the AU decision would require them to do; their support was critical in order to ensure the necessary nine affirmative votes in the Council. It also brought the US fully on board for military engagement and ultimately pushed the remaining skeptical members of the UNSC towards abstention rather than vetoing the Resolution (Bellamy and Williams 2011, 846). Policy gatekeeping can easily lead to unrestrained regional autonomy if the respective RO does not abide by multilateralism in principle and is unwilling to operate within the multilateral framework of the UN setting.

Thus, the quest for greater effectiveness in the handling of regional issues could run against the perspective of global governance and caution is required vis-à-vis the scope and exact terms of ROs-UN interactions (Smith and Weiss 1997, 595-6).

CONCLUSION

The main challenge for the UN in the years ahead is to confront a wide range of threats and hostilities of a much more complex nature than those it experienced for many years. It has to do so in a context of international fluidity as a result of an ongoing systemic re-calibration that is mainly owed to the ascendance of new and powerful players. For those aspiring to institutionalized international cooperation and collective action to address global challenges, the good news is that the UN has seemingly left behind the catastrophic early years after the collapse of the stable bipolar world and has been in a process of transformation and reform. The bad news is that this process is arduous and very time- and energy-consuming. Still, a UN agenda has emerged that reflects the quest for a principle-based multilateralism and will eventually increase the organization's effectiveness. This agenda comprises a new set of governing rules for the UN decision-making process, mainly targeting the UNSC in an attempt to render it a legitimate multilateral structure of authority. To achieve that, the much desired reform efforts should take into consideration key principles, such as representation, inclusiveness, transparency and accountability. Any reforms that encode great power dominance or prerogatives of the past with little reference to these principles are in danger of sentencing the UN to oblivion. Furthermore, the agenda comprises a norm-based comprehensive framework for UN action, both for inter-state and intra-state security threats. In this framework the role of ROs is increasingly important. ROs can contribute to the fostering of multilateralism as a form of global governance since they constitute regional multilateral orders themselves. However, it is necessary to examine in depth the scope of this emerging intersecting multilateralism and identify its functionalist or normative base. The former entails an instrumental logic of cooperation whereas the latter points to a deep-trenched understanding of the need for cooperative global action that ties well with principle-based multilateralism.

REFERENCES

Alagappa, M. 1997. "Regional institutions, the UN and international security: A framework for analysis." *Third World Quarterly* 18 (3): 421-442.

Alger, C. 2007. "Widening Participation." In *The Oxford Handbook on the United Nations,* edited by T. Weiss and S. Daws, 701-715. Oxford: Oxford University Press.

Barnett, M. 1995. "Partners in peace? The UN, regional organizations, and peace-keeping." *Review of International Studies* 21 (4): 411-433.

Bellamy, A. and P. Williams. 2011. "The New Politics of Protection? Côte d' Ivoire, Libya and the Responsibility to Protect." *International Affairs* 87(4): 825-850.

Bennett, L. and J. Oliver. 2002. *International Organizations. Principles and Issues.* 7th ed., New Jersey: Prentice Hall.

Blavoukos, S. and D. Bourantonis. 2017. "Nested Institutions." In *The Palgrave Handbook of Inter-Organizational Relations in World Politics*, edited by R. Biermann and J. A. Koops, 303-317. London: Palgrave/Macmillan.

Blavoukos, S. and D. Bourantonis, D. 2014 "Do sanctions strengthen the international presence of the EU?" *European Foreign Affairs Review* 19 (3): 393-409.

Bourantonis, D. 2005. *The History and Politics of UN Security Council Reform*. Abingdon: Routledge.

Brantner, F. and R. Gowan. 2009. "Complex engagement: The EU and the UN system." In *EU and International Organizations*, edited by K-E Jørgensen, 37-60. London: Routledge.

Brosig, M. 2011. "Overlap and interplay between international organisations: theories and approaches." *South African Journal of International Affairs* 18 (2): 147-167.

Bruhl, T. and V. Rittberger. 2001. "From International to Global Governance: Actors, Collective Decision-making, and the United Nations in the World of the Twenty-first Century." In *Global Governance and the United Nations System*, edited by V. Rittberger, 1-47. Tokyo: United Nations University Press.

Caporaso, J. A. 1992. "International Relations Theory and Multilateralism: The Search for Foundations," In *Multilateralism Matters: The Theory and Practice of an Institutional Form*, edited by J. G. Ruggie, 51-90. New York: Columbia University Press.

Carr, E. H. 1946. *The Twenty Years' Crisis*, 2nd edn, London: Macmillan.

Charbonneau, B. 2009. "What is so special about the European Union? EU-UN cooperation in crisis management in Africa." *International Peacekeeping* 16(4): 546-561.

Clark, P. and J. Wilson. 1961. "Incentive systems: A theory of organizations." *Administrative Science Quarterly* 6 (2): 129-166.

Claude, I. 1966. "Collective legitimization as a political function of the United Nations." *International Organization* 20 (3): 367-379.

Diehl, P and B. Frederking (eds) 2010. 4th edition, *The Politics of Global Governance. International Organizations in an Interdependent World*, Boulder: Lynne Rienner.

Evan, W. 1965. "Toward a theory of inter-organizational relations," *Management Science* 11 (10): 217-230.

Fassbender, B. 2004. "Pressure for Security Council Reform." In *The UN Security Council. From the Cold War to the 21st Century*, edited by D. Malone, 341-355. Boulder: Lynne Rienner.

Finnemore, M. 2005. "Fights about Rules: The Role of Efficacy and Power in Changing Multilateralism." *Review of International Studies* 31 (S 1): 187-206.

Franck, T. 1990. *The Power of Legitimacy among Nations*, Oxford: Oxford University Press.

Galaskiewicz, J. 1985. "Interorganizational relation." *Annual Review of Sociology* 11: 281-304.

Hettne, B. and F. Söderbaum, 2006. "The UN and regional organizations in global security: competing or complementary logics?" *Global Governance* 12 (3): 227-232.

Hill, C. 2005. "The European dimension of the debate on UN Security Council membership." *The International Spectator* 40 (4): 31-39.

Hurd, I. 2002. "Legitimacy, Power and the Symbolic Life of the UN Security Council." *Global Governance* 8(1): 35-51.

Hurd, I. 1999. "Legitimacy and Authority in International Politics." *International Organization* 53(2): 379-408.

Karns, M. and K. Mingst. 2010. *International Organizations. The Politics and Processes of Global Governance.* Boulder: Lynne Rienner.

Kaunert, C. and M. Della Giovanna. 2010. "Post 9/11 EU counter-terrorist financing cooperation: differentiating supranational policy entrepreneurship by the Commission and the Council Secretariat." *European Security* 19 (2): 275-295.

Katzenstein, P. J. (ed.) 1996. *The Culture of National Security: Norms and Identity in World Politics.* New York: Columbia University Press.

Keohane, R. 1990. "Multilateralism: An Agenda for Research." *International Journal* 45(4): 731-764.

Kingah, S. and L. Van Langenhove, L. 2012. "Determinants of a regional organisation's role in peace and security: the African Union and the European Union compared." *South African Journal of International Affairs* 19 (2): 201-222.

Kirchner, E. and J. Sperling (eds) 2007. *Global Security Governance. Competing Perceptions of Security in the 21st Century.* Abingdon: Routledge.

Knight, W. 2002. "The Future of the UN Security Council: Questions of Legitimacy and representation in Multilateral Governance." In *Enhancing Global Governance. Toward a New Diplomacy*, edited by A. Cooper, J. English, and R. Thakur, 19-37. New York: United Nations University Press.

Koops, J. 2013. "Inter-organisational approaches." In *The Routledge Handbook on the European Union and International Institutions: Performance, Policy, Power*, edited by K-E. Jorgensen and K. Laatikainen, 71-85. London: Routledge.

Koops, J. 2009. "Effective inter-organizationalism? Lessons learned from the standby high readiness brigade for UN operations (SHIRBRIG)." *Studia Diplomatica* 62 (3): 81-90.

Koremenos, B., C. Lipson, and D. Snidal. 2001. "The Rational Design of International Institutions." *International Organizations* 55(4): 761-799.

Laatikainen, K. 2010. "Multilateral leadership at the UN after the Lisbon treaty." *European Foreign Affairs Review* 15 (4): 475-493.

Laatikainen, K. and Smith, K. (eds.) 2006. *The European Union at the United Nations. Intersecting Multilateralisms.* Houndmills: Palgrave/Macmillan.

Léonard, S. and C. Kaunert. 2012. "Combating the financing of terrorism together? The influence of the United Nations on the European Union's financial sanctions regime" In *The Influence of International Institutions on the EU. When Multilateralism Hits Brussels*, edited by O. Costa and K-E Jørgensen, 111-134. Houndmills: Palgrave Macmillan.

Levine, S. and White, P. 1961. "Exchange as a conceptual framework for the study of interorganizational relationships." *Administrative Science Quarterly* 5 (4): 583-601.

Luck, E. 2007. "Principal Organs," In *The Oxford Handbook on the United Nations*, edited by T. Weiss and S. Daws, 653-674. Oxford: Oxford University Press.

Martin, L. 1992. "The Rational State Choice of Multilateralism." In *Multilateralism Matters: The Theory and Practice of an Institutional Form,* edited by J. G. Ruggie, 91-121. New York: Columbia University Press.

March, J. G. and J. P. Olsen. 1998. "The Institutional Dynamics of International Political Orders." *International Organization* 52(4): 943-969.

Nollkaemper, A. 2009. "The European courts and the Security Council: between 'dédoublement fonctionnel' and the balancing of values: - three replies to Pasquale De Sena and Maria Chiara Vitucci." *European Journal of International Law* 20 (3): 853-887.

Oliver, C. 1990. "Determinants of interorganizational relationships: Integration and future directions." *The Academy of Management Review* 15 (2): 241-265.

Pierson, P. 2000. "The Limits of Design: Explaining Institutional Origins and Change." *Governance* 13(4): 475-499.

Report of the High-Level Panel on Threats, Challenges and Change. 2004. *A More Secured World: Our Shared Responsibility*. New York: United Nations.

Rittberger, V. (ed). 2001. *Global Governance and the United Nations System*. Tokyo: United Nations University Press.

Ruggie, J. G. 1992. "Multilateralism: The Anatomy of an Institution." In *Multilateralism Matters: The Theory and Practice of an Institutional Form*, edited by J. G. Ruggie, 3-47. New York: Columbia University Press.

Schermerhorn, J. 1975. "Determinants of interorganizational cooperation." *The Academy of Management Journal* 18 (4): 846-856.

Smith, E. and Weiss, T. 1997. "UN task-sharing: towards or away from global governance?" *Third World Quarterly* 18(3): 595-619.

Suchman, M. 1995. "Managing Legitimacy: Strategic and Institutional Approaches." *Academy of Management Review* 20(3): 571-610.

Tacsan, J. 1997. "Searching for OAS/UN task-sharing opportunities in Central America and Haiti." *Third World Quarterly* 18 (3): 489-508.

Thakur, R. 2006. *The United Nations, Peace and Security. From Collective Security to Responsibility to Protect*. Cambridge: Cambridge University Press.

Thakur, R. and Langenhove, L. 2006. "Enhancing global governance through regional integration." *Global Governance* 12 (3): 233-240.

Viljoen, F. 2011. "Human rights in Africa: Normative, institutional and functional complementarity and distinctiveness." *South African Journal of International Affairs* 18(2): 191-216.

Weiss, T. and S. Daws (eds). 2007. *The Oxford Handbook on the United Nations*. Oxford: Oxford University Press.

Weiss, T. and R. Thakur. 2010. *Global Governance and the UN: An Unfinished Journey*. Bloomington: Indiana University Press.

Woods, N. 1999. "Good Governance in International Organizations." *Global Governance* 5(1): 39-61.

In: Global Governance
Editor: Sagarika Dutt

ISBN: 978-1-53612-969-4
© 2018 Nova Science Publishers, Inc.

Chapter 7

A COMMENT ON GLOBAL GOVERNANCE, MULTILATERALISM AND THE MANAGEMENT OF INTERNATIONAL TRADE

Christopher Farrands

Principal Lecturer in International Relations
at the Nottingham Trent University, Nottingham, UK

ABSTRACT

The global governance of international trade is in question as it has not been for a long time. The multilateral trading order seems to be in crisis, especially since the failure of the Doha round of multilateral trade talks in the 2000s. The WTO was created to manage world trade but a growing proportion of world trade is also managed through bilateral trade agreements. The main objective of the GATT/WTO was the reduction of tariffs and the promotion of freer trade relations through a multilateral approach. It was also grounded in the idea of a rules based system rather than a results based system. The negotiation of these rules has, therefore, become a highly political process given their particular impacts. All sides try to swing the rules in ways that they think (or hope) will have effects which work in their favour. The world trade system was created by the US but the election of Donald Trump as US President in 2016 has formed a powerful challenge to the idea of a relatively open rules based liberal world trade order, and it is not the only threat to this system of world trade.

INTRODUCTION

The world trade system is in many ways a paradigm case of what both critics and supporters usually mean by 'global governance'. Thus there are many state actors, most but not all now members of the World Trade Organisation (WTO). The WTO does not 'manage' world trade alone – there are other stakeholders and other agreements that have compelling interests in the security and growth of world trade, not least the G20, OECD, regional organisations and UN economic agencies, as well as a host of non-governmental organisations (NGOs) and business lobbies. A growing proportion of world trade is managed through bilateral trade agreements. These are sometimes seen as a profound threat to a multilateral world trading order, but a pure multilateral trading order has never existed and bilateral agreements, especially between some of the most powerful players, have always mattered alongside whatever multilateral regime existed. More basically, one should remember that trade is largely done between firms, not by governments or institutions. And most trade is done by the largest multinational firms, dealing with each other. Around 18% of all world trade is intra-trade, meaning that it is international –it crosses national boundaries-but is done within a single company (or its subsidiaries). Governments make the rules of global trade through negotiations which are largely managed by consensus, which sounds relatively comfortable; but rule making is very tough and the process of reaching a global consensus on a particular rule may well involve baskets of side deals, bilateral carve-ups or special interest mediation before the final text is settled. And global trade negotiations through the WTO are by no means the only institutional arrangements through which world trade is managed: there are bilateral agreements, between states or between blocs of states, as well as regional arrangements such as the (very different) free trade agreements (FTAs) involved in the

European Union, the South East Asia Treaty Organisation, the South American trade deal, Mercosur, and others.

This is a 'paradigm case' of global governance in the specific sense that there is no 'world government of trade', no single central organisation makes the rules; but the rules succeed in carrying a certain authority, and procedures once agreed have generally proved to be binding. Dispute procedures have evolved since the WTO's predecessor, the General Agreement on Tariffs and Trade (GATT) was set up at Havana in 1947, but they remain widely used even if they are also frequently criticised. One central idea behind this very complex system is that it is a 'rules based' rather than a 'results based' system. That is to say that the whole structure works through a set of rules which it is pretended are neutral in their effects; but everyone involved knows that the rules have particular impacts, and therefore when the rules are negotiated or revised, all sides try to swing the rules in ways that they think (or hope) will have effects which work in their favour. However the election of Donald Trump as U.S. President in 2016 has formed a powerful challenge to the idea of a relatively open rules based liberal world trade order, and it is not the only threat to the governance system which evolved between 1947 and 1994, as this paper will explain later.

THE ISSUES THAT THE SYSTEM OF GOVERNANCE OF WORLD TRADE GIVES RISE TO

It must also be recognised that the governance system of world trade has presided over the production of global inequalities on a very significant scale even while it has helped to promote a period of significant, steady growth. The present system disadvantages and marginalises smaller firms and producers as it benefits from and reflects the lobbying power of the largest companies. It also disadvantages many consumers and disrupts local markets in the global south on which the prospect of development turns. It does this even though at the same time it creates global supply chains which have often brought important benefits in terms of greater choice and lower prices for consumers. It is not even controversial to argue that it has deleterious environmental effects as a by-product of large scale production and in the disposal of waste materials. It can have perverse impacts on the distribution of investment. It used to be possible to argue that whatever the harmful side effects of the way world trade was managed, trade was a positive sum game in which each side benefitted even if some gained systematically more than others. In 2017, it has become much harder to make that case, which more radical liberal, structural Marxist and Gramscian critics, as well as others, have always contested. Following the failure of the main lines of the Doha Round of multilateral trade talks in the 2000s, how can we evaluate the difficulties of the world trade system and its governance? Is the multilateral rules based open system of world trade still fit for purpose?

A further point to raise is whether the growth of complexity of world trade is something that the WTO system is able to manage at all. This relates first of all to the complexity of trade agreements which no longer look primarily to the reduction of tariffs and tariff equivalents, and which aim instead to regulate other aspects of trade which are much more difficult to measure and much easier to politicise. At the same time, trade has become more complex because of the evolution of ever more complex supply chains and logistical systems. And governments have created, often under powerful domestic pressure, increasingly difficult instruments for their management of world trade, some of which thread their way nervously along the border of what is acceptable at all under WTO rules, and some of which clearly overbalance into the straightforwardly unacceptable. These may form the grounds for disputes under WTO procedures, but national governments do not even need to be particularly unscrupulous to recognise that WTO disputes take a minimum of about six years to complete, i.e., resolve. They can initiate proceedings or allow them to be started against them in the knowledge that a rapid judgment or solution is unlikely. And however one assesses the work of the world trade system as a whole or the WTO more specifically, it is important to remember that it is first of all a negotiated order which relies on the willingness of states to enter and conduct negotiations in good faith. If there seem to be non-negotiable issues or disputes –which do of course arise in the world of sovereign actors- then the most sophisticated institutional machinery may be nugatory. Effective negotiation depends on a willingness to compromise and resolve disputes, however difficult or long drawn out they may be. Some of the main criticisms of the world trade system seem to this author at least to be well grounded; but of those criticisms, some may also fail to recognise the complex negotiation procedures between states and other actors which make any kind of agreement possible.

THE GROWTH OF BILATERAL NEGOTIATIONS AND TRADE AGREEMENTS

It is not especially original now to observe that multilateral trade agreements have been in difficulty for some time. Nor is it very remarkable that there has been a growth of bilateral negotiations leading to a flowering of various kinds of bilateral as well as regional agreements to manage trade issues. Even before the election of Donald Trump in November 2016, one of the main bases of the liberal international order of the last sixty years appeared to be under threat. And from a liberal point of view, all this matters very much: stable expanding trade relations not only form a basis for economic growth and the possibility of rising incomes and rising standards of living; they also form one of the bulwarks of international security, providing at least a measure of guarantee of avoiding the much more conflictual, nationalist, mercantilist global order of the 1930s (and before that the 1870s and the years immediately preceding World War One).

But it might still be important to ask whether the shift from multilateral to bilateral trade agreements is really quite so harmful. Perhaps, first of all, the form does not matter so much as the content of the agreements reached. And if the prospect of a global multilateral deal sank with the Doha Round of WTO talks, perhaps some level of agreement is preferable to ongoing deadlock? It may also be sensible to argue that the grand format of rounds of tariff reduction which worked so well after 1947 for the GATT and the WTO simply has not proved workable when tariffs have been cut so far that they matter only a little in actual trade by comparison with regulations and agreements on standardisation of product types as well as safety standards and so on, which are all much less susceptible to global 'round' negotiation structures. And from the perspective of the global south, it might also be claimed that whether a trade agreement is multilateral or bilateral does not matter very much if whatever the agreement is reflects a dominant hegemonic set of interests dictated by lobby groups from large firms in leading countries (now as likely to include Nigeria, Indonesia, China or Brazil as any of the more 'traditional' hegemonic actors in world trade). Smaller trade actors find themselves in weak positions in all kinds of trade talks, excluded unless they accept conditions imposed by others.

For all these reasons, the global governance of international trade is in question as it has not been for a long time, and for all these reasons, its future matters in security and financial terms as well as in terms of a more narrowly defined commercial agenda. In this paper, it is not possible to unpack all these issues, but it is possible to make a foray into the main debate, and in particular to ask whether the spread of bilateral and regional agreements matters if we accept that the last few global multilateral trade deals have failed by quite a long way to live up to the expectations held for them.

THE TRANSFORMED GLOBAL CONTEXT

The balance of power in the world economy shifted significantly before the financial crisis of 2007-10, but perhaps the change was partially concealed until that upheaval. After 2010, it became impossible not to recognise that very real changes had taken place in the core structures of power relations. The United States remained the largest actor, the largest trader and a key locus of financial power. The European Union remained the second most powerful economy but the largest trading power. But China had become almost as significant as those two actors, not only because of the size of its exports but because a sustained export surplus over many years had led to a steady inflow of funds into both state and private coffers. India, Indonesia and Brazil lagged behind, and each had its own domestic constraints on rapid growth as a trading power, but all three had become significant players in trade diplomacy as well as in actual exchange, and all three had ridden the tide of growing complexity of supply chains. In particular, India's electronics, IT and software sectors had become powerful through the outsourcing of services including finance and IT security, as well as through Indian business's purchase of assets in Europe and the United States. Japan, weakened in the 1997 Asian crisis, nonetheless remained a significant player. The United States and European Union had managed to combine a competitive rivalry with a duopoly of power through world trade talks in the 1980s and 1990s, including in the transfer from the GATT to the WTO. But from 1995 onwards, the other major trading powers increasingly fought back against this hegemony. The two traditional hegemons were no longer able to go into a huddle in trade negotiations and come out with an outcome which satisfied their joint interests and ignored or slapped down the others. This was most evident in the outcome of the 2003 Cancun Summit. The outcome was a deadlock because the main global south governments refused to accept either the agenda or the process pushed through by the US and EU.

Evaluation of the work and effectiveness of the WTO trade system inevitably hinges at least in part on the assessment of the global context. Those writers (mainly from the US) who believe that the brief moment when the US enjoyed a genuine dominant position after the end of the Cold War has in fact been prolonged into the present tend to have high expectations for the US and low expectations for the institutional effectiveness of multilateralism. Those who remain staunchly liberal in their economic thinking tend to underestimate the extent to which managing the WTO system is as much a juggling of political interests and modalities. The world economy is not a free market system. It is dominated by large state actors and very large oligopolistic multinational companies. Power is concentrated in a relatively few hands, although that now includes significant players from what used to be called the 'developing world': Brazil, India, Indonesia and China as well as other members of the G20 group. How one understands the geopolitics and balance of interest between these major players provides a framework for debates about how effective world trade governance is, or can be.

THE SUCCESSES OF GATT AND WTO

Trade agreements under the GATT and WTO have aimed to unwind the growth of tariff based protectionism which was at a level when GATT was founded (1947) which was undoubtedly a serious obstacle to trade and welfare growth. This project succeeded and made a significant contribution to gains from trade, while trade growth was consistently higher than world GDP growth and played an important part in driving world GDP growth. It has always been true that the benefits of this growth were distributed unevenly; it has always been true that primary producers and especially economies which relied mainly on agricultural exports gained less than those which produced manufactured goods. It has also been increasingly the case that those countries (and firms) which relied on intellectual property ownership and complex service exports gained more from trade than those which could only buy in those goods. But however asymmetrical the gains, it used to be assumed that gains accrued to both sides, as liberal theory which understood trade as a positive sum game argued. More than this, as Baldwin (2016) has recently maintained, the system which was constructed and which the World Trade Organisation oversees, has been a rules based one in which rules were agreed and then managed the trade system rather than a results based system in which the results of trade dictated how the system was managed.

Neither the General Agreement on Tariffs and Trade nor the World Trade Organisation which succeeded it in 1995 are strictly speaking (i.e., in international law) organisations. That is to say that while they have both authority and international personality, they do not have their own international authority to 'rule' their members —members retain sovereignty within the organisation as well as having the sovereign right to withdraw from it. But by consensus both have acquired a capacity to create law and to create binding procedures for judgment, something which goes beyond the intentions of the (mainly British and American) diplomats who created the GATT in 1947.

One objection to the argument at issue here is that the governance of international trade has been trundling along for the last twenty years without a major collapse. There have been major technological transformations and at least two financial crises (the East Asian crisis of 1997 as well as the global 2007-10 collapse), but trade has continued to grow under the existing governance regime. What has proved very difficult is the negotiation of *new* global rules. The WTO system has managed existing trade pretty well, has succeeded in absorbing the significant impact of the growth of new members, most obviously China, and has responded to the other problems in the world economy with a firm if not entirely regular pattern of growth, reflecting the growth of exports and consumer demand in more rapidly growing emerging markets even while the US, the EU and other OECD economies were weak. This is a potent argument: the WTO system is not a liberal bicycle which has to keep moving steadily 'forward' or it will fall over. But there are real difficulties in assuming that even while new global trade deals have been so difficult the existing system can continue to function effectively. One major risk is that the expectation of continuing growth from continuing trade is not a law or necessary feature of global relations; it is perfectly possible to imagine scenarios where trade stops driving global growth, and one does not have to imagine a mega-breakdown such as the one that occurred in 1929-32 to see how this would be possible. But in any case, as successive WTO annual reports have forcefully argued, the world trade system, although not a bicycle, needs to be resilient and roadworthy. It needs regular maintenance and frequent adaptation to new conditions and new membership, as well as regular rule maintenance to counter the new tricks national trade managers devise to find ways around the rules without actually breaking them.

There is also a boundary issue in these conversations. It is a conceptual boundary, but also an important practical one. Trade can be studied by narrowly focussed economists and practised by highly qualified negotiators, often with a legal background. But trade is about welfare in the broadest sense, including jobs, investment, incomes and wellbeing, as well as environmental impacts.

The WTO system works effectively in a number of respects, and its advocates have some good grounds to hold that the organisation is capable of providing a framework of rules which manages global trade as well as it can be done given the powerful political restraints from large and important actors, under pressure from enormously powerful lobbies and regional as well as trade association interests. But there are all the same some compelling arguments against the complacency that this view suggests.

While the WTO system works pretty effectively to manage differences between the large economies, including today some of the large developing countries as well as the major developed country economies, it is much harder to defend the role it has had for smaller developing countries. This is something WTO officials are as aware of as anyone else. Some of the reasons for its failure have changed over time; others have dogged the GATT and WTO since the 1950s.

KEY ISSUES IN WTO AS A NEGOTIATING FORUM AND GOVERNANCE SYSTEM

The WTO trade system appears to have stalled as a negotiating forum after many years of relative success in the GATT. This may not be surprising. The GATT system faced a world dominated by nationalist thinking as a hangover from before the Second World War, and there was plenty of opportunity to reach agreement on tariff reductions in industrial goods before turning to the more difficult agendas which the Uruguay Round identified as the future agenda of the soon-to-be born WTO. The WTO always was going to have a more difficult set of agendas and issues to address. When one factors in the substantial increase in the number of parties, the increasing complexity of patterns and structures of trade, and the intractability of issues in agriculture, intellectual property, services and dispute settlement processes in particular, it is even less surprising that negotiations after 1995 stalled. And all that is without taking account of the shifted balance of power and the decline of hegemony discussed earlier in this chapter.

All the same, before one concludes that the negotiation of the new WTO agenda after 1995 was simply a reach too far, it might be valuable to hold three thoughts in mind. Firstly, the negotiations in the GATT system between 1947 and 1980 were far from easy as the image suggested here tends to imply. Secondly the GATT system was itself a compromise and not at all the negotiating framework leading actors (the US and UK) originally desired. Thirdly, the level of complexity in trade negotiations sets an enormous premium on technical expertise in the matters at hand. They take a long time to 'settle' and demand intellectual mastery of great detail. Some countries have the capacity or political structures which allow that detailed work to be done more than others; some quite large actors lack the capability, and others have learned quickly how to make the existing system and its negotiating and legal frameworks work for them – China being a key example.

This section tends to point towards a rather simple conclusion, that the WTO governance system might work well as a system of multilateral international management but has largely failed as a system of renewal through negotiation, and that where there have been more successful trade negotiations they have been bilateral (either between individual states or between blocs) outside the WTO framework. There is something in this; but it is very much an incomplete account, and it ignores several important issues.

Mainly because the key issues facing trade negotiators have proved increasingly intractable, the agenda of global trade talks has remained broadly the same since the last years of the GATT. It is this intractability which has invited alternative approaches to trade policy management, including the shift towards bilateral agreements. It has also created a context where governments have pursued an increasing number of trade disputes both through the WTO's own procedures and through the newly created procedures in other institutional arrangements such as regional organisations.

The essence of the GATT/WTO system is partly the reduction of tariffs and the promotion of freer trade relations through a multilateral approach. But it is also grounded in the idea of a rules based system rather than a results based system as the object of negotiation. This has already been partially eroded. But some key actors are very anxious to shift the basis of trade talks to a results based system in which trade is treated much more as a zero sum negotiation rather than a positive sum negotiation, and this in turn makes effective negotiation much more difficult to achieve and much more difficult to assess in its effects.

THE IMPACT OF THE TRUMP ADMINISTRATION

Trump's election in November 2016 was as much a shock to international economic institutions as it was in domestic politics, to NATO or to stable security relations. Trump campaigned openly on an anti-multilateralism agenda, denouncing previous agreements including those which had brought China into the WTO in 1999 (concluded by the Clinton administration), the TTIP agreement with the European Union, the Trans-Pacific Partnership (TPP) and especially the NAFTA agreement with Canada and Mexico. Trump claimed that all these agreements cost US jobs, which they may have done. He ignored the significant benefits these agreements brought for employment in other sectors as well as for consumers and shareholders. He also ignored the likelihood that jobs 'returned' to the mainland United States from Mexico, China or wherever would quite possibly be taken by automated systems: Trump promised jobs to poorly qualified blue collar workers which were much more likely to be taken by robots than by those workers, unless they were heavily upskilled, something he neither mentioned nor promised to fund throughout his election campaign. Despite all of this, the emergence of the Trump government has had significant impacts even at this early stage.

It is not so much what the Trump government has actually done as what it seems to want to stand for which poses the greatest threat to the global trading system. What it has done is to repudiate the North American Free Trade Agreement (NAFTA), and then suggest that it wants to renegotiate the deal rather than reject it outright. It has withdrawn from the Trans-Pacific Partnership trade deal made after considerable difficulty with nineteen other partners who have resolved to continue with the agreement without the United States, a move which may isolate and weaken the US rather than strengthen it. And it has attacked the Trans-Atlantic trade and services agreement negotiated over a long period of time with the European Union, a deal which was already coming apart at the seams because of widespread opposition in Europe well before Trump was inaugurated. How far one draws conclusions from these actions relatively early in the administration's life depends partly on whether one believes Trump's rhetoric during his election campaign and listens to the most extreme right wing nationalist voices in the White House (such as the 'alt right' publicist Steven Bannon), or whether one listens more to other voices in the Administration and in Washington. In particular, while Trump is popular in some parts of the Republican Party and in his base in the middle and south of the US, his trade policies have to pass scrutiny in Congress, have to be scrutinised by the International Trade Commission (which owes its primary allegiance to Congress not to the presidency) and by powerful business lobbies. These lobbies may back Trump's tax cutting plans and ambitions for carbon energy, but are much more skeptical of the impact of his rhetoric on trade and investment. Trump has appeared to want to support some economic sectors (infrastructure and construction as well as some automobile firms) while attacking and seeking to undermine others, including the high tech sectors which are a primary source of jobs and growth as well as those car makers who import significant volumes of components from outside the US. But in doing this Trump would seem to be trying to undermine patterns of trade and investment which have been very deeply embedded for more than forty years. His aim is obviously to try to create a large number of jobs quickly to satisfy his political base and meet some of his electoral promises. It is not yet clear either that he understands the details of the economy enough to achieve this or that he is able to manage the process without profound and potentially damaging side effects. For example, repatriating car industry jobs is more likely to create work for robots than for semi-skilled labour, while creating a surge in infrastructure building may well create a surge in imports of materials as well as a shortage of skilled labour to achieve the core aim. However welcome investment in the poor road and rail system in the US may be, it is not something that can be switched on even in the four years of a presidency.

But the most important issue with Trump's proposed trade policy with its 'America First' slogan, and very limited substance, is that it seems to aim to undermine the whole idea of a rules based global trade system. The trade system which has evolved over the last seventy years was designed first and foremost to avoid the experience of the 1930s when major economies fought a series of tariff wars, introducing tough regulations as well as high tariffs in pursuit of exactly the kind of economic nationalism which Trump has campaigned for. He threatens his neighbours in the belief that in any trade conflict they will be far more damaged than the United States. While this may be true, trade wars with Mexico and Canada, as well as with Brazil and Argentina and others, will certainly cause both problems for jobs and problems for investment, all the more so since (unlike the 1930s) there are plenty of alternatives for the Latin American countries. They do not have to buy US food products, although it is cheaper right now for them to do so. They do not have to sell manufactures in the US, although again a readjustment would be costly, and they can buy and sell elsewhere in the world. For a number of Latin American countries, China and Australia are already important trade partners. They also have an institutional structure (Mercosur) through which they can develop intra-

American trade if they choose to make it work more effectively, which would not need to take a long time.

The wider threat to a rules based system is one which is recognised very clearly, not only in Tokyo and Brussels, but also in Beijing. Even for India, which is building a closer security relationship with the United States and which has often presented itself as the major challenger to the status quo in international trade disputes, the dismantling of the multilateral framework from which it has gained quite a lot in the last two decades poses more of a threat than an opportunity.

The challenge which the Trump administration sets for trade lies also in its apparent desire to renegotiate agreements which the United States has entered in good faith and which its partners will be all the more reluctant to change. In January 2017 the BBC economics journalist Mark Broad asked whether Trump would mean "'the end of world trade" (BBC Business News online, 25 January 2017). He concluded that although this kind of rather apocalyptic question is worth asking, the answer is still 'no'. And although China may well be a part of the problem, he suggests that technological innovation is a much greater cause of the loss of jobs and the growth of trade deficits in the US –along with many other established industrial countries. Politicians in the US (and elsewhere) may not recognise that workers whose jobs disappear are also consumers who benefit from lower prices and greater choice. And that may be rational while consumers are much less effectively organised than labour or capital. But Broad also reports that many economists think the way to reduce the US deficit and create more jobs is for the US to sell more in China rather than to buy less because of tariffs or other restrictions. And that requires that the negotiations between the two great economic blocs focusses on greater access in Chinese markets, which would also support Chinese consumers and perhaps promote greater satisfaction with the political as well as the economic system. Broad's conclusion that there may be a 'Trump problem' but there is also a 'China problem' not only makes sense, it is also reflected in the different but similarly powerful trade restrictions (especially on certain products and on inward investment in India and some other emerging economies).

THE POSSIBILITY OF 'JUSTICE' IN A WORLD TRADING SYSTEM

Irrespective of the objectives of individual governments, and beyond the specific criticisms of many broadly liberal scholars, the WTO system has been widely seen as a system which promotes and embeds injustice and inequality in the world economy. Some scholars understand the WTO as a part of a larger system of hegemonic dominance (O'Brien et al, 2000; Cox, 1996). Non-governmental organisations have perhaps been the most compelling critics of the WTO system. They have argued that the economics underpinning theories of free trade do not actually work, and are often intellectually empty as well as harmful in their practical consequences. One reason for this is that international markets simply do not conform to the basic assumptions of a 'free trade' model: they are highly oligopolistic, barriers to new entrants are typically very high, and knowledge is imperfectly shared and unavailable. Large companies dominate world trade as much in agricultural products as in manufactures or services, and they have disproportionate lobbying power. Governments listen to trade associations representing larger firms more than to small business groups; even if they claim to listen to the latter it is generally only when it suits them. Large lobbying institutions permeate the fabric of life in Washington and Brussels, as they do in New Delhi, Ankara, Brasilia and Ottawa. It is in this context that the smaller developing and developed countries find themselves outside the magic circle and excluded from influence in major trade debates. That may include some G20 members (Argentina, Mexico) but as the NGO campaigners rightly show it includes most of all the smaller and poorer members of the world community.

CONCLUSION

The seemingly ordered world trade system of the last seventy years has in many respects remained in flux. It has never completed the potential wished for it by its creators. Led by the United States, the system was significantly changed when the WTO was created. But ever since then, US political and business leaders have lined up to repudiate the system which they created, which is to say that was created mainly by leading US business and farming lobbies rather than by government policy. The Trump Administration has piled into the existing system but has much less power to change it than its pronouncements often pretend, unless, that is, they want a trade and monetary conflict which would damage the US economy as much as it would harm the countries, including Mexico, Canada, China, India and Vietnam, that the Trumpistas say they want to target. The dilemma in world trade policy has become much bigger and much more complex than the question of bilateral vs multilateral negotiating platforms and agreements.

Viewed in a longer term perspective, the governance of the world trade system by a triopoly of the WTO agreements, large scale but not universal multilateral agreements (such as TPP), and bilateral deals in a variety of forms remains strongly entrenched. It is embedded in the institutional relations of governments and administrators and it reflects a series of compromises worked out over seventy years which satisfy leading state interests while meeting minimal expectations from others sufficient to prevent them from defecting from the regime.

REFERENCES

Baldwin, Richard and Patrick Low. 2009. *Multilateralizing Regionalism: Challenges for the Global Trading System.* Cambridge: Cambridge University Press.

Baldwin, Richard. 2016. "The World Trade Organization and the future of multilateralism." *Journal of Economic Perspectives* 30 (1): 95-116.

Bayne, Nicholas and Stephen Woolcock (eds). 2011. *The New Economic Diplomacy: Decision Making and Negotiation in International Economic Relations*, 3rd ed., Farnham: Ashgate.

Cox, Robert W. with Timothy J. Sinclair. 1996. *Approaches to World Order*. Cambridge: Cambridge University Press.

Decreux, Yvan and Lionel Fontagné. 2015. "What Next for Multilateral Trade Talks? Quantifying the Role of Negotiation Modalities." *World Trade Review* 14 (1):29-43.

Hoekman, Bernard M. and Petros C. Mavroidis. 2015. "WTO 'à la carte' or WTO 'menu du jour'? Assessing the Case for Plurilateral Agreements." *European Journal of International Law* 26 (2): 319-343.

Kapstein, Ethan B. 2008. "Fairness Considerations in World Politics: Lessons from International Trade Negotiations." *Political Science Quarterly* 123 (2): 229-245.

O'Brien, Robert, Anne Marie Goetz, Jan Aart Scholte and Marc Williams. 2000. *Contesting Global Governance, Multilateral Economic Institutions and Global Social Movements*. Cambridge: Cambridge University Press.

Ross, Robert S. and Jo Inge Bekkevold (eds). 2016. *China in the Era of Xi Jinping: Domestic and Foreign Policy Challenges*. Washington DC: Georgetown University Press.

Steffek, Jens and Ulrike Ehling. 2008. "Civil society participation at the margins: The case of the WTO." In *Civil Society Participation in European and Global Governance: A Cure for the Democratic Deficit? (Transformations of the State)*, edited by J. Steffek, C. Kissling and P. Nanz, 95-115. London: Palgrave Macmillan.

Stevens, Christopher. 2006. "The EU, Africa and Economic Partnership Agreements: Unintended Consequences of Policy Leverage." *The Journal of Modern African Studies* 44 (3): 441-458.

Sylla, Ndongo Samba. 2014. "On the Inequalities of the International Trade System." In *The Fair Trade Scandal: Marketing Poverty to*

Benefit the Rich by N. S. Sylla, 8-33. Athens, Ohio: Ohio University Press.

Trebilcock, Michael J. and Robert Howse. 2005. *The Regulation of International Trade*, 3rd ed., London: Routledge.

Woll, C. 2013. "Global Companies as Agenda Setters in the World Trade Organization." In *The Handbook of Global Companies*, edited by John Mikler, 257-271. London: Wiley.

Zeng, Ka and Wei Liang (eds). 2013. *China and Global Trade Governance: China's First Decade in the World Trade Organization.* London: Routledge.

In: Global Governance
Editor: Sagarika Dutt

ISBN: 978-1-53612-969-4
© 2018 Nova Science Publishers, Inc.

Chapter 8

THE RISE OF ISLAMISM IN THE CONTEMPORARY WORLD: A SOUTH ASIAN PERSPECTIVE

Kunal Mukherjee

Lecturer in International Relations at Lancaster University,
Lancaster, UK

ABSTRACT

The world shaking events of 9/11 and the more recent terrorist attacks in London and Manchester, UK, in the first half of 2017, have once again put Islamism or political Islam onto the centre stage of international affairs. Islamism is an extremely politicised version of Islam associated with a minority of Muslims which sees itself in a state of perpetual conflict with the western world, non-Muslims such as Hindus and Sikhs, and also other Muslims who are seen as insufficiently pious by Islamist ideologues. The rise of Islamism and transnational Islamist networks is turning out to be one of the most serious challenges of the 21st century. The aim of this chapter is to give readers an overview of the rise of Islamism and how it has changed its character with the passage of time, and how Islamist networks exist and operate in a globalised and more contemporary context. The chapter then moves on to its case studies which include the Muslim majority countries of South Asia, and Britain.

INTRODUCTION

The world shaking events of 9/11 and more recently the rise of ISIS and the 2017 terror attacks in London and Manchester have once again put Islamism or political Islam onto the centre stage of world affairs.[22] In the first instance, Islamism should not be confused with Islam. Whilst the former is a violent form of religiosity, the latter is a peace loving religion. Islamism is a political ideology and is often compared with the other 'isms' of the previous century like Fascism, Marxist- Leninism and Nazism. It is an extremely politicised version of Islam associated with a very small number of Muslims who see themselves in a state of perpetual conflict with the western world or western Christendom, non-Muslims like Hindus, Buddhists, Sikhs and Jains and also with other Muslims who are seen as too westernised or secularised or insufficiently religious from the Islamist standpoint (Mukherjee 2009, 17). Thus, the conflict by and large for Islamists exists at these three levels. Islamist ideologues do not in any way represent ordinary Muslims, just as Hindu nationalist groups in contemporary India are not representative of ordinary Hindus. Most Islamist groups see their own version of Islam as the only true path to Islam and other Muslims who are not following that path are seen as heretical. Needless to say, Islamist ideologues have a very narrow way of viewing the world. Lifestyles and values which are not in keeping with the Islamist view point are viewed unfavourably and as threatening. Islamism may be considered a form of 'Rejectionism', which is a way of thinking which is critical of the very notion of global governance, and represents a somewhat intolerant worldview (Sinclair 2012, 152-55). It is the aim of this chapter to look into the root causes and rise of Islamism in the contemporary world with a focus on South Asia and Britain.

---

[22] The spate of terrorist attacks in Europe (including the UK) in recent years makes it necessary to revisit global Islamism, especially as the rise of ISIS and the radicalisation of Muslim youth have been identified as the principal causes. ('Houses of Parliament attack: four dead including police officer', *the Guardian*, 22 March 2017; 'Manchester attack: What we know so far', BBC News, 12 June 2017; 'London terror attack: what we know so far', *the Guardian*, 5 June 2017).

There are two major strands of Islamism. In this connection, mention maybe made of Middle Eastern Wahhabism and South Asian Deobandism. These two categories, however, should not be seen as water tight compartments or in black and white terms. This is because in events like 9/11, the two strands often merge together and come as one after resolving their differences. The Wahabi tradition which originated in central Arabia in the mid-1700s is associated with Mohammed Abdul Wahhab and is often seen as the more stringent variety out of the two which goes back to the Koranic text for answers to solve contemporary Muslim problems. Wahhabi Islamist ideologues are generally seen as more puritanical in their approach when compared with their South Asian Deobandi counterparts. The term, Deobandism comes from the name, Deoband, which is a small town in north India, where an Islamic seminary, Dar-ul-Uloom (House of Knowledge), came into existence during the times of British colonialism in the mid-1800s (Abbas 2014, 66). The reason why this seminary came into existence was to protect Islamic values from the onslaught of western Christian values since this was the time in India when Christian missionaries were busy with their proselytization campaigns, openly denigrating indigenous south Asian religious traditions and forcefully converting people to Christianity. Thus, the founders of the Deobandi tradition who were Mohammed Qasim Nanatawi and Rashid Ahmed Gangohi took a defensive approach to protect Islamic cultural values from the attacks that came from the Christian missionaries (MetCalf 1982). Benazir Bhutto writes, 'Deobandis worry about western influence on Muslim values and argue that instead of becoming westerners, Muslims must keep their own identity' (Bhutto 2008, 52). The rise of South Asian Islamism should also be seen as a response to the imposition of an aggressive western modernity by the East India Company, which was one of the main pillars of the British Empire in the sub-continent, the other main pillar being the Christian missionaries. Just as most Middle Eastern Islamist groups like Hamas, Hezbollah and the ISIS follow the Wahhabi tradition, most South Asian Islamist groups like the Taliban, Jamat I Islami, Tablighi Jamat, Lashkar e Taiba, Jaish e Mohammed, Tehrik I Taliban of Pakistan, Sunni Tehrik follow the Deobandi tradition. Whilst solving contemporary problems, Deobandi ideologues are known to consult the fiqh or Islamic jurisprudence in addition to the Koranic text. The differences between Wahabism and Deobandism are both theological and cultural (Cesari 2004, 93). The Deobandi group are also seen as more flexible in their approach and they recognise other categories and groups within the *ummah* or world-wide Muslim community other than their own. For instance, they recognise the Sufi tradition which is associated with Islamic mysticism. The reason for this flexibility could be because South Asia was subjected to Islamisation at a much later date than Saudi Arabia, where the religion is believed to have survived in its pristine form. Thus, it is important to note that within Islamism, there are some groups which are more extremist than others, and it should be noted that all Islamists do not think in the same way. There are moderate Islamist groups, more extremist ones and those who fall in between. Most of these groups are not homogeneous and are highly fragmented.

THE HISTORICAL BACKGROUND

Scholars who have analysed and looked at the historical side of Islamism have identified three distinct phases. Let us first look at the historical side of Islamism and then we can look at Islamism in a more contemporary context. This will help us to set the context before we move on to the details of the South Asian situation. Islamism went through three distinct phases which have been identified as Islamic Revivalism, Islamic Reformism or Islamic Modernism and finally Islamic Radicalism (Edwards 2005; Chouerri 1990). The rough dates for the first phase are from 1750 to 1850. The rough dates for the second phase are from 1850 till 1950, and the final phase is seen as a post 1950 phenomenon.

When we look at the first phase of Islamic revivalism, we are basically looking at three great Islamic empires which were on the verge of collapse and disintegration. In this context, mention maybe made of Mughal India, Safavid Iran and Ottoman Turkey. These empires in the mid-1700s were on the brink of collapse and were about to crumble. At this point of time in history, all three empires were going through a phase of political turmoil, agricultural stagnation, demographic dislocations and dispersive movements. This was a time of political, economic and social crisis and people were moving around to better their situation, so that they could extricate themselves from the problems and the turmoil that they were grappling with. Most of these movements emerged in the peripheral parts of these empires where the central authorities did not have much control and the social basis of these movements was predominantly tribal (Choueiri 1990, 15-29). The Faraizi movement from Bengal in southern Asia is a good example of a revivalist movement. Because this was a phase of turmoil, revivalist ideologues tried to push Islam back onto the centre stage and argued that religion in its pristine form could provide solutions to the problems which Muslim people were facing. These ideologues had a very dichotomous approach to the world and saw the world in very binary terms. They divided the world into dar-ul-harb and dar-ul-Islam. Dar-ul-harb was enemy territory and dar-ul-Islam was seen as the true land of Islam. As a true Muslim, one was expected to migrate from dar-ul-harb or enemy territory or land of the infidel to the nearest Muslim land following the prophetic tradition called hijra. Mohammed Abdul Wahab from Arabia is the chief ideologue associated with this phase. Revivalist thinkers, however, failed to come up with suitable answers and hence the phase fizzled out and paved the way for the second phase to come into existence, which is called Islamic Reformism.

Islamic reformism or Islamic modernism is the second phase as far as the historical side of Islamism is concerned and the rough dates for this phase are from 1850 till 1950. These movements emerged in the wake of European colonial expansion and were a response to external pressure. Reformist thinkers were far more accommodating than their revivalist precursors. They had high regard for western philosophy and the European Enlightenment and they tried to use the European path to development and modernity in an Islamic context to help Muslims with the economic and political problems that they were facing. Mohammed Abduh from Egypt is the chief ideologue associated with this phase (Ibid.). Reformists, however, failed to come up with answers which paved the way for a vacuum which was filled in by the third phase called Islamic Radicalism.

Islamic radicalism is the third phase and is a post Second World War phase. Once again this was a phase of political and economic turmoil. The participants of this phase encompassed recent rural migrants to the cities, shopkeepers, peasants, school teachers, merchants and artisans and hence this phase is inextricably linked with the tensions, anxieties and ambitions of these different social groups and categories (Ibid.). Due to the economic challenges these groups were facing at the time, they made an attempt to move to the nearest urban centres to better themselves. According to Burke, 'In 1979, in Egypt, Iran and elsewhere, Islamic radicalism was drawing most of its recruits from the recently urbanized and often impoverished lower-middle classes that had resulted from massive population growth and economic development' (Burke 2007, 61). This phase was also the last attempt to create an Islamic totalitarian state and was seen as a response to the rising tide of nationalism which was dividing the historic land of dar-ul-Islam. This phase was strongly associated with countries of the Middle East and North Africa, and the chief ideologue associated with this phase was Sayyid Qutb, once again from Egypt. Sayid Qutb's impact on Islamist thought has been huge. He used the word, 'Jahilya' in a new and different way. Jahilya originally refers to the pre Islamic phase in Arabia when people worshipped stones, rivers, trees and idols. It is seen as a phase of ignorance and darkness by present day Islamist groups (Esposito 2003, 154). This is the original meaning of Jahilya. However, Qutb spoke of the new Jahilya. He argued that the Muslim world in the post Second World War phase was increasingly being besieged by the west, particularly by the Americans, and the US was exploiting Muslim resources to suit their own American interests. Furthermore, American culture was also having a decaying impact on the morals and lifestyles of the Muslim youth. According to Qutb, the Muslim youth were getting drawn into an American way of living and were being influenced by American pop music, and Hollywood films. The Muslim youth were increasingly rejecting Islamic clothing and dressing in a non-Muslim way, more in keeping with the way people dressed in the west in jeans and casual wear. American influence was having an eroding impact on the Islamic lifestyle which was practised by Muslims. The Muslim youth were getting distracted and getting drawn into McDonaldisation and Americanisation. He also spoke of sexual degeneration, homosexuality, alcoholism, drugs and sexual promiscuity. This was the new Jahilya according to Qutb. It had a political/economic side to it referring to American political hegemony in the Middle East and also the exploitation of Middle Eastern resources by the Americans to further American interests regionally as well as globally. But there was also a social-cultural side to the word Jahilya which referred to the impact America was increasingly having on the life styles of the Muslim youth, through films and music. This was pushing the Muslim youth away from the true path of Islam to a path of moral degeneration and cultural decay. The only way out of this state of decline according to Qutb was through *jihad* which would liberate Muslims (Milton-Edwards 2011, 155).

When we look at the above three phases, by and large what we see is that as the forces of modernity and globalisation sweep across traditional Muslim societies, it opens up opportunities for some, but it leaves others feeling excluded. Not everyone benefits from the modernisation process and from globalisation. The forces of modernity undermine traditional social norms, tear the bonds which exist between communities and also sharpen class differences. At first we see how the more reactionary elements in traditional societies try to bring about a marriage between tradition and modernity, but when that marriage does not work out and fails, some groups resort to violence and an Islamist movement is born. This is one of the classical explanations put forward by scholars working in the area of religious fundamentalism, that not just Islamism but any religious fundamentalist movement is a response to modernity and the modernisation process (Armstrong 2001, 140). There are of course other explanations and theories which argue that the rise of Islamism is a response to racism in the west (Afshar 2006; Abbas 2007), a response to poverty and economic deprivation (Pipes 2003), a response to oppressive political regimes (Rashid 2002), a response to globalisation (Stern 2003, 40-41) and a response to western foreign policy in the Muslim world

(Ahmed 2005/6, 41-45; Yaqoob 2007, 286). Most explanations of Islamism argue that it is a response to this or that and tend to be reactive explanations.

Although Wahab, Abduh and Qutb are seen as the chief ideologues who have contributed to the rise of Islamism down the ages, there are other thinkers, and politicians who have also contributed. A Nabhani from Jordan, Hasan al Bana and the Muslim Brotherhood from Egypt, Mawdudi and the Jamat I Islami from South Asia are a few examples of other religious thinkers. General Zia from Pakistan is an example of a military personnel or a political figure who also contributed to the process of Islamisation especially in South Central Asia in the early-mid 80s. In addition to politicians and religious thinkers, other major political developments like the Iranian Revolution of 1979 have also contributed to the rise of Islamism in the contemporary world (Esposito 1990).

THE CONTEMPORARY CONTEXT

Now that we have looked at the historical side of Islamism, let us look at how Islamism exists in a more contemporary context. We can then turn our focus to the South Asian situation. Scholars like Olivier Roy have used the word 'neo fundamentalism' to understand Islamism in contemporary times. This term was used in his celebrated book, 'Globalised Islam', which was published in the year 2004 (Roy 2004). He uses the word 'de-territorialisation' to understand contemporary Islamist movements and argues that Islamist groups and movements which were previously confined to a particular territory have now become global, transnational and this has happened as a result of globalisation, the use of technology and better communication systems. In other words, Islamist movements which were previously confined to a particular geographical territory have now become global. For instance, the Jamat I Islami or the Tablighi Jamat which are both south Asian in origin and were initially confined to South Asia now have their daughter versions in Britain. The Hizb ut Tahrir which was founded in the Middle East shortly after the Second World War and was previously confined to the Middle East now also has its daughter version in Britain. There are also off shoots of the Hizb ut Tahrir that have been operating in Britain in the early 90s. Roy also talks about how websites and technology have been used to spread Islamist messages.

American analyst Marc Sageman has built on Roy's argument and talks about the use of chat forums in addition to the internet and websites (Sageman, 2008). Sageman argues that the threat is no longer from foreign fanatics but from the alienated youth in the west who have been radicalised through Islamist websites and chat forums. It is commonly believed that leaders generate ideas and that disciples are passive recipients, but Sageman gives us a picture the other way round. These days, global Islamist networks are not evenly distributed, and the growth of the internet has transformed the dynamic of this evolving threat. This idea is in keeping with the new security agenda which argues that since the ending of the Cold War, there are new enemies, new challenges and new threats. Since 2000, there has been a shift from face to face interactions to interactions on the internet. In other words, there has been a shift from offline interactions to online interactions. Through chat forums, the Islamist discussions may revolve around how Muslims are being oppressed in different parts of the world by non-Muslim powers e.g., Kashmiri Muslims are being oppressed by the Indian government, Uyghur Muslims are being oppressed by the Chinese government, Britain and America have been oppressing Muslims throughout the Middle East and South Central Asia, and Israel has been oppressing Muslims in Palestine. In this connection, Daniel Byman writes 'Al Qaeda also used its training camps in Afghanistan to support various insurgent and terrorist groups throughout the Muslim world, helping fighters in Kashmir, Yemen, the Philippines, and elsewhere' (Byman 2015, 53). Through these chat forums, the 'ummah' or the world wide Muslim community becomes a reality, and something worth fighting for. Bomb making instructions can be downloaded from different websites. So although from our standpoint here in the west, Islamists may easily be categorised as terrorists, from the standpoint of people who they are trying to defend, they are seen as freedom fighters or liberators. Most of the Muslim youth who are found in these chat forums in the western world have been subjected to racism in their youth. They are the alienated youth and have been subjected to socio economic marginalisation. There is a sense of disillusionment (amongst the alienated youth) with Britain and America who talk about liberalism and democracy but in reality freedom is only for ethnic majorities and not for ethnic minorities. The internet has been used because of the increasing hostile monitoring of Mosques in recent times in the western world. Gender separation amongst Islamists is starting to disappear because of the use of the internet. Present day Islamist networks consist of both online and offline elements and thus the situation has become very complicated and unevenly distributed. For a long time, the British and American government missed out the point that home grown Islamists in the west are actively seeking out Al Qaeda rather than the other way round. According to Sageman, it is the internet which makes leaderless jihad possible (Sageman 2008).

THE SOUTH ASIAN SITUATION

Now that we have discussed the definition of Islamism and looked at its historical background and seen how it exists in a more contemporary globalised context, let us turn to the situation in South Asia. In this section of the chapter, we will be looking at Islamism in the Muslim majority countries of southern Asia, namely, Afghanistan, Pakistan and Bangladesh. We will first of all take up Afghanistan and Pakistan together, which is often called the AFPAK region collectively, and then we will look at the situation in Bangladesh.

THE AFPAK: AFGHANISTAN AND PAKISTAN

It is believed by many that at the time of 9/11, more Al Qaeda operatives lived in Pakistan than in any other country, which is why South Asia deserves special attention in this chapter. Daniel. S. Markey writes, 'The mastermind of 9/11, Khalid Sheikh Mohammed, was born to

Pakistani parents and captured in Rawalpindi in 2003, near Pakistan's capital. Eight years later, and just seventy miles to the north, U.S. Navy SEALs raided Osama bin Laden's compound in the Pakistani town of Abbottabad. No one can doubt that Al Qaeda's roots in Pakistan run chillingly deep' (Markey 2013, 11).

However, when one looks at the rise of Islamism in Pakistan, one really needs to take up the two countries of Afghanistan and Pakistan together collectively for discussion since the developments in the two countries in relation to Islamism are strongly intertwined with each other. It became clear by 2005 that the Taliban phenomenon was not just confined to the Pashtun areas of Afghanistan, but that it had also become Pakistan's most 'debilitating challenge' (Malik 2010, 152). Afghanistan and Pakistan are collectively referred to as the AFPAK region by the American security establishment in the post 9/11 phase and as a single theatre of operations. The term 'AFPAK' became increasingly popular when President Obama made it clear that the future of Afghanistan was inextricably linked with that of neighbouring Pakistan (Schofield 2010, 9). The demarcating line which separates the two countries is called the Durand Line, which was founded by Sir Mortimer Durand in the year 1893. It was a figure by the name of Abdur Rahman who had signed an agreement with the then British signatory of British India, Sir Henry Mortimer Durand, to delineate the 1610 mile long Afghan-Indian border. Since the Durand line split Waziristan, and thus the Waziri and Mehsud tribes, it sowed the seeds of instability in the border region (Hiro 2011, 27). Whilst Pakistan recognises this as the demarcating line, the Afghans do not. Afghans see this demarcating line as illegitimate and argue that there should be no border amongst Muslims (Paliwal 2016, 195). Since 9/11, after American intervention in Afghanistan, there has been a huge influx of Afghans into Pakistani territory crossing the Durand line which has paved the way for a new set of ethnic conflicts between the original inhabitants of Pakistan and the new arrivals from neighbouring Afghanistan. The influx of refugees from Afghanistan to Pakistan happened not only in the post 9//11 period with the onset of American bombing, but also when the Soviets invaded Afghanistan in the late seventies and early eighties. 'By the end of 1980, almost one million Afghans had come to Pakistan as refugees. By 1988, the number of refugees reached three million' (Haqqani 2016, 211).

Pakistan has recently been called 'The Warrior State' by scholars because it has been at war with itself since its creation in 1947 (Paul 2014, 2). Although there are multiple layers of conflict within Pakistan, one major area of conflict is between Islamists and secularists. The debate between the two groups revolves around what should be the path towards development and modernity for Pakistan: should it be along western secular lines or should it be along the lines of Sharia law.

The 9/11 Commission sees the AFPAK region as the new epicentre of radical Islam. Areas which have come under special focus include the FATA or the Federally Administered Tribal Areas, Balakot and Waziristan (Beg 2009, 149). 'The JUI (Jamiat-ul-Ulema-e-Islam) madrasas or religious schools/seminaries in the NWFP/North West Frontier Provinces and Baluchistan were prominent breeding grounds for the Taliban' (Shafqat 2009, 293). When we look at the rise of Islamism in the AFPAK, scholars tend to trace its origins to the rise of General Zia in Pakistani politics, who funded and trained the Afghan mujahedeen along with the American CIA, when Afghanistan was invaded by the Soviets in 1979. The Soviet invasion lasted for a full decade and ended in 1989. During this time General Zia in Pakistan and the American CIA supported the Afghan resistance to check the spread of Soviet Communism. 'The CIA shared responsibility for running the Afghan war with the ISI (Inter-Services Intelligence), and each year (1981-88) the former provided 640 million dollars for Afghan covert operations' (Hilali 2002, 301). Hein. G. Kiessling writes, 'months before the invasion of Soviet troops in Afghanistan in July 1979 President Carter had agreed to covert assistance to the Afghan resistance against the communist regime in Kabul' (Kiessling 2016, 48).

During Zia's time we also see the rise of Islamic seminaries or madrasas, which are often viewed unfavourably by sections in the American security establishment. 'Madrasa networks in the FATA/Federally Administered Tribal Areas, the Pashtun regions and the rest of Pakistan provided a constant stream of recruits during the years the Taliban held power in Afghanistan' (Siddique 2014, 73). Zia changed the motto of the Pakistani army, replacing Jinnah's formula, 'Faith, Unity and Discipline', with 'Imam, Taqwa, Jihad-fi-sibilillah' which refers to Faith, Piety and Holy War (Jaffrelot 2015, 468). Many see these Islamic seminaries along the AFPAK border as the new recruiting grounds or breeding grounds of Islamist terrorism. This, however, is contested. Some of the groups operate not just in the AFPAK, but also elsewhere in South Central Asia, including the Lashkar e Taiba, the Lashkar e Jhangvi, the Sunni Tehrik, the Taliban, Jaish e Mohammed, and the Tehrik I Taliban of Pakistan. Many of these groups have also participated in the conflict in Kashmir, which is a contested territory primarily between India and Pakistan. It should be noted that all these Islamist groups do not think and operate in the same way. Some are more extremist than others.

Most theories in relation to Islamism have argued that Islamism is a response to this or that and are reactive explanations. In the case of Afghanistan, it is most certainly seen as a response to the Soviet invasion of Afghanistan and the oppression associated with it. Musharraf writes, 'The trauma started in 1979 with the invasion of Afghanistan by the Soviet Union' (Musharraf 2006, 274). The rise of Islamism in this part of the world needs to be understood in this context. As one author notes: 'The earliest resistance to the Soviets arose through the loosely structured Harakat-i-Inquilab Islami Party headed by Maulvi Mohammed Nabi Mohammedi' (Rasanayagam 2010, 177). Islamist groups could be easily mobilised when the cause of Islam was threatened. The reason why the Soviets invaded Afghanistan in 1979 was because they had a fear of being encircled by other powers, and Afghanistan could potentially act as a good buffer zone for Russia. The Iranian Revolution of 1979 also had a destabilising impact on regional security which could have precipitated the Soviet invasion of Afghanistan. To integrate Afghanistan into the mother country, a Russification programme followed, which proved to be very oppressive both politically and economically. As a part of the Russification programme, Communist indoctrination started early and young men were uprooted from Afghanistan and sent to Russia to feel more Russian,

Russian language was introduced in Afghan schools, Afghan teachers were expected to talk about Russian-Afghan friendship, text books were prepared by Soviet advisors, the Soviets controlled the news programmes, Russian films were screened regularly, the Soviets followed a policy of Divide and Rule and they exploited regional Afghan resources to suit the needs of the mother country. As the situation became increasingly oppressive both politically and economically, there was resistance from below supported by Pakistan and the Americans, and hence we see the rise of the mujahedeen. It is widely believed that a lot of the south Asian Islamist groups emerged from the mujahedeen.

After the invasion came to an end and after the ending of the Cold War in 1989/90, the mujahedeen lost their purpose and were no longer employed to fight against the Soviets. But they still had easy access to weapons which had been provided to them by the CIA and General Zia during the 70s and 80s. So much of the post 90s Islamist violence was possible because of what happened during the earlier Cold War phase. This sits very well with one of the features of Kaldor's, 'new wars' thesis when she argues that many of the conflicts in the post 1990s period were a result of the consequences of the Cold War (Kaldor 2006). So it is against this backdrop that the Taliban came into existence. Although there has been some confusion about whether the Taliban is a group, movement or an ideology, it is certain that their roots are intrinsically tied up with the Soviet legacy. The word, 'taliban', comes from the word 'talib', which refers to a student from a humble background. Because most of the Taliban leaders were from a Pashto background and because the areas that they took charge of were also predominantly Pashto, this was one of the reasons why they could come into power and stay in power for so long. Analysts often talk about this as the common ethnicity factor. Only three countries in the Muslim world recognised the Taliban as the legitimate rulers after they captured power in Kabul in 1996 and these countries were Pakistan, Saudi Arabia and the United Arab Emirates (Steele 2011, 219). The Taliban, ideologically, follows *deobandism* and was supported by Pakistan's Frontier Constabulary and the National Logistics Cell. 'Pakistan did not create the Taliban, but the Taliban could not have survived amongst Afghanistan's warring factions without the support of Islamabad' (Rashid 2002, 212). With the passage of time, offshoots of the Taliban spread all over the AFPAK region. Islamist terrorist networks which have had their origins in the AFPAK have attacked India several times. In this connection, mention maybe made of the 2008 attacks, when the iconic Taj Mahal hotel came under assault in Mumbai along with the attacks on the Jewish centre, and the Central Railway Station in Mumbai. 'In 2001, five men believed to be affiliated with organisations in Pakistan attacked the Parliament in New Delhi, launching a direct assault on the seat of Indian democratic governance. Eight years prior, in March 1993, an Indian criminal don, Dawood Ibrahim, facilitated by Pakistan's ISI/Inter-Services Intelligence, orchestrated a series of bomb explosions in Mumbai that left 257 people dead' (Perkovich and Dalton 2016, 1). It is now evident that the terrorist attack on the Parliament House was carried out collaboratively by Pak based and supported terrorist outfits, namely, Lashkar-e-Taiba and Jaish-e-Mohammed (Singh 2013, 246).

This analysis of Islamism in the AFPAK would not be complete without some mention of western intervention in the region post 9/11, and how western intervention has exacerbated the already strained situation. 'With lower Manhattan in ruins, not only President Bush, but almost all members of Congress, and a great majority of Americans believed that a military response to 9/11 was the proper course of action' (Shlapentokh, Woods and Shiraev 2005, 180). Western intervention in the region took place in the form of Operation Enduring Freedom and Overseas Contingency Operations. Although post 9/11, western governments initially focussed on Iraq and Afghanistan, many of these Islamist groups had regrouped into neighbouring Pakistan after the bombing had started. 'The US military campaign in 2001 involved mainly the CIA, Special Operations Forces and air power' (Bali 2012, 31). This influx of Islamist groups and ordinary Afghans into Pakistan brought them into conflict with the original residents of Pakistan. The CIA's operations in the region were vast, complicated, expensive and counterproductive (Rashid 2009, 131). They funded the warlords who in turn recruited hundreds of militia men. They acted as ground forces, spies and bodyguards for the Americans. This only created further mayhem. The CIA Special Operations Force set up bases along the Pakistan border, and this was done to gather intelligence about Al Qaeda. They hired Pashto tribesmen as well, paying these men about 200 dollars a month along with bonuses. These mercenaries were called the Afghan Militia Force and were being hired as late as 2006. The Special Operations Force also had the authority to hire about a hundred of these men who would then act as interpreters, guard their camps and act as drivers for the Americans. The AMF commanders received cash, weapons and communications equipment and often sold the weapons of the Taliban on the black market. These commanders became a destabilising force in the countryside since they saw themselves as unaccountable to anyone. The war lords were fragmented and not a unified group. They fought to have control over drugs, tolls and weapons which only added to the crisis situation. Needless to say, western intervention in the AFPAK since 9/11 has had an adverse impact on regional South Asian as well as global security, paving the way for further instability. In the later stages of American intervention in the AFPAK region, 'as its use increased, the drone became a symbol of America's war on terror' (Ahmed 2013, 1). Its main targets appeared to be Muslim tribal groups living in the AFPAK and other countries like Yemen and Somalia. 'Incessant and concentrated strikes were directed at what was considered the ground zero of the war on terror, Waziristan, in the tribal areas of Pakistan' (Ibid.). These communities, some of the poorest and most isolated in the world, had become the targets of the 21st century's most advanced kill technology. Very recently in April, 2017 it was reported in the Telegraph, a Kolkata based newspaper, that the 'American forces dropped one of the largest conventional bombs ever used in combat on what they described as a tunnel complex used by the Islamic State militants in Nangarhar's Achin district' (*The Telegraph*, 15th April, 2017, p5). Achin is separated from Pakistan by a range of high mountains. This was one of the areas where the Taliban militants and groups associated with Al Qaeda fled when the Americans intervened in Afghanistan in late 2001. There are many Afghans who view Washington with deep suspicion and unfavourably and see the on-going American presence in Afghanistan as nothing short of an occupation of their country. However, there are others who view American intervention since 2001 favourably, fearing that the alternative would be a return to strict Islamist rule associated with the Taliban.

This problem of Islamist terror in the AFPAK region has continued till 2017. In an article entitled, 'Taliban raid kills 140 at Afghan base' which came out on Sunday, the 23rd of April, 2017, in the Kolkata based newspaper, the Telegraph, it was reported that at least 140 Afghan soldiers were killed by Taliban militants disguised in military uniforms and this incident came to be known as one of the deadliest attacks ever on an Afghan military base (*The Telegraph*, 23rd April, 2017, p3). This attack occurred on the 22nd of April in the northern city of Mazar I Sharif. In addition to the 140 soldiers who were killed, there were many more who were injured and badly hurt. This attack clearly shows us the on-going struggle of the Afghan government, backed by the international community, against the Taliban insurgency that has gripped Afghanistan for more than ten years now. In another article entitled, '22 killed in Pak Mosque attack', which came out in the Telegraph on Saturday, the first of April, 2017, it was reported that a 'bomb apparently targeting a mosque in Pakistan's north western city of Parachinar killed at least 22 people today and wounded dozens in an attack claimed by the Pakistani Taliban' (*The Telegraph*, 1 April 2017, p2). Thus, the future of the AFPAK region still seems to be fraught with much peril and uncertainty.

THE RISE OF ISLAMISM IN BANGLADESH

Now that we have looked at the rise of Islamism in the AFPAK region and the more frontier parts of the Indian subcontinent, let us now turn to South Asia proper, and focus on Bangladesh. Before we look at the rise of Islamism in present day Bangladesh, let us first take a brief look at the history of Islam in this part of South Asia, which will help to set the context.

The spread of Islam to the more eastern parts of the subcontinent happened during the middle ages. It was a figure by the name of

Muhammad Bhaktiyar Khalji who was responsible for bringing Islam and Turkish rule to Bengal, much of which is present day Bangladesh, in the Middle Ages. Khalji made his raids into the heart of Bengal in early 1200. The Turkish elite at that time came into close contact with the local people which is probably one reason why Islam spread so rapidly in Bengal. This is in contrast to the surrounding areas of Delhi where a predominantly Hindu stamp remained despite the fact that the Delhi-Agra part of South Asia has been the seat of Muslim rule for centuries. Islam spread to Bengal due the efforts and preachings of wandering dervishes or pirs called qalandars (Sengupta 2011, 82). They preached universal brotherhood and direct communion with God and the other fundamentals of Islam but mixed it up with local customs, traditions and practices, which is why it appealed so much to the masses. Instead of taking a hardliner top down approach and doing away with local traditions, these wandering dervishes preached monotheism, mass prayers, social egalitarianism and discouraged image worship and mixed the basic tenets of Islam with local traditions (Ibid). On some occasions these wandering dervishes would take to arms as well to spread the message of Islam. Whilst the sword of Islam did have a role to play in converting people, one of the main reasons why many so called lower caste Hindus converted to Islam is because Brahmanical Hinduism was becoming increasingly oppressive. The rigidities of the case system for instance, and the cruel treatment of women, widows in particular were facets of the Hindu tradition which the common people were becoming highly dissatisfied with. In addition to this, Islam also spread to Bengal because of the mass migration of Muslim traders, officials and soldiers from north India to Bengal and also because it was easier to find job opportunities in the Muslim government and bureaucracy at the time if you were Muslim. In Bengal, Islam is basically a syncretic fusion of Islam with local Hindu traditions. There are shrines all over Bengal where both Hindus and Muslims pray side by side. Islam is thus marked by a high degree of flexibility here and is very accommodating of other religious practices. The Sufis and the Vaishnava poets from Islam and Hinduism emphasised the common areas between the two dominant religions which helped in bridge building and bringing people together. So if this is the history of Islam in Bengal, which is by and large one of peaceful coexistence, why has there then been a rise in Islamist violence in recent years? Some analysts argue that Islamist violence in Bangladesh has been so much on the rise in recent times that it might very well become the next Afghanistan (Karlekar 2005).

After partition, which took place in 1947, Bangladesh was a part of Pakistan and was then called East Pakistan. It remained as East Pakistan till the Liberation War broke out in 1971, which is the year when former East Pakistan seceded from West Pakistan with Indian assistance and became the independent country of Bangladesh. The reason for this secession was because Bengali Muslims were not being fairly represented in political and military circles. There was economic discrimination and West Pakistan was also imposing their cultural values and language on the Bengali people, all of which was increasingly becoming oppressive. After 1971 though, Bangladesh has not had an easy journey and has slipped into military dictatorships on two occasions firstly under Zia ur Rahman from 1976 till 1981, and then under Mohammed Ershad who was in power from 1982 to 1990. Like their Pakistani counterparts, both these generals also used religion to further their own agenda and brought religion back to the political forefront. The military brought back religion based identity politics. Basic political reform started to take place from the post 90s period with Khaleda Zia and Sheikh Hasina (Jahan 2000).

It has been argued by scholars such as Ali Riaz that although Bangladesh historically has had a strong culturally embedded vibrant public sphere which has consisted of a multiplicity of publics and that the idea of a public sphere was based on secular rationality, the situation is now changing, and attempts are increasingly being made to create an Islamist public sphere (Riaz 2013, 299). What Riaz means by an Islamist public sphere is 'a space for debates informed by Islamic texts and interpretations to foreground Islam in daily lives and create counter publics' (Ibid.). This is happening as a result of the growth of Islamist parties within the country. 'Globally unnoticed, on 17th August 2005, Bangladesh experienced its own 9/11 in a shockwave of terror when a relatively unknown Islamist group, Jamaatul Mujahideen Bangladesh

(JMB), detonated 500 bombs simultaneously across the country' (Hasan 2011, 98). At every bombing spot pamphlets had been left with demands of establishing the law of Allah in the country by getting rid of the current democratic system, claiming that 'democracy and constitutions are sources of polytheism' (Ibid.). The JMB then went on to attack the Bangladesh judicial system by several suicide bomb attacks on the third and eighth of October and fourteenth November, 2005, murdering four judges to emphasise on the seriousness of their demand. On-going tensions between the Bangladesh government and two influential Islamist parties, the Jamaat I Islami Bangladesh (JIB) and the Hizb ut Tahrir Bangladesh (HTB) opened up a space for a dialogue to take place between the two sides about the role of political Islam in Bangladesh's public life. Recently, atheist bloggers were hacked to death and public intellectuals and writers such as Taslima Nasreen have been driven out of the country because of their more secular ways.

The Jamat I Islami Bangladesh is one of the largest and most active Islamist parties in contemporary Bangladesh. Earlier it operated under the name Jamat I Islami East Pakistan, led by Mawdudi, the well-known south Asian revivalist thinker of the 20th century. After former East Pakistan seceded from West Pakistan in 1971 and became the independent country of Bangladesh this party could not operate within the official political discourse because secularism was decreed as one of the new state's principles. There are also strong accusations that members of this party were actually involved in helping the Pakistani army kill Bangladeshi freedom fighters in order to maintain the unity of one Muslim country. After the murder of the first Bangladeshi President, Sheikh Mujibar Rahman, in 1975, the military seized power and stayed in power till 1990 and allowed the JIB to operate. The JIB leaders had strong connections with Middle Eastern countries and the military regime was heavily dependent on foreign aid which primarily came from the Middle East, oil rich Islamic countries. Therefore, to win the approval of these oil rich Islamic countries the military regimes in Bangladesh allowed Islamist parties to operate freely and to have a say in politics. The aim of the JIB has been to bring about changes in all spheres of public life on the basis of the guidance revealed by Allah and exemplified by His Prophet Mohammed. The JIB is supported by different groups such as students, intellectuals, the military and civil servants. It also became the main ally of the BNP/Bangladesh National Party before 2008. However, the JIB is currently under pressure because the Bangladeshi Awami League party under Sheikh Hasina has vowed to bring war criminals, a number of whom were strongly associated with the JIB, to face a war crimes trial. 'During her previous term in office (December 2008-January 2014), Sheikh Hasina was proactive in cracking down on radical Islamists and emphasising the secular principles of the country's founding' (Curtis, Florance, Lohman and Philips 2014, 10).

The HTB/Hizb ut Tahrir emerged as a global Islamist party shortly after the Second World War. It was founded by An Nabhani in Jordan. It works at all levels of society to restore to Muslims a means of living an Islamic life under the shade of the Caliphate. It has operated throughout the Muslim world, but is also banned in certain countries like Saudi Arabia, Pakistan, Syria, Tunisia, Lebanon, Egypt, Turkey and Libya. It is believed that an individual by the name of Golam Mowla, a lecturer of Management at Dhaka University, went to London in 1993 for his PhD studies and was introduced to discussions on the Hizb ut Tahrir at Regent's Park Mosque in London. After he returned to Bangladesh, in 2000, Mowla set up an office at a coaching centre in the capital city of Dhaka to disseminate the ideas of the Hizb ut Tahrir, and this paved the way for the formation of Hizb ut Tahrir Bangladesh. The HTB has supporters from both students and the academic community in Bangladesh. Mohiuddin Ahmed, another academic also led the HTB for a while. Finally, by the end of 2009, the party was banned for carrying out anti-government activity (Hasan 2011).

The JMB as mentioned earlier made its presence felt by detonating 500 bombs simultaneously in 2005 throughout Bangladesh, and they have claimed responsibility for further acts of extremism and violence, including suicide bombings in courts, and throwing grenades at foreign diplomats. Following pressure from donors, the group was banned, and in 2007 seven members of the organisation were executed following a trial. However, the execution of top members of the JMB did not mean the end of this Islamist movement.

Some analysts believe that Bangladesh was swept by a wave of Islamic militancy from 1999 till the year 2005, but that it cannot really take root in the country (Khan 2011, 51). For instance, Khan argues that Bangladesh saw a rise in Islamic militancy because of foreign ideology and tactics that was brought to Bangladesh by some returnees from the Afghan War against the Soviet occupation in the 1980s, which we have discussed already in the earlier section on the AFPAK. These veterans had imbibed Islamist ideology whilst in Afghanistan, but when they returned from Afghanistan to Bangladesh, they thought they could transplant the same fanatical ideology in Bangladesh. Khan argues, 'The relative ease by which the Bangladesh government's anti-terrorism campaign crushed this outbreak of Islamist militancy demonstrated how the militants had misunderstood Islam in the Bangladesh context, a context in which Islam is intimately interwoven with deeper traditions of tolerance and secularism in that culture' (Ibid., 64). It is true that Bangladeshi culture is tolerant and has been accommodating of other traditions like Hinduism, which we discussed earlier in this section. However, recent events have clearly shown us that Islamism in contemporary Bangladesh is most certainly on the rise. Bangladesh has attracted international media attention because of Islamist terror attacks, many of which took place in 2015, particularly after the killing of many bloggers by a local Islamist group associated with the AQIS, Al Qaeda in the Indian Subcontinent, and the murder of foreign nationals, responsibility for which has been claimed by the Islamic State (Riaz 2016). 'Although Bangladesh has clocked an average seven per cent growth in the past few years and made significant achievements on several human development indices, it has drawn more attention in recent times for terror related incidents' (Purohit 2017, 7). On March 29th, more than a thousand students marched on the campus of Dhaka University against terrorism. In March, 2017, a family of eight including children blew themselves up after the police stormed a hideout of the neo Jamat ul Mujahideen Bangladesh (neo JMB) in Nasirpur after a two day stand-off (*The Telegraph*, 2017, p3). The blast was so powerful that that it tore the bodies into pieces, making it very difficult for the police to ascertain exactly how many people were inside the militant den in Moulvibazar Sadar upazila, Nasirpur (Ibid). The militants in the hideout belonged to the pro-Islamic State neo JMB. In late March of 2017, six people including two police officers were killed and over forty wounded in two bomb blasts in the north eastern city of Sylhet. It was reported on the 28th of March in 2017 in *The Telegraph* that the IS claimed responsibility for this act of terrorism in Sylhet (*The Telegraph*, 2017, p2). Thus, from the discussion above it is quite clear that the future of Bangladesh, like the AFPAK region, is fraught with much peril.

THE RISE OF GLOBAL ISLAMISM: THE BRITISH CONTEXT

Now that we have looked at the specificities associated with the South Asian situation, let us turn to the rise of global Islamism, focussing on Islamism in the west, especially the British context. It was argued earlier that Islamist movements which previously had a territorial basis have now become de territorialised and supranational as a result of globalisation, better communication systems and technology (Roy 2004). Islamist groups which originated in South Asia now have a presence in Britain amongst the south Asian diaspora (Lewis 1994). Just as the public face of Islam and Islamism in France is dominated by North African groups from countries like Algeria, Tunisia and Morocco, the public face of British Islam and Islamism has been dominated by groups from the Indian subcontinent (Kepel 1997). This has happened partly because of Britain's connections with ex colonial territories. Most of the Islamist terrorists in the British context have been of south Asian descent, although not all (Abbas 2007, 6). In the post war period, Britain needed cheap labour from ex colonial territories like South Asia to work in Britain for reconstruction and development. Since the 50s we have seen waves of migration taking place from South Asia to Britain especially from Mirpur in Azad Kashmir, Pakistan, Gujarat in India and Sylhet in Bangladesh. As these flows of migration have been happening we also see the arrival of different Islamist groups and ideologues, who have played a crucial role in the radicalisation of the British Muslim youth.

When we look at the British context more closely and try to analyse the 7/7 bombings or the more recent attacks which have taken place in Manchester and London in 2017, we need to locate them in the context of social exclusion, economic marginalisation and racism, which the British Muslim youth are often subjected to on a regular basis. Sadek Hamid argues that people join Islamist groups in Britain 'for a number of different reasons such as a search for shelter from racism and Islam-o-phobia, the negative impact of geo-politics and social dislocation and group identity' (Hamid 2007, 150). One of the most powerful arguments which has come up in several pieces of scholarship on Islamism in Britain is that Islamism is a response to racism (Afshar 2006). As Marc Sageman mentions in his *Leaderless Jihad* (2008), it is the alienated youth who are drawn to Islamic radicalisation. Racism today does not exist the way it used to twenty years ago. It has changed its character with the passage of time as most things do. Racism today exists in more subtle and indirect ways. The days of direct racism are by and large over although that may happen too. The British Muslim youth, for instance will find it harder to get jobs, punishments meted out to British Muslims and ethnic minorities more generally are much harsher than those meted out to their white counterparts when in prison, and treatment of minorities is often very unfair when they try to access public services. There is a sense of disillusionment with the broader British establishment amongst ethnic minorities in Britain especially amongst south Asian groups. The system seems to work well for the white majority, but not for south Asian Muslims. Not just the British Muslim youth, but ethnic minorities more generally are subjected to discrimination and injustice in Britain on a daily basis. It is this structural violence which needs urgent attention. Many ethnic minorities feel that Britain is not a liberal democracy for them but a democracy that suits the needs of the white majority. Often in employment, the few ethnic minorities who may hold a senior position are not taken seriously. Well known scholar on Islamic radicalism in Britain, Tahir Abbas in his edited book, 'Islamic Political Radicalism: A European Perspective' writes, 'In

Western Europe, indigenous born Muslims can often experience a complex and dislocated existence. Post war immigrant groups who were either invited or came searching for improved economic opportunities have found their young growing up in societies that exhibit prejudice, discrimination and racism towards minority Muslim communities' (Abbas 2007, 3). Issues of racism never get addressed and the perpetrators often go unpunished. What makes matters worse is when people from the ethnic white majority make excuses for racism and choose to ignore it making the British Muslim youth feel like second class citizens. Currently, the atmosphere in Britain is politically charged with a sense of Islam-o-phobia, primarily because of negative depictions of Islam and the Muslim world on British television. Acts of terrorism in the UK or anywhere in the western world are often blown out of proportion whereas terrorist attacks in the Muslim world do not receive the same kind of attention and do not get a similar coverage, which makes people in the west often forget that people in places like Pakistan are also victims just as much as they are[23]. Lives lost because of western intervention in Muslim countries is an area that is not covered by the western media in the same way. The western media also gives the impression that the west is a force for good in the world and the east is a force for evil thereby pandering to all sorts of orientalist understandings of world politics and stereotypical imaging (Said 1978/1997, and Guny 1996). In recent years it has also given the impression that it values the lives of people in the west more than the lives of people living in parts of the Muslim world. This message especially comes across to British Muslims when terrorist attacks abroad in the Muslim world do not get the same kind of coverage, whereas attacks in the west are often blown out of proportion and over emphasised. This sort of biased approach deepens the cleavage which already exists between ethnic minorities and ethnic majority communities in Britain. Thus, the media is known to pander to western prejudices. Negative stories sell newspapers

---

[23] For example, on 16 December 2014, gunmen affiliated with the Tehrik-i-Taliban (TTP) massacred over one hundred school children at an army run school in Peshawar ('Pakistan Taliban: Peshawar school attack leaves 141 dead', BBC News, 16 December 2014, http://www.bbc.co.uk/news/world-asia-30491435; 'Taliban massacre school kids', *The Statesman*, Kolkata, 17 December 2014).

and journalists often have a profit motive. Negative images of the Muslim world and of ethnic minorities within Britain have only added fuel to the fire and increased racial tension in contemporary Britain. In a democracy, the media is supposed to act as checks and balances on the government. However, many ethnic minorities especially from the Muslim community feel that it acts as a divisive force in Britain, separating them from the white majority. Needless to say, television has a powerful impact on the minds of people and when these negative images are constantly shown, the racism gets worse and the British Muslim youth feel even more excluded. Furthermore, the global war on terror is seen by most Muslims in Britain as a war against Islam. The anti-terror laws directed primarily at ethnic minorities in Britain which were introduced shortly after the 7/7 bombings in London have most certainly exacerbated the situation. Abbas writes, 'After 9/11, and certainly after 7/7, a whole host of factors have negatively impacted on British Muslims' (Ibid.). Some of these include increasing anti-terrorist measures, increased policing powers, and racial and ethnic profiling in the criminal justice system just to mention a few. When the British Muslim youth see Britain and America dropping bombs on Muslim lands their sense of loyalty for Britain is likely to weaken since many would feel strongly about their collective sense of Islamic identity associated with the *ummah* or the world wide Muslim community. Western foreign policy in the Middle East and South Central Asia spearheaded by Britain and America and British high handedness and repression against its own minority communities has added to the crisis and only strengthened transnational Islamist groups paving the way for further radicalisation in the 21st century.

The way forward for Britain is not to further crackdown on Islamist groups and the British Muslim community more generally, but to look more closely and pay careful attention to this problem of structural violence and issues of racism. Playing the blame game will not help. As a democracy, Britain has a responsibility for looking after its ethnic minorities. The current state of a lot of minorities in Britain from where large numbers of terrorists or potential terrorists come is a sorry state of affairs. Ethnic minority issues are often very sensitive and need to be dealt with more sympathy rather than following a policy of high handedness and repression. Violence breeds more violence so a policy of crackdown which Britain has followed so far can never be the solution. The media would need to stop depicting negative images of the East and the Muslim world in particular. The media would need to be more balanced in their approach rather than sensationalising these very sensitive issues. The media and the government can collectively play a constructive role in bridge building and bringing communities together. Social policy workers working on ethnic minorities in Britain and issues of multiculturalism would need to do more collaborative work with security analysts who are dealing with issues of terrorism. Finally, the state centric militaristic approach which both Britain and America have taken since 9/11 to deal with global Islamism and transnational terrorist networks needs to stop. Western intervention in far off Muslim countries is often viewed very unfavourably by British born Muslims and ethnic minorities living closer to home[24].

REFERENCES

Abbas, A. 2014. *The Taliban Revival: Violence and Extremism on the Pakistan-Afghanistan Frontier*. New Haven and London: Yale University Press.

Abbas, T. (ed.). 2007. *Islamic Political Radicalism: A European Perspective*. Edinburgh: Edinburgh University Press.

Afshar, H. 2006. "Islam and Democracy." *Democracy Series*: Hansard Society.

Ahmed, S. 2005/6. "Post 7/7: Is Legislation Enough?" *New Civilization*, Winter.

---

[24] See Christopher Hope, 'Corbyn: UK wars to blame for terror', *The Daily Telegraph*, 26 May 2017, p.1. Hope writes that the Labour leader, Jeremy Corbyn, is a consistent opponent of British military intervention and recently said that Britain had not fought a just conflict since 1945.

Ahmed, A. 2013. *The Thistle and the Drone: How America's War on Terror Became a Global War on Tribal Islam*. Noida: Harper Collins Publishers.

Armstrong, K. 2001. *Islam: A Short History*. London: Phoenix Press.

Bali, S. 2012. "Afghanistan and the War on Terror." In *South Asian Security: 21ˢᵗ Century Discourses*, edited by Sagarika Dutt and Alok Bansal, 29-46. London and New York: Routledge.

Beg, S. 2009. "Pakistan's Tribal Areas: A Battle for Jihad." In *Religion, Conflict and Military Intervention*, edited by R. Durward and L. Marsden. Farnham, Surrey: Ashgate.

Bhutto, B. 2008. *Reconciliation: Her Final Words on Islam, Democracy and the West*. London: Pocket Books.

Burke, J. 2007. *Al Qaeda: The True Story of Radical Islam*. London: Penguin Books.

Byman, D. 2015. *Al Qaeda, The Islamic State, and the Global Jihadist Movement*. Oxford: Oxford University Press.

Cesari, J. 2004. *When Islam and Democracy Meet*. Basingstoke: Palgrave Macmillan.

Chouerri, Y. 1990. *Islamic Fundamentalism*. London: Pinter.

Curtis, L., C. Florance, W. Lohman, and J. Philips. 2014. "Pursuing a Freedom Agenda Amidst Rising Global Islamism," *The Heritage Foundation, Special Report*, No.159.

Edwards, B. 2005. *Islamic Fundamentalism since 1945*. London: Routledge.

Esposito, J. 1990. *The Iranian Revolution: Its Global Impact*. Florida: Florida International University Press.

Esposito, J. 2003. *The Oxford Dictionary of Islam*. Oxford and New York: Oxford University Press.

Guny, A.1996. *Images of Islam in 18ᵗʰ Century Writings*. London: Grey Seal.

Hamid, S. 2007. "Islamic Political Radicalism in Britain: The Case of Hizb-ut-Tahrir." In *Islamic Political Radicalism: A European Perspective* edited by T. Abbas, 145-159. Edinburgh: Edinburgh University Press.

Haqqani, H. 2016. *Pakistan: Between Mosque and Military*. Gurgaon: Penguin Viking.

Hasan, M. 2011. "Democracy and Political Islam in Bangladesh." *South Asia Research* 31(2): 97-117.

Hilali, A.Z. 2002. "The Costs and Benefits of the Afghan War for Pakistan." *Contemporary South Asia* 11(3): 291-310.

Hiro, D. 2011. *Jihad on Two Fronts: South Asia's Unfolding Drama*. New Delhi: Harper Collins Publishers.

Jaffrelot, C. 2015. *The Pakistan Paradox: Instability and Resilience*. Gurgaon: Random House India.

Jahan, R. 2000. *Bangladesh: Promise and Performance*. London: Zed Books.

Kaldor, M. 2006. *New Wars and Old Wars*. Cambridge: Polity.

Karlekar, H. 2005. *Bangladesh: The Next Afghanistan?* New Delhi: Sage Publications.

Kepel, G. 1997. *Allah in the West: Islamic Movements in America and Europe*. Cambridge: Polity Press.

Khan, M. 2011. "Islamist Militancy in Bangladesh: Why it failed to take root?" *Journal of Policing, Intelligence and Counter Terrorism* 6(1): 51-64.

Kiessling, H. G. 2016. *Faith, Unity, Discipline: The ISI of Pakistan*. Noida: Harper Collins Publishers India.

Lewis, P. 1994. *Islamic Britain*. London: I. B.Tauris.

Malik, I. 2010. *Pakistan: Democracy, Terror and the Building of a Nation*. London: New Holland Publishers.

Markey, D. S. 2013. *No Exit from Pakistan: America's Tortured Relationship with Islamabad*. New Delhi: Cambridge University Press.

MetCalf, B. 1982. *Islamic Revival in British India: Deoband, 1860-1900*. Princeton, New Jersey: Princeton University Press.

Milton-Edwards, B. 2011. *Contemporary Politics in the Middle East*. Cambridge: Polity.

Mukherjee, K. 2009. "Islamism and Neo Fundamentalism" In *Religion, Conflict and Military Intervention*, edited by R. Durward and L. Marsden, 17-31. Farnham, Surrey: Ashgate.

Musharraf, P. 2006. *In the Line of Fire: A Memoir*. London: Pocket Books.

Paliwal, A. 2016. "Pakistan-Afghanistan Relations since 2001: There are no Endgames" In *Pakistan at the Crossroads: Domestic Dynamics and External Pressures*, edited by C. Jaffrelot, 191-218. Gurgaon: Random House India.

Paul, T. V. 2014. *The Warrior State: Pakistan in the Contemporary World*. Gurgaon: Random House India.

Perkovich, G. and T. Dalton. 2016. *Not War, Not Peace: Motivating Pakistan to Prevent Cross Border Terrorism*. New Delhi: Oxford University Press.

Pipes, D. 2002. *Militant Islam Reaches America*. London and New York: W.W.Norton.

Purohit, D. 2017. "In Dhaka Varsity, signs of 'no fear'. " *The Telegraph*, Calcutta/Kolkata, 29th March, 2017.

Rasanayagam, A. 2010. *Afghanistan: A Modern History*. London: I.B.Tauris.

Rashid, A. 2002. *Jihad: The Rise of Militant Islam in Central Asia*. New Delhi: Penguin Books.

Rashid, A. 2009. *Descent into Chaos: Pakistan, Afghanistan and the Threat to Global Security*. London: Penguin Books.

Riaz, A. 2013. "The New Islamist Public Sphere in Bangladesh," *Global Change, Peace and Security* 25(3): 299-312.

Riaz, A. 2016. "Who are the Bangladeshi Islamist Militants?" *Perspectives on Terrorism* 10(1): 2-18.

Roy, O. 2004. *Globalised Islam*. London: Hurst.

Sageman, M. 2008. *Leaderless Jihad*. Philadelphia: Pennsylvania University Press.

Said, E. 1978. *Orientalism*. New York: Random House.

Said, E. 1997. *Covering Islam: How the Media and the Experts determine how we see the rest of the world*. London: Vintage Books.

Schofield, V. 2010. *Afghan Frontier: At the Crossroads of Conflict*. London: Tauris Parke Paperbacks.

Sengupta, N. 2011. *Land of Two Rivers: A History of Bengal from the Mahabharata to Mujib*. New Delhi: Penguin Books.

Shafqat, S. 2009. "The Kargil Conflict's Impact on Pakistani Politics and Society." In *Asymmetric Warfare in South Asia: The Causes and Consequences of the Kargil Conflict*, edited by P. Lavoy, 280-308. Cambridge: Cambridge University Press.

Shlapentokh, V., J. Woods, and E. Shiraev, (eds.). 2005. *America: Sovereign Defender or Cowboy Nation?* Aldershot: Ashgate.

Siddique, A. 2014. *The Pashtuns: The Unresolved Key to the Future of Pakistan and Afghanistan*. Gurgaon: Random House India.

Sinclair, T. J. 2012. *Global Governance*. Cambridge and Malden (USA): Polity Press.

Singh, J. 2013. *India at Risk: Mistakes, Misconceptions and Misadventures of Security Policy*. New Delhi: Rainlight/Rupa Publications.

Steele, J. 2011. *Ghosts of Afghanistan: The Haunted Battleground*. London: Portobello.

Stern, J. 2003. *Terror in the name of God: Why religious militants kill?* New York: Harper Collins.

The Telegraph (Kolkata), 2017, 'Family blew themselves up after police stormed den: 8 killed in Bangla raid', p.3.

The Telegraph (Kolkata), 23.04.2017, 'Taliban raid kills 140 at Afghan base', p.3.

The Telegraph (Kolkata), 1.04.2017, 'Taliban claim responsibility for raid: 22 killed in Pak Mosque attack', p.2.

The Telegraph (Kolkata), 15.04.2017, 'Reactions mixed in Afghan village after bombing', p.5.

The Telegraph (Kolkata), 28.03.2017, '4 Militants Killed in Bangla Operation, p.2.

Yaqoob, S. 2007. "British Islamic Political Radicalism" In *Islamic Political Radicalism: A European Perspective*, edited by T. Abbas, 279-294. Edinburgh: Edinburgh University Press.

In: Global Governance
Editor: Sagarika Dutt

ISBN: 978-1-53612-969-4
© 2018 Nova Science Publishers, Inc.

Chapter 9

COUNTERTERRORISM IN A GLOBALISED WORLD: CHALLENGES, THREATS AND WAYS FORWARD

Natasha Underhill [*]

Lecturer in International Relations,
The Nottingham Trent University, Nottingham, UK

ABSTRACT

The aim of this chapter is to critically re-address the main issues facing a truly globalised fight against terrorism as outlined by Wyn Rees (2014) in his work 'Counter-Terrorism' in *Handbook of Governance and Security* both challenging and supporting his main ideas and arguments. The chapter will follow the topic areas covered by Rees, beginning with an outline of global governance in context, identifying its key characteristics and providing a clear indication of its strengths and weaknesses as a process. The chapter then moves on to contextualising the current terrorist threat as well as the counterterrorism approaches currently being implemented. Following this there will be a case study of the US and EU in terms of their role in counterterrorism. Finally, the

---

[*] Natasha Underhill is also the course leader for the BA Hons (International Relations) degree programme.

chapter ends with an overview of the main challenges facing counterterrorism today and the ways in which global governance may be able to aid in addressing these challenges.

INTRODUCTION

Counterterrorism has, it seems, never been so pertinent to security matters than in the period since 9/11. It was at this point that the threat from terrorism truly became a global issue in the eyes of the global community. Since then, there have been numerous challenges to counterterrorism policies, processes and actions that have many questioning whether or not we need to re-think our approaches to counterterrorism to suit the more globalised world in which we live. Global governance has long been heralded as the ideal model under which the world should function. The question remains, however, how much room is there in the fight against terrorism for global governance structures? Can this global governance approach ever actually work in this regard? Some would argue that the fight against terrorism is first and foremost a domestic issue that feeds outwards to the regional context before becoming an issue to be dealt with globally. Others would say that in order to truly fight against terrorism there needs to be a global governance type system that provides a unified approach to dealing with terrorism while prescribing ways to prevent its reoccurrence. This challenge is being made all the more difficult with the rapid changes taking place within the international system such as Brexit and the future of the EU, the election of Trump as President of the United States of America (USA) and the global spread of religiously motivated terrorism led by Islamic State. The aim of this chapter is to assess, building on and challenging in places the work of Rees, the main issues facing a truly globalised fight against terrorism. It will begin by outlining global governance in the context of security. Identifying its key characteristics and providing a clear indication of its strengths and weaknesses as a process. The chapter will then move on to contextualising the current terrorist threat as well as the ways in which we are currently dealing with this. It will focus here mainly on the threat from Islamic State and similar groups as well as touching upon the current counterterrorism measures that are taking place to target the group. The chapter will then move on to focus on a case study of the US and EU in terms of their role in counterterrorism. This will be a comparative section of sorts with both the regional and global platforms within which each of these actors function, taken into consideration. Finally, the chapter will end with an overview of the main challenges facing counterterrorism today and the ways in which global governance may be able to aid in addressing these challenges. The aim is not to develop a new counterterrorism policy, but to try to understand the limitations of the current approaches while recommending some alternative ways in which we can move closer to a universally acceptable counterterrorism application.

GLOBAL GOVERNANCE IN THE CONTEXT OF SECURITY

According to Keohane (2002), governance is 'the processes and institutions, both formal and informal that guide and restrain the collective activities of a group'. This definition does not take into account the global aspect so, building on this, Finkelstein (1995, 368-9) argues that global governance is defined as 'governing, without sovereign authority, relationships that transcend national frontiers. Global governance is doing internationally what governments do at home'. It can also be defined as 'any purposeful activity intended to "control" or influence someone else that either occurs in the arena occupied by nations or, occurring at other levels, projects influence into that arena' (Ibid). Global governance as a process is challenging enough in and of itself in terms of trying to develop and implement a system that would be acceptable to every nation state in the world. However, it becomes even more complicated when it is applied to security. According to Rees (2014, 452), 'the presence of a hegemonic state may play a special role in creating and shaping patterns of security governance. A hegemonic state has the power to offer inducements for other countries to engage in cooperative behaviour and, at the other end of the spectrum, can impose penalties on recalcitrant countries that refuse to do so. Hegemons can help to establish international organisations that become the repositories of security governance and they can also play a critical role in generating security norms to which other states will align. Realists view governance structures as reflecting the interests of such strong powers and caution against seeing governance mechanisms as more than a temporary phenomenon.' This argument is never more relevant than when applied to the context of the US.

The US takes its role as world leader in the realm of security extremely seriously, especially in regards to setting norms and standards that are applied to all aspects of security. This means that in regards to the process of security governance, it becomes an almost top-down approach filtering from US aims and objectives rather than a multipolar-developed process that takes into account a more widespread set of issues within the security realm. The US, in its role as security governance leader, uses its influence often times in a negative way, imposing its norms and standards rather than allowing others to challenge, build upon or reinterpret its ideas to suit their own security needs. This has led to a backlash against the US, as it is now seen as being more of a dictator-like promoter of security governance rather than a partner in the process. This has become even more apparent since the election of Donald Trump and his extremely aggressive and antagonistic approach not just to global governance but to international relations in general. Rather than leading with such a narrow-minded and realist approach as the US has been inclined to do, security governance should instead represent 'an attempt to bring together countries and coordinate their response to "the increasingly complex challenges of governing in a globalising world" (Webber et al. 2004: 5)' (cited in Rees 2014, 452). A question emerges, however, when it comes to the threat from terrorism. Does this model fit or do we need to address terrorism in a different way in terms of the application of global governance?

According to Rees (2014, 452), the issue of countering terrorism, 'presents a special challenge in this regard. By its very nature terrorism is an amorphous and complex security problem. In some cases, it is state-centred, as countries are accused of employing terrorist methods, while in others they are alleged to fund and support terrorist groups. But in most cases, terrorism concerns the activity of sub-state actors. Terrorism tends to be clandestine in nature and crosses the traditional divide between internal and external security. For example, it may be planned by sub-state groups within one country but perpetrated as attacks in a neighbouring country. As a result, it is difficult to counter by mechanisms that are designed to regulate interstate activity.' This is an extremely interesting approach to the issue of terrorism and Rees does have a valid argument in terms of the difficulties emerging from tackling the terrorist threat. Terrorism as a threat is often specific to each state that is being targeted. Take the group Islamic State for example. Within the Middle East, more specifically Syria and Iraq, the aim of the group is to incite sectarianism, create massive instability, develop its caliphate by capturing and controlling territory, and challenging the legitimacy of the governments in power, to name but a few. Moving to Europe then, the aim is to promote fear, carry out attacks and force states such as the UK and France into action within the Middle East through counterterrorism campaigns. The aim with this would be to draw them into a ground battle where the group would be able to cause mass casualties, create chaos and force the hand of these states into strong-handed reactions that may lead to civilian casualties. This all then feeds into the propaganda campaigns that can bolster support for the group and prolong their survival. As a result, as noted by Rees (2014), it becomes extremely difficult then to apply a singular counterterrorism approach as there are completely different aims and objectives on both sides. As the US is a lead actor in this process, for example, it would not really have the same focus or security objectives that the Iraqi government would have thus making it almost impossible for the two to agree on one core counterterrorism approach.

In addition, there is the issue of actually defining terrorism as a phenomenon in and of itself. Terrorism is, and has always been a contested subject with declarations that one man's terrorist is another man's freedom fighter highlighting just how important perception can be in creating a threat and categorising a group. As a result there is no universal agreement on the definition of terrorism which should come as no surprise. One of the main problems that emerges when trying to create this universally accepted definition is that the international community, and more specifically the West, has a long history of competing views on who to designate as terrorists. 'Some states feel more threatened by terrorism than others, thereby rendering governance of the issue problematic. Diverging security agendas have made terrorism a security priority for western states, particularly over the last decade, but this is not shared by the rest of the world. Even within the West, there are countries that perceive little threat to their own security and are reluctant to enact robust security measures' (Rees 2014, 453). This designation is often times dependent on the level of support for a cause, level of sympathy for the group or level of threat perception facing the state. The main danger here is that without a set of specific criteria that can be applied equally to all groups, there will never be a clear definitional understanding of the concept of terrorism. Essentially, by categorising one group as terrorist and another as rebel group even though both are using the same tactics, methods, and have the same aims and objectives but one of the groups is more supportive of Western policies than the other, we are really diluting the value of the term terrorist and causing a lack of clarity as to who the terrorists actually are. Simply because we do not support the leadership or aims and objectives of one group over another is not ground enough to label one group as terrorist and the other not.

As well as this, 'up until the end of the Cold War, terrorism was largely a national affair. Individual countries experienced ethno-nationalist challenges from groups prepared to use violence, but this rarely spilled over borders and affected the wider international community' (Rees 2014, 453). The shift from more localised terrorism or regional groups to a more global terrorist threat has in a way forced us closer to trying to develop a global approach to terrorism. The problem is, however, that states such as the US have a very limited history of terrorism in the domestic context and therefore are not fully equipped to address the threat of terrorism outside of the post-9/11 context. The dangers of this is that many of the traits of the more traditional ethno-nationalist or separatist terrorist organisations such as the IRA and ETA such as fights for independence, removal of a perceived oppressor or fight for autonomy have been ignored in favour of focusing on religion as being the main cause of terrorism. This is especially significant when it comes to understanding the terrorist organisations that have emerged from the conflicts in the Middle East as many of those groups, Islamic State included, are using these issues as ways to garner support. Religion is simply a tool that is used by these groups to unify a community and to legitimize their actions.

The reality behind the aims and objectives of these groups is mostly political and economic and thus by focusing solely on the issue of religion, the West specifically is failing to adequately address the underlying root causes as to why groups such as al-Qaeda and Islamic State have been able to emerge in the first place. This means that we will never successfully be able to remove the threat from terrorism as our approaches are much too limited and do not take into account all aspects of the threat from terrorism. Therefore, this limited approach to counterterrorism as well as the domination by the West in the process of developing a global counterterrorism policy that is acceptable to all affected by the threat means that there has been little progress in developing an international governance-based organisation or approach. There remains no dedicated international organisation that can lead on counterterrorism cooperation. The UN Security Council takes on some of this responsibility but, as we will note later, is bound by the difference of opinions between the Permanent 5 members (US, Russia, China, UK, France) who, with the power of the veto, can control when and where intervention takes place. What results is a completely disjointed, state-centric approach to counterterrorism which means that unless the threat is facing that specific state there will be little to no action taken thus often prolonging conflict and facilitating the expansion of terrorist networks.

BILATERALISM IN A POST-9/11 WORLD

Bilateral cooperation in relation to counterterrorism policy development and implementation is a feature that cannot be overstated in relation to its significance. These long-standing relationships that have been developed over time are key to the success of counterterrorism policies. However, since 9/11 the US has often dismissed bilateralism in favour of an overly aggressive unilateral stance. Rees notes that the USA has played a unique role in encouraging other countries to enter into bilateral cooperation situations often through coercion or force. According to Rees, bilateralism has been at the heart of counterterrorism cooperation, which reflects what he terms a self-interested approach to international relations and global governance whereby countries share information in threats and challenges within a cooperative system of sharing (Rees, 2014). This approach has been, especially since 9/11, a core feature of the global fight against terrorism. There have been some issues, however, facing the success of this more multilateral, cooperative approach. Since then the US has taken the lead in the global fight against terrorism and bilateralism was pushed to the background in favour of a more dominant and unilateral approach.

The creation of a globally focused counterterrorism operation has been and remains to be a challenging process. By the very nature of the threat of terrorism, counterterrorism efforts in the global context tend to challenge state sovereignty as they require that changes to domestic policy as well as foreign policy are made in order to adequately address the threat. These globally focused counterterrorism operations have essentially blurred the lines between the domestic and the international in many areas including highly sensitive issues including intelligence sharing, immigration policy development and border security. In an increasingly globalised world, interdependence and interconnectedness has changed the ways in which states understand the concept of sovereignty and the ways in which they are willing to protect this. According to Krasner (1983), there are four core features of sovereignty that need to be considered. Firstly, when a state enjoys international legal sovereignty, it is recognised by other states as a legal entity. Secondly, Westphalian sovereignty establishes a state's territorial boundary and asserts that the state has sole control over legitimate behaviour within its territory. Thirdly, interdependent sovereignty means that the state has the ability to control movements across its borders. Finally, domestic sovereignty or autonomy asserts that the state and its rulers have the capacity to make policy and control developments within their jurisdictional territory. Essentially what this means is that sovereignty is linked to the notion that states are independent and autonomous from each other and it is this feature of the modern international system through which policy development and interactions take place, often making cooperation a difficult thing to achieve. In an increasingly globalised world, however, the degree to which states can remain completely autonomous has been challenged. This independent stance has been challenged even further by the shared threat from terrorism. According to Biswas (2009), balancing security, interdependence and sovereignty is particularly challenging due to the fact that security related issues such as countering terrorism are seen as being particularly relevant to the immediate interests of the state.

9/11 resulted in the securitisation of relationships between states to a degree not seen since the Cold War. Jervis (1978) notes that given the anarchic structure of the international system constant mistrust and uncertainty about the motivations of others perpetuates insecurity among states. This rationale, though now dated, still stands and if anything has become more relevant in the post-9/11 world. In order to try to achieve a coherent level of global governance and global cooperation institutions such as the UN were developed to act as a mechanism to constrain the behaviour of the dominant global powers such as the US and Russia but this is not often successful (Barry and Bratt, 2009). The US, for example, completely bypassed the UN in its decision to proceed with the invasion of Iraq as part of its Global War on Terrorism (GWOT). This GWOT that emerged post-9/11 further re-structured the international security agenda. It enabled the US to convince its allies to follow in its path to the creation of a new global security model. One of the most significant aspects of this was the threatening and forceful stance taken by President George W. Bush who famously declared that 'either you are with us or you are with the terrorists' (Bush 2001). This placed a lot of countries, even some of the closest allies of the US, into a precarious situation. They either agreed with and supported the policies implemented by the US or were open to targeting by the US as a possible terrorist ally. This form of forceful cooperation always has its limits and impacts negatively on the idea of global governance and multilateral and bilateral relationships. Additionally, through its Regional Strategic Initiative, and its 'Anti-Terror Assistance Programs' the US has encouraged countries to adhere to its counter-terror norms through the use of tools such as the provision of financial aid and training (Perl 2007, 24). Rees notes that although the power of the US has harnessed other countries to its counterterrorism priorities, its unilateralism and the controversial nature of its policies have provoked a backlash which has impacted on its stance as world superpower. Many of the policies engineered by the Bush administration have been repudiated and condemned by the wider-international community and this has been even more of an issue since President Trump has taken over from a more liberal and globally focused Barack Obama. Trump apparently wants to isolate the US, making it more insular and dominant as a global power. At the same time, he wants to project US power and dominance especially in the realm of counterterrorism and the fight against Islamic State. Interestingly though, even with his overly aggressive stance on the position of the US as being the world power, he is willing to portray his administration as being a cooperative one with those countries who agree with his policies. This is especially relevant to the relationship between the US and UK. Rees (2014) notes that much of this cooperation, however, remains quite informal and opportunistic. It relies on the ability of the US to forge personal relationships between the security authorities of each side. This leads to the concept of regional governance in the context of counterterrorism.

ISSUES FOR GLOBAL GOVERNANCE IN COUNTERTERRORISM

The GWOT has had a significant impact on the way in which the global community view international security. The process of global governance is an invaluable tool in the continued fight against terrorism. Global governance is a phenomenon that provides rules, norms and institutions that are, in theory, supposed to aid in the creation of a more unified world. According to Woods (1999), 'at the conceptual level global governance is a structure that is predicated on tolerance and a willingness to recognise and manage differences and reconcile self to other, and us to them. It is assumed to be a process in which all international actors have equal opportunities to participate in transnational networks, institution building, norm entrepreneurship, regime creation and the management of global change.' However, in reality global governance actually assumes that there is a power politics dimension to the global system and that this largely reflects the interests and preferences of the great powers first and foremost.

According to Makinda (2010), international institutions are those that create the rules, functions, practices and limitations of the global community in relation to a number of key areas including international law, diplomacy and religion as well as security. Even though institutions such as the UN and NATO exist to provide the above, the US in the post 9/11 world has increasingly acted unilaterally providing the rationale that it cannot be constrained by the norms and standards sets by these institutions as they are limiting its ability to carry out its GWOT. The dangers associated with this unilateral activity is that it can actually serve to weaken international norms and the institutions created to protect which in turn can play into the hands of the very terrorist organisations that we are trying to fight against. It is extremely important to note that counterterrorism measures if not properly conceived, developed and carried out can in fact facilitate the emergence of more terrorism and in turn create a never-ending cycle of terrorism and counterterrorism. Building on this, Huntington (1993) argued that 'The West in effect is using international institutions, military power and economic resources to run the world in ways that will maintain Western predominance, protect Western interests and promote Western political and economic values.' This in turn promotes an unbalanced system whereby the dominant states benefit the most and the weaker are often forced to simply agree and follow. Rees (2014) argues that governance in counterterrorism through institutions such as the UN is extremely difficult to implement owing to the very real diversity of views within the organisation. This means that universal agreement over such issues as counterterrorism has been notable by its absence within the UN framework. This has, therefore, resulted in a limited ability to shape international behaviour.

It has not all been negative, however, and the UN has often times heralded successful resolutions in relation to counter-terrorism governance. There have been 16 conventions and protocols passed and implemented that reflect attempts to address some of the principal features of terrorism since the 1970s through the UN system, including international agreements against the hijacking of commercial aircraft, prohibition of hostage-taking, the suppression of bombings, the protection of nuclear materials and efforts to counter terrorist-financing (Rees 2014). An additional strength of the UN is that it is able to interact with more legitimacy, in the eyes of the international community, with a broad range of international regulatory bodies to oversee the development of global security measures. The term legitimacy here is key as many view a unilaterally-acting US as a threat not as an ally and this can lead to challenges and an overall backlash to its approaches to counterterrorism. However, as noted by Rees (2014, 460), 'even within the West there has been disagreement over the UN's relative importance. While European governments have been all too aware of the deficiencies of the UN, they have remained committed to the principle of multilateralism'. By contrast, the USA has believed that it must be capable of acting even when others remain passive (Daalder and Lisay, 2005). President Bush regarded the UN as being weak or *'having failed the test' in relation to its decision on the invasion of Iraq and demanded that it should not get in America's way* (Ibid.).

What, then, are the implications for the blatant disregard of international norms and institutions in relation to global governance and the continued global fight against terrorism? Makinda (2010) states that 'without norms and institutions there would be no sense of order, security and justice…If the most powerful state does not want to be constrained by international norms and institutions, global governance is seriously undermined, and the war on terror loses purpose except as a demonstration of allegiance to the US'. This essentially makes other states feel inadequate and in a position of coerced agreement in areas of global governance where they may not feel confident or compliant thus triggering possibly aggressive responses to the US. In addition, the US in taking such a defiant stance is undermining its 'claims to be a responsible manager of global affairs...and is also indirectly threatening certainty, stability and order in international society because its actions might encourage aspiring great powers to emulate it' (Makinda, 2010). What the US needs to consider is that global governance actually has more capacity to address the most threatening issues facing the world including terrorism and the factors that can give rise to it such as poverty, lack of education and state failure. Where then does regional governance sit in the ongoing fight against terrorism?

ISSUES FOR REGIONAL GOVERNANCE IN THE CONTEXT OF COUNTERTERRORISM

In addition to global governance and cooperation in the fight against terrorism, regional action is critical to a successful counterterrorism campaign. It has even been argued that this is a more appropriate level for cooperation because it combines the ability to meet the transnational threat of terrorism while enabling actors to configure their efforts to the specific cultures of the states concerned (Rees 2014). According to Rees (2014, 462), in relation to 'regional counter-terrorism cooperation, ... areas with the highest incidence of terrorism, such as the Middle East and South East Asia, have the least cooperation'. This may be 'because states within a region have very different experiences of terrorism and are therefore reluctant to invest effort and resources to fight the phenomenon...few countries outside of the West share its preoccupation with terrorism, except for those that have their own domestic terrorist problems.' Various regional organisations have incorporated counterterrorism provisions within their terms of reference but these are usually unambitious in their scope. This sounds like an extremely sensible approach to understanding the impact of regional actors however it must be noted that in the current counterterrorism campaign many regional bodies are not doing as much as they could be, examples including the Arab League and ASEAN. These failures may be linked to the fact that regional cooperation can reflect the shared priorities of groups of states within an organisation and will not necessarily reflect the needs of those outside of that region often then resulting in challenges to policy development and implementation.

Taking ASEAN as an example here, the organisation has adopted numerous policies and initiatives in the fight against terrorism within its regional sphere which would to the outside world be viewed as a signal of intent from the group. In reality, however, ASEAN is a group with a varied membership of nations without a shared history of terrorism, different languages and religions and differing priorities in relation to the fight against terrorism. This essentially makes the group almost inept as it cannot agree internally on what the best unified approach is for its own members let alone develop an approach that can be implemented further afield into the global community. Rees (2014, 463) further outlines the case of the African Union (AU) noting that 'in the case of West Africa there is no regional framework to facilitate cooperation. Terrorism has not been accorded the same level of priority here as it has in the developed world. The region requires a broader range of responses to terrorism, rather than just seeing it as a security problem…The AU has turned its attention to countering terrorism as the threat has increased.' This reactive rather than proactive creation of counterterrorism policy more often than not results in ineffective policies that are outdated even before they are implemented. These examples alone show that within regional organisations there is no real uniformity to the development of counterterrorism policy which leads to a disjointed and often contradictory counterterrorism approach.

According to Rees (2014, 464), 'the only regional organisation that has taken substantive steps towards counter-terrorism action has been the EU… The EU is a multi-level actor in which its member states have granted it a broad range of competences, including in Common Foreign and Security Policy (CFSP) and in Justice, Liberty and Security (JLS).' The EU is the only regional organisation that has been successful in moving towards a substantive counterterrorism policy and implementation process. Since 9/11 specifically the EU has become a key actor in counterterrorism policymaking and in turn has increased the capability and competency of its members in relation to the implementation of shared security policies. In the post-9/11 environment, following attacks such as the London, Madrid, German, and Belgian attacks, the member states of the EU have become much more focused in their national counterterrorism laws and have in turn fed those upwards and outwards to be used in a more coherent and unified approach to counterterrorism. In 2008, the EU expanded its definition of terrorism in a more formal context and criminalised three new offences: Public provocation to commit a terrorist offence, recruitment for terrorism and training for terrorism (McNamara 2011). Additionally, an EU-wide Solidarity clause was adopted, similar in style to NATO's Article 5, whereby member states would act jointly if one of them became a victim of a terrorist attack and that they shall mobilise all instruments at their disposal including military resources as needed.[25] Building on this, the EU in November 2005 agreed on a Counterterrorism Strategy that outlined four key strategic pillars that would outline the EU's counterterrorism policy: prevent, protect, pursue and respond.[26]

However, even with these seemingly largescale successes, the EU remains constrained in its ability to successfully implement these policies in a uniform manner and is also dependent on states for the sharing of criminal intelligence which can be a challenge when states are not only trying to protect themselves regionally but also, and for some more importantly, domestically (Rees 2014). Renard (2012), in fact, notes that an estimated 90 per cent of counter-terrorism activities in Europe remain at the national level. In fact, since 2004, the EU has prioritized its response to terrorism through the lead role placed on civilian agencies, which means that the EU as an institution was now required to engage in cross-pillar coordination in order to act with purpose against the terrorist threat using the civilian context as an extra layer to its process. This often did not work

---

[25] EU (2005) 'Declaration on Combating Terrorism' March 25, 2005 www.consilium.europa.eu/uedocs/cmsUpload/DECL-25.3.pdf.

[26] Council on European Union (2011) 'The European Union Counterterrorism Strategy' http://register.concilium.eu.int/pdf/en/05/st14/st14469-re04.en05.pdf.

as planned as states have disagreed as to the extent they are willing to implement counterterrorism policies. This also links with the EU-US relationship in relation to counterterrorism which is seen as being the strongest in the global context. In fact, the EU views itself as being so successful in relation to counterterrorism that it has exported its model of counterterrorism governance to countries in its region, both allies of the EU and those who are direct neighbours of the organisation. The main tool used to ensure compliance has been the principle of conditionality whereby states have been expected to adopt its counterterrorism norms and practices as part of the accession process (Rees 2014). This differs massively from the approach of pressure and coercion taken by the US therefore making the EU a more legitimate partner to work with in the fight against terrorism.

CONCLUSION

Rees (2014, 467) sums up well the challenges facing the ongoing fight against terrorism in relation to global governance, stating that 'Governance is an apt description for the means by which counter-terrorism cooperation takes place within the international system. It captures the essence of a patchy and incomplete pattern of activity that is conducted on many different levels and by a range of different actors. There are overlapping competences between organizations and states and no single framework in which priorities are determined...It reflects the reality that terrorism remains a contested concept over which there is no unanimity within the international community.' However, he adds that patterns of cooperation are still evolving, and the ways in which such issues as Brexit and the Trump administration's continued unilateral stance on the GWOT will develop, will all have significant impacts on the future success of any EU counterterrorism policy development.

It is extremely difficult to counter a threat such as terrorism that is so fluid in nature, one that early traverses borders and that challenges the stability of states all over the world. The only way in which the GWOT can be a success is if it is truly universal. This means that a system of supranational governance needs to be agreed upon and put into place with the support of all nations across the globe. This of course will be a challenge when countries such as the US and Russia take it upon themselves to act as they see fit to protect their own security first before taking into account global security. As can be seen from the current system, elements of the global governance type system that has emerged stem from the priorities of the USA. Other elements have emerged from bilateral relationships between states that are opposed to terrorism but are also reluctant to commit themselves to formal multilateral patterns of cooperation (Rees 2014). The result of this disjointed and often fractured set of frameworks and approaches to counterterrorism is a range of norms that are adhered to by many, but not all, states thus not having a solid enough base to become a truly unified global framework to use to develop a truly universal counterterrorism policy.

REFERENCES

Barry, Donald and Duane Bratt. 2009. "Defence against Help: Explaining Canada-US Security Relations." *American Review of Canadian Studies* 38 (1): 63-89.

Biswas, Bidisha. 2009. "Bilateral Cooperation and Bounded Sovereignty in Counter-terrorism Efforts." *Border Policy Research Institute Working Paper No. 5.*

Council on European Union (2011) *'The European Union Counterterrorism Strategy'* http://register.concilium.eu.int/pdf/en/05/st14/st14469-re04.en05.pdf.

Daalder, Ivo and James Lisay. 2005. *America Unbound: The Bush Revolution in Foreign Policy.* New Jersey: John Wiley and Sons.

EU (2005) *'Declaration on Combating Terrorism'* March 25, 2005 www.consilium.europa.eu/uedocs/cmsUpload/DECL-25.3.pdf

Finkelstein, Lawrence S. 1995. "What is Global Governance?" *Global Governance* 1(3) (Sept-Dec): 367-372.

Huntington, Samuel P. 1993. "The Clash of Civilizations?" *Foreign Affairs* 72 (3): 22-49.

Jervis, Robert. 1978. "Cooperation under the Security Dilemma." *World Politics* 30 (2): 167-214.

Keohane, Robert O. and Joseph S. Nye. 2000. "Globalisation: What's New? What's Not (And So What?)" *Foreign Policy* 118: 104-119.

Keohane, Robert O. (ed). 2002. *Power and governance in a partially globalized world.* London and New York: Routledge.

Krasner, Stephen. 1983. 'Security Regimes' in *International Regimes.* Ithaca: Cornell University Press.

Makinda, Samuel M. 2010. "Global Governance and Terrorism." *Global Change, Peace and Security* 15 (1): 43-58.

McNamara, Sally. 2011. "The EU-US Counterterrorism Relationship: An Agenda for Cooperation." *The Heritage Foundation* March 2011 www.heritage.org/europe/report/the-eu-us-counterterrorism-relationship-agenda-cooperation.

Perl, R. 2007. "International terrorism: threat, policy and response." *Congressional Research Service Report for Congress.* Washington DC: Library of Congress.

Rees, Wyn. 2014. "Counter-Terrorism." In *Handbook of Governance and Security*, edited by James Sperling, 452-469. Cheltenham, UK and Northampton, USA: Edward Elgar.

Renard, Thomas. 2012. *"EU Counterterrorism Policies and Institutions after the Lisbon Treaty."* Centre on Global Counterterrorism Cooperation, Policy Brief, September 2012.

Webber, M., S. Croft, J. Howorth, T. Terriff and E. Krahmann. 2004. "The governance of European security." *Review of International Studies* 30(1): 3-26.

Woods, N. 1999. "Good Governance in International Organizations." *Global Governance* 5 (1): 39-61.

In: Global Governance
Editor: Sagarika Dutt

ISBN: 978-1-53612-969-4
© 2018 Nova Science Publishers, Inc.

Chapter 10

GLOBAL GOVERNANCE AND WORLD ORDER: PERSPECTIVES, CHALLENGES AND OUTLOOK

Sagarika Dutt

Senior Lecturer in International Relations and Subject Leader,
Nottingham Trent University, Nottingham, UK

ABSTRACT

Governance today is about the plurality of the modes of control that lead to 'the production of fragmented and multidimensional order within the state, by the state, without the state, and beyond the state' (Levi-Faur 2012, 3). Our study of order, as well as change, is enhanced by the adoption of an interdisciplinary perspective on governance that allows 'interpretations of the regulatory challenge from different disciplinary backgrounds'. Thus world order is not simply order among states but wider than that, and it is maintained by a hybrid of different systems of regulatory control, or governance. However, can global governance activities be justified with reference to the common good?

INTRODUCTION

This chapter revisits the theoretical aspects of the study of global governance and is partly based on a review of the *Oxford Handbook of Governance,* with a focus on global governance, international order and world order. Braithwaite (2012, vi) makes the point that 'a political science that clings to a preoccupation with government, marginalising the study of governance, restricts its relevance beyond the politics of settled western democracies, risking irrelevance in understanding moments of political transition'. The Arab spring that started in 2010[27], the Velvet Revolution in Czechoslovakia (1989); the Rose Revolution in Georgia (2003); Ukraine's Orange revolution (2004); and Kyrgzstan's Tulip Revolution (2005) are just some examples of political transition that brought a sea change in the politics of these countries in the 20th and 21st centuries. As chapter one of this volume notes, governance is about steering. Braithwaite writes that 'As in France, England and Boston, in Egypt, Libya and Yemen there is a struggle among very different political forces on the street to steer the crowd'. He gives the example of Libya where the Gaddafi family remains the key node in the governance of his tribe and of western Libya, while a variety of rebel leaders are key nodes of the networks governing the east. The political forces in today's world include networks, ideologies, religious sects, tribal powerbrokers and much more. Of course, international and regional institutions play a role as well in governance. In the case of Libya, NATO governed the skies above the east and the west, enforcing a UN no-fly zone. But the governance of the ground was also shaped by NATO, hence the use of the concept of networked governance.

---

[27] Ambassador Wael Al-Assad argues that the revolutions in the Arab world were hailed by many as the 'Arab Spring' but the reality is different. A lot of problems and challenges that were inherited from the ousted regimes will have to be dealt with. 'But before we get there, and for the time being, the Arabs are now suffering the agony of self-discovery and the pains of transformation. But this is the price nations often pay in their transformative moments'. Ambassador Wael Al-Assad, Representative of the Secretary-General for Disarmament and Regional Security, League of Arab States, "The agony of transformation in the Arab world." In *After the Spring, Prospects for the Arab World in 2013*, edited by Prof. Gareth Stansfield, Prof. Sir Paul Newton KBE, 13. London: UNA-UK.

Levi-Faur (2012, 3) explains the approach taken by the *Oxford Handbook of Governance* in these words: 'In this handbook, governance is an interdisciplinary research agenda on order and disorder, efficiency and legitimacy all in the context of the hybridization of modes of control that allow the production of fragmented and multidimensional order within the state, by the state, without the state, and beyond the state. The plurality of the modes of control reflect and reshape new ways of making politics, new understanding of institutions of the state and beyond the state and allow us to explore new ways for the control of risks, empowering citizens and promoting new and experimentalist forms of democratic decision-making'. The relevance of this scholarship to our research lies in the theorising of governance as 'a broad concept that is central to the study of political, economic, spatial, and social order in general and to the understanding of the dynamics of change of capitalist democracies in particular'.

THE VALUE OF AN INTERDISCIPLINARY PERSPECTIVE

The academic literature on governance makes it abundantly clear that it isn't just Political Scientists who are interested in governance. According to Levi-Faur (2012) an analysis of over 9,000 papers published on the topic of governance between 2006 and 2009 revealed that they were published in a wide variety of academic journals and that included journals from a range of disciplines such as Economics, Management, Political Science, Business, Environmental Studies, Public Administration, Planning and Development, Geography, Business and Finance, International Relations, Law, Urban Studies, Sociology and so on. This, therefore, makes it possible to adopt an interdisciplinary perspective on governance that has a heuristic value. Governance is a fluid concept rather than a 'clearly identifiable political construct, institutional framework, or historical period'. Zumbansen (2012, 83-84) argues that governance 'points to a reorientation of the language used by a discipline to address architectures of order, hierarchies of norms and values, organizational principles as well as distinct competences and authorities from an uncertain and evolving vantage point. Crucially, governance exposes the tedious relationship between form and substance, which is the paradoxical, mutually irreducible relation between organizational architecture and normative justification and legitimacy'. As this book attempts to illustrate, discourses on governance have led to new research in the field of international relations that have benefitted from the reorientation that Zumbansen refers to.

Zumbansen (2012, 84) argues that 'Governance breaks down boundaries between otherwise distinct discourses, disciplines and theories of order and calls the hitherto employed reference frameworks into question. In cutting across disciplinary boundaries and by reaching deep into the learned semantics of conceptualizations of order, governance signals a fundamental transformation in the communication about the determinants of ordering, including its political, legal, economic, religious nature. The significance of the term lies in its horizontal and vertical irritation of disciplinary discourse as it forces us, on the one hand, to think about the connections between "different" analytical and conceptual frameworks and, on the other, to take seriously the exhaustion of individual disciplines' vocabulary and established patterns of construction. The key to understanding governance then lies in accepting its interdisciplinary and transformative natures'. Thus not only is the concept of governance a bridging element, 'any reference to governance now prompts the inclusion of competing disciplinary interpretations of the regulatory challenge from different disciplinary backgrounds' (Ibid., 92).

PERSPECTIVES ON THE STATE IN THE AGE OF GOVERNANCE

Levi-Faur (2012) distinguishes between four different perspectives on the state in the age of governance. The first of these perspectives conceptualises governance as the hollowing out of the state. This means that there has been a shift from government to governance whereby power and authority drift away upwards towards transnational markets and political institutions, and downward toward local or regional government, domestic business communities and non-governmental organisations. Sorensen and Torfing (cited in Levi-Faur 2012, 10) suggest that 'Although the state still plays a role in local, national and transnational policy processes, it is nevertheless to an increasing extent "de-governmentalized" since it no longer monopolizes the governing of the general well-being of the population in the way that it used to do'. The second perspective can be described as 'degovernancing'. Levi-Faur (2012, 11) writes that 'Like the concepts of deregulation and debureaucratization, it is about the intended and unintended outcomes of limiting the ability to govern via centralized administrative and political mechanisms. Degovernancing is about the hollowing out of the state but also the hollowing out of alternative spheres of authority such as business-to-business regulation, civil regulation, and transnational regulation'. He goes on to say that this perspective sees good governance as 'no governance' or 'minimal governance' and the preferred mode of control is that of the market.

The third perspective is 'state-centred governance' which 'combines a recognition of the shift and transformation in the organization of the state, the limitations of its policy capacities and the importance of private actors in the policy process and in global governance more generally, with the suggestion that the state is still the most important and central actor in politics and policy'. There are variations within this perspective that can be identified with different authors (Levi-Faur 2012, 12). The fourth perspective can be referred to as Big Governance or from Big Government to Big Governance i.e., the growth and expansion of alternative modes of governance via increasing reliance on regulation. The shift from Big Government to Big (regulatory) Governance is a result of the growth of regulatory functions of public institutions, alongside the growth in the regulatory functions of other modes of governance. In Levi-Faur's (2012, 13) view, 'This perspective explores the relations between governments and governance from the perspective of regulation and with regard to the consolidation of what might best be called regulatory capitalism'. It draws on the governance literature to discuss the decentralization and diversification of politics and policy beyond the state, and draws on the regulation literature to discuss the expansion of regulatory governance and especially the notion of the regulatory state. 'By bringing the regulation and governance perspectives together an important aspect of the current capitalist order is becoming clearer: the growth and indeed explosion in the demand and supply of rules and regulation via hybrid modes of governance' (Levi-Faur 2012, 13).

On the subject of world order which is the focus of this chapter, *The Oxford Handbook of Governance* argues that 'We need to conceptualize a world order where governance is increasingly a hybrid of different systems of regulatory control; where statist regulation co-evolves with civil regulation; national regulation expands with international and global regulation; private regulation co-evolves with social regulation; voluntary regulations expand with coercive ones; and the market itself is used or mobilized as a regulatory mechanism' (Levi-Faur 2012, 14). International Relations scholars view governance as denoting a shift from 'anarchy'[28] to 'regulation' at the global level and as producing more order and stronger institutions. On the other hand those who are interested in domestic politics associate it with a 'softer order' that 'replaces stagnating bureaucracies and centralized state controls with softer and collaborative forms of policy-making' (Levi-Faur 2012, 7). Thus governance, according to this perspective, is not about hierarchy but about the decentralization of power and the creation of decentralized, informal, and collaborative systems of governance (Levi-Faur, 2012, 9). The following sections examine different views on global governance and world order expressed by different authors, before reaching a conclusion about the future of global governance.

---

[28] The term 'anarchy' does not imply chaos, but in Realist theory it means the absence of political authority. It can also refer to a system operating in the absence of any central government. (Baylis, John, S. Smith and P. Owens. 2011. *The Globalization of World Politics*, 559. Oxford: Oxford University Press)

GLOBAL GOVERNANCE AND WORLD ORDER

The study of international relations has always focused on relations between sovereign nation-states and as a result Realism and Neo-realism emerged as major theoretical frameworks for examining the nature of relations between these states. But the study of international political economy and global political economy is more interested in the growth of interdependence between states, the role of the market, and non-state actors of all kinds, for example Multinational Corporations. This gave rise to the concept of 'complex interdependence'[29], as discussed by Keohane and Nye (1977), as well as international regimes and other international institutions to manage complex interdependence. Regimes are defined as 'sets of governing arrangements that affect relationships of interdependence' and that include 'networks of rules, norms, and procedures that regularize behaviour and control its effects', in 'a given issue-area' (Keohane and Nye 1977, 19). On the other hand, as Rosenau (1992, 9) points out, 'governance in a global order is not confined to a single sphere of endeavour. It refers to the arrangements that prevail in the lacunae between regimes and, perhaps more importantly, to the principles, norms, rules, and procedures that come into play when two or more regimes overlap, conflict, or otherwise require arrangements that facilitate accommodation among the competing interests.' The need for global governance is explained by Arie Kacowicz (2012, 686) who argues that 'in an age of globalization there is an increasing need for global governance', as there was a functional need for international regimes and other international institutions to manage complex interdependence, in the previous period. This is because globalization has led to a process of deterritorialization, as

---

[29] The concept of complex interdependence suggested that the world had become more pluralistic and that there were more actors involved in international interactions and that they had become more dependent on each other. Complex interdependence has four characteristics: (1) increasing linkages among states and non-state actors; (2) a new agenda of international issues with no distinction between low and high politics; (3) a recognition of multiple channels for interaction among actors across national boundaries; and (4) the decline of the efficacy of military force as a tool of statecraft. Complex interdependence scholars would suggest that globalisation represents an increase in linkages and channels for interaction, as well as in the number of interconnections. (Baylis, John, S. Smith and P. Owens. 2011. *The Globalization of World Politics*, 121. Oxford: Oxford University Press)

social, political, and economic activities are increasingly 'stretched' across the globe (Baylis and Smith 2011, 18). They are no longer organized solely according to a strictly territorial logic. The boundaries of national economic or political space are no longer demarcated by territorial borders. For example, some large companies may have their headquarters abroad or outsource their production to other countries. However, as Baylis and Smith (2011, 19) argue, 'globalization is a process that involves a great deal more than simply growing connections or interdependence between states. It can be defined as "a historical process involving a fundamental shift or transformation in the spatial scale of human social organization that links distant communities and expands the reach of power relations across regions and continents"'.

As stated earlier in this chapter, International Relations scholars view global governance as denoting a shift from 'anarchy' to 'regulation' at the global level and as producing more order and stronger institutions. Arie Kacowicz (2012) argues that global governance should be understood in terms of a continuum of governance ranging from international order (Bull's anarchical society) to world government. In his book, *The Anarchical Society, A Study of Order in World Politics*, Bull (1995, 3-4) argues that men look for order in social life. But the order they are looking for is not simply any pattern or regularity in the relations of human individuals or groups, 'but a pattern that leads to a particular result, an arrangement of social life such that it promotes certain goals or values'. He mentions three goals, life, truth (i.e., promises made will be kept), and property, which he considers to be the elementary, primary or universal goals of social life. Thus, by order in social life he means 'a pattern of human activity that sustains elementary, primary or universal goals of social life such as these'.

However, his main interest in this book is to inquire into the nature of order in world politics, and in particular into the society of sovereign states through which order is maintained. He seeks to answer three questions: What is order in world politics? How is order maintained within the present system of sovereign states? Does the system of sovereign states still provide a viable path to world order? While he does not make a distinction between world politics and international politics, he does make a distinction between international order and world order. By international order, he means 'a pattern of activity that sustains the elementary or primary goals of the society of states, or international society', and by world order he means 'those patterns or dispositions of human activity that sustain the elementary or primary goals of social life among mankind as a whole'. International order is, therefore, order among states. States are independent political communities which possess a government and exercise sovereignty over a piece of territory and the population inhabiting it. When two or more states have sufficient contact between them, and sufficient impact on one another's decisions, causing them to behave as parts of a whole, at least to some extent, a system of states is formed. A system of states becomes a society of states when 'a group of states, conscious of certain common interests and common values, form a society in the sense that they conceive themselves to be bound by a common set of rules in their relations with one another, and share in the working of common institutions'(Bull 1995, 13). Attempting to answer the second question, how is order maintained within the present system of sovereign states, Bull argues that while a balance of power may help to limit violence, within international society, order is the consequence not merely of contingent facts such as this, but of a sense of common interests in the elementary goals of social life; rules prescribing behaviour that sustains these goals; and institutions that help to make these rules effective. Finally, the third question is answered under the sub-heading 'The states system and world order'. Bull argues that 'The states system will indeed prove dysfunctional if states are not able to preserve and extend the sense of common interests, common rules and common institutions that have moderated their conflicts in the past'. If there is a descent into a Hobbesian state of war the goal of world order will not be achieved (Bull 1995, 284).

GOVERNMENTALITY AND SELF-GOVERNANCE

The concept of governmentality, as opposed to sovereignty, can help us to explore and examine governance in a different way. Innes and Steele (2012, 716) draw on the concept of governmentality introduced by Michel Foucault and developed by other scholars and theorists. They write: 'We conceptualize regulation not as the "command and control" of populations, but rather as notions of responsibilizing individuals through new instruments of management that emerge from the market-driven logic of neoliberal governance'.

Foucault conceptualised governmentality not in terms of laws imposed on men but in terms of tactics, including using laws themselves as tactics, to achieve certain ends. 'These tactics can be thought of as "a form of political power that consists of various technologies, mentalities, and rationalities of governing others and oneself"' (Innes and Steele 2012, 717). Governance is not necessarily state-centred as power can emanate and power relations can be formed from the actions and practices of a variety of non-state actors. Although governmentality can be applied at the state level and to understand the state-citizen relationship, understandings of global governance incorporate a multitude of supra-state and sub-state actors, which represent the agents that self-govern as well as the agencies that disseminate the rules and tactics. Innes and Steele (2012, 717) argue that 'the "governance of the self" is key to governmentality – as a notion of "regulation" operating in governmentality is key to self-regulation – it is an embedded logic of "responsibility" to perform actions representing the self within fields of governmental power relations'.

The use of the term governance rather than government suggests decentralization and the incorporation of different actors within a network of governance, and also allows the identification of governance as a multilevel and multijurisdictional, rather than a hierarchical, process. This can be adapted to the study of global governance as multilevel governance and will be discussed later in this chapter. Explaining the theory of governmentality with a focus on the subject, or 'the self-to-self relationship', Innes and Steele (2012, 717) argue that it 'offers unique insight into how these interactions operate at the level of the agent, be it individuals, groups, states, or other corporate actors. Rather than looking at the institutions of governance, governmentality focuses on the tactics that the array of global actors employ to achieve self-governance at the level of the governed'.

Explaining this further Innes and Steele (2012, 717-18) argue that governmentality 'is attached to the mechanisms of a form of global governance that is predicated upon the assumptions of the neoliberal economic system. Indeed, Foucault's lectures on governmentality analysed the rise of neoliberalism, and following work adopted neoliberalism as the framework to understand rationalities of government. The mechanisms and tactics that characterise governmentality can be broadly understood as regulation and rules of conduct that encourage self-governance. They are managed through statistical and actuarial technologies. The agents of regulation are not understood in a top-down hierarchical way, but comply with a horizontal or networked understanding of power relations that are mobile, transformable, and reversible. Self-governance is encouraged through tactics that shift responsibility for behaviour to the subject. These tactics reward certain types of behaviour and punish others, provoking individuals, states, or other agents to assume responsibility for their compliance with a particular type of behaviour or set of norms that are informed by a liberal rationality of governance'.

Thus the Foucauldian concept of disciplined conduct differs from disciplinary power in that the conduct is managed rather than enforced and is related to a conceptualisation of global behaviour as fuelled by potential risk rather than threat. At the international level, 'rankings' can be seen as a tactic of governmentality because the disciplining in question is not applied by 'formal and restrictive hierarchies'. States are not obliged to take part in the governance indicator data and they are not formally punished for negative results or deviant behaviour. But a high ranking will encourage investment and lead to economic growth, while a low ranking will deter potential investors, and could also prevent developing countries from qualifying for aid until their corruption and democracy scores improve. The issue of good governance was addressed in chapter one and Innes and Steele's arguments contribute to this debate.

FORMS OF GLOBAL GOVERNANCE

Kacowicz (2012, 691) writes that 'following Rosenau (2002) and Risse (2009), for analytical purposes we can establish a typology of six forms of global governance, according to three categories: formal structures (hierarchical); informal structures (non-hierarchical); and mixed formal and informal structures (such as public-private networks and partnerships). The directional flows of authority may be unidirectional (either vertical, top-down or bottom-up; or horizontal, non-hierarchical). Alternatively, the direction can follow multiple flows of authority transmission, both vertical and horizontal. The actors involved might include governments, transnational corporations (TNCs), IGOs, NGOs, business alliances, and public-private, and private-private partnerships. While traditional IR are best typified in Table 1 by cell #1, global governance is best typified in the hybrid of mixed formal and informal structures and multidirectional flows of authority in cell #6. We should add that all the cells in Table 1 represent different forms and ways of global governance'. This typology is summarized in the table (adapted from Rosenau 2002 and Risse 2009).

From the reading of the table, Kacowicz argues, 'we can get a better understanding of the multi-level character of global governance as well as the multiplicity of the relevant political actors and institutions. Furthermore, we should locate the complex processes of global governance within an imaginary continuum running from the traditional form of international order (the Westphalian system of sovereign states) all the way to the utopian ideal of a world government.'

Table 1. A typology of global governance

	Unidirectional: vertical or horizontal flows of authority	Multidirectional: vertical and horizontal flows of authority
Formal Structures	*Top-down (hierarchical)* [Cell # 1] Governments of nation-states and supranational institutions (IGOs); TNCs (corporate hierarchies); contracting out and outsourcing	*Network governance* [Cell # 2] Governments of nation-states; international institutions (IGOs); NGOs; business alliances; contracting out and outsourcing
Informal Structures	*Bottom-up governance* [Cell # 3] Impact of civil society and networks of advocacy; NGOs and INGOs; positive incentives and bargaining	*Side-by-side governance* [Cell # 4] NGOs and INGOs; governments; positive incentives and bargaining; international regimes; private interest government/ private regimes; private- private partnerships
Mixed formal and informal structures	*Market-type governance* [Cell # 5] Governments of nation-states, IGOs; elites; markets; mass publics; TNCs, public-private networks and partnerships	*Web/network governance* [Cell # 6] Governments of nation-states; IGOs; elites; mass publics; TNCs; NGOs; INGOs; networks of advocacy; civil society

THE CONTINUUM OF GLOBAL GOVERNANCE

International Order → World Society → World Order → New Medievalism → World Government

Maintaining the distinction Bull makes between international order and world order, Kacowicz writes that world order is a wider category of order than international order. Its units of order are not just nation-states, but rather individual human beings, and this enables us to assesses the degree of order on the basis of the delivery of certain kinds of public goods (such as security, human rights, basic needs, or justice) for humanity as a whole. While different conceptualisations of world order may be found in the IR literature, since the 1990s, following the end of the Cold War and the advent of the contemporary age of globalisation, many contemporary scholars prefer to use the term global governance and global democracy in a conscious effort to expand the epistemic community of academics and practitioners who embrace the key assumptions and principles of world order. Kacowicz (2012, 694) writes that 'As a matter of fact, global governance incorporates the same problematique of world order, heading in the direction of distancing or deviance from world anarchy and chaos. Thus the concept here becomes more normative than analytic, or at least carries a strong normative bias.'

GLOBAL GOVERNANCE AS MULTI-LEVEL GOVERNANCE

Michael Zurn's chapter in the *Oxford Handbook of Governance* entitled 'Global Governance as Multi-Level Governance' complements the chapters discussed above but is written from a slightly different perspective. He begins his chapter with a definition of global governance. It refers to the 'entirety of regulations put forward with reference to solving specific denationalized and deregionalized problems or providing transnational common goods' (Zurn 2012, 731). By 'denationalized' problems he means problems which reach beyond national borders. By the entirety of regulations he means the 'substantial norms, rules, and programs, the processes by which norms, rules, and programmes are adopted, monitored and enforced, as well as the structures in which they operate'. First of all, this is a comprehensive definition and not dissimilar to definitions offered by other authors, as discussed in chapter one.

Secondly, he makes a distinction between 'government' which refers to one public actor, and governance which 'describes an activity independent of the numbers and kinds of actors carrying it out'. This leads to a discussion of global governance as multi-level governance, and more than just inter-governmental co-ordination, a system in which the global level possesses some authority of its own, and is characterised by the interplay of different levels, rather than working independently from other governance levels.

Zurn's notion of a multi-level governance system is not based on the Westphalian system of territorial states that are sovereign actors and have a monopoly on political authority. In the Westphalian system 'international institutions are considered as instruments of the territorial state, without possessing political authority in their own right'. Zurn's notion of multilevel governance is based on political authority beyond the nation-state, for example supranationalization which may lead to 'obligations for national governments to take measures even when they have not agreed to do so'. This, therefore, contradicts the consensus principle and the principle of non-intervention associated with the Westphalian system of states. Zurn (2012, 731) argues that the 'whole notion of a multi-level governance system is based on the idea that segmentary differentiation of similar states, each of which controls a certain territorially defined part of the world, gets replaced by a concept that is at least to some extent characterized by functional and stratificatory differentiation'.

He also argues that the growing authority of international institutions is reflected in the increase in the number of international agreements concluded under the aegis of the UN. He writes that 'underlying this increase is a corresponding growth in the issue areas to be dealt with by international institutions. For a long time, security issues and economic relations have dominated as the focal points of international cooperation; today, however, international institutions deal with a much broader range of issue areas' (Zurn 2012, 732). He also mentions 'the new authority-generating quality of international institutions at different phases of the policy cycle'. Explaining a policy cycle, he writes that a policy cycle 'is a sequence of distinct phases in the life-course of a regulation. At the international level, we can differentiate between the following phases:

- agenda-setting,
- decision-making,
- implementation/rule interpretation,
- monitoring,
- enforcement,
- evaluation/new agenda-setting.

A policy cycle begins when there is a growing need for regulation at the international level and there are growing demands on international institutions to accommodate this need. The process of decision-making, usually majoritarian decision-making, enhances the authority of international institutions, as does the monitoring and verification of international rules by actors who are not directly under the control of states, for example the International Atomic Energy Agency (IAEA) processes information on treaty compliance in relation to the Nuclear Nonproliferation Treaty. Similarly, transnational non-governmental organisations (NGOs), often in collaboration with societal actors, undertake informal, independent regulatory monitoring, for example, human rights organisations like Human Rights Watch monitor internationally standardised human rights. In the area of rule enforcement, the international community has increasingly begun to respond to cases of gross violation of human rights with military force and economic sanctions.

Finally, in the field of policy evaluation and related agenda setting non-state actors have begun to compete with states, for example, transnational NGOs and international secretariats, as well as knowledge bodies affiliated with the secretariats of international organisations, like the Intergovernmental Panel for Climate Change (IPCC). Zurn argues that the normative pressure resulting from the authority of such knowledge bodies and agenda-setting actors weakens the ability of individual governments to oppose international norm development processes. It can be concluded, therefore, that in many issue areas, the global level has achieved a certain degree of authority and has thus partially replaced the consensus principle of the traditional international system. It may be argued that this has, therefore, to some extent, become the basis of world order. But it also needs to be acknowledged that if global governance is conceived as multilevel governance (i.e., constituted by the interplay of different levels and organisations, whereby each level and organisation cannot work unilaterally), each of these levels exercises authority and there is, therefore, a need to coordinate decisions between different levels.

Thirdly, Zurn argues that while governance activities are justified with reference to the common good, they do not necessarily serve it. Thus this raises the issue of interest, i.e., in whose interest is global governance being promoted? Zurn gets around this question by arguing that 'international regulatory governance often aims actively at achieving normatively laden political goals when handling common problems of the international community. In this sense, governance presupposes some common interests and goal orientations beyond the nation-state, at least in a rudimentary form, without – of course – denying the persistence of fundamental conflicts' (Ibid., 730-31). Other authors are more critical about global governance. For example, in his chapter entitled 'Politics in a floating world: Toward a critique of global governance' in *Approaches to Global Governance Theory* edited by Martin Hewson and Timothy Sinclair, Robert Latham (1999, 30) asks 'Does a focus on global governance risk, however, well intended, legitimizing and thereby further empowering actors leading existing international institutions simply because they are the best placed and most capable governors?' He rightly points out that we want global governance to be effective, but we also want it to be just, and to lead to a just world order and the possibility of governing well. 'Yet we have only an open, fluid (if not nascent) social context ("the global community") against which to hold governors' (Ibid.). While some critics may argue that global governance suffers from a democratic deficit, it could also be argued that global governance is simply an academic concept that tries to make sense of the laws, norms, rules, policies and institutions that shape international behaviour, and analyse the emergence of different forms of international and transnational regulatory governance. Djelic and Sahlin (2012) write that traditionally regulatory issues have been approached, in political science and in the international relations literature, from a state-centred perspective. However, since the financial and economic crisis that started in 2008, there have been calls for more regulation and order at the transnational level. Djelic and Sahlin (2012) describe this as a period of consequential reregulation or reordering, through the proliferation of soft law which increasingly had a transnational reach.

Possibly one of the best critiques of global governance is provided by Craig Murphy (2005) in his chapter entitled 'Global Governance: Poorly done and poorly understood' in the *Global Governance Reader* edited by Rorden Wilkinson. His main contention is that global governance has not dealt with moral questions very well. One of the examples he provides of the failures of the international community to prevent human suffering is the Rwandan genocide. The Tutsi population of Rwanda was systematically slaughtered by the Hutus despite a widely ratified UN Genocide Convention and ample early warning provided to the UN Secretariat and the Security Council by its own officers in the field. In more recent years, the suffering of the Rohingya people of Myanmar has been an issue that the UN has highlighted but not been able to end[30]. There is plenty of evidence to suggest that global governance is 'likely to remain inefficient, incapable of shifting resources from the world's wealthy to the world's poor, pro-market, and relatively insensitive to the concerns of labour and the rural poor, despite the progressive role that it recently may have played in promoting liberal democracy and the empowering of

---

[30] According to UN spokesman, Stephane Dujarric, the number of Rohingya refugees who fled Myanmar to Bangladesh since late August (2017) has reached 480,000, challenging efforts to care for them. The Office for the Coordination of Humanitarian Affairs (OCHA) says that this brings the total number of Rohingya refugees in Bangladesh to more than 700,000 people. Meanwhile, UN Secretary-General, Antonio Guterres, will brief members of the UN Security Council on what he says is ethnic cleansing in Myanmar, as the Council considers taking action to end the violence. ('UN chief to brief Security Council as Rohingya refugee numbers climb', UN Wire, 27 September 2017 and 'Guterres: Rohingya crisis "a humanitarian and human rights nightmare" ', UN Wire, 29 September 2017)

women' (Murphy 2005, 90). The reason is that global governance is ultimately more concerned with economic issues. As Murphy (2005, 98) argues, it is a response to the 'overall logic of industrial capitalism' and its pressure towards larger and larger market areas, that can be summed up as economic globalisation.

CONCLUSION

But as the chapters in this book have shown more needs to be done to improve global governance so that the world achieves the goals the international community wants to achieve. These include international peace and security, and sustainable development. The gap between the rich and the poor, both in terms of countries and communities, is still too wide. There are many different ways in which this gap can be narrowed down and these need to be explored. The reduction of poverty is a political commitment that all international actors must make and will entail the mobilisation of resources and the adoption of policies that deliver results. The Sustainable Development Goals are more wide ranging than the Millennium Development Goals and more ambitious. But they highlight the issues that global governance needs to address. At the same time, the work of the UN and its specialised agencies, funds and programmes such as UNDP in achieving them emphasise the importance of global public goods. Without the work of the World Health Organisation (WHO) or the Food and Agriculture Organisation (FAO), or for that matter the IAEA, the world would be worse off and this needs to be appreciated by everyone whether they believe that there is a future for global governance or are deeply sceptical about it.

REFERENCES

Al-Assad, Wael. 2013. "The agony of transformation in the Arab world." In *After the Spring, Prospects for the Arab World in 2013*, edited by Prof. Gareth Stansfield and Paul Newton, 13. London: UNA-UK.

Braithwaite, John. 2012. "Foreword." In *The Oxford Handbook of Governance*, edited by David Levi-Faur, v-ix. Oxford: Oxford University Press.

Bull, Hedley. 1995. *The Anarchical Society – A Study of Order in World Politics*. Basingstoke and London: Macmillan Press Ltd.

Djelic, Marie-Laure & Kerstin Sahlin. 2012. "Reordering the World: Transnational Regulatory Governance and its Challenges." In *The Oxford Handbook of Governance*, edited by David Levi-Faur, 745-758. Oxford: Oxford University Press.

Innes, Alexandria Jayne & Brent J. Steele. 2012. "Governmentality in Global Governance." In *The Oxford Handbook of Governance*, edited by David Levi-Faur, 730-744. Oxford: Oxford University Press.

Kacowicz, Arie M. 2012. "Global Governance, International Order, and World Order." In *The Oxford Handbook of Governance*, edited by David Levi-Faur, 686-698. Oxford: Oxford University Press.

Keohane, R. O. & J. S. Nye. 1977. *Power and Interdependence*. Boston and Toronto: Little, Brown and Co.

Krasner, Stephen D. 1982. "Structural causes and regime consequences: regimes as intervening variables." *International Organization 36* (2): 185-205.

Latham, Robert. 1999. "Politics in a Floating World, Toward a critique of global governance." In *Approaches to global governance theory*, edited by Martin Hewson and Timothy J. Sinclair, 23-53. Albany: State University of New York Press.

Levi-Faur, David. 2012. "From "Big Government" to "Big Governance"?" In *The Oxford Handbook of Governance*, edited by David Levi-Faur, 3-18. Oxford: Oxford University Press.

Murphy, Craig N. 2005. "Global Governance: Poorly Done and poorly Understood." In *The Global Governance Reader* edited by Rorden Wilkinson, 90-104. London and New York: Routledge.

Risse, T. 2009. Notes on 'global governance' and prospects for Israeli-German academic exchange. In *In the spirit of Einstein: Germans and Israelis on Ethics and International Order*, edited by A. M. Kacowicz,

57-70. Jerusalem: The Leonard Davis Institute for International Relations and the Einstein Center, Hebrew University of Jerusalem.

Rosenau, James N. & Ernst-Otto Czempiel (eds.). 1992. *Governance without government: order and change in world politics.* Cambridge: Cambridge University Press.

Rosenau, James N. 2002. "Governance in a new global order." In *Governing Globalization: Power, Authority, and Global Governance,* edited by D. Held and A. McGrew, 70-86. Cambridge: Polity.

Sørensen, E. & J. Torfing. 2005. "Democratic anchorage of governance networks." *Scandinavian Political Studies 28*: 195-218.

Zumbansen, Peer. 2012. "Governance: An Interdisciplinary Perspective." In *The Oxford Handbook of Governance*, edited by David Levi-Faur, 83-96. Oxford: Oxford University Press.

Zürn, Michael. 2012. "Global Governance as Multi-Level Governance." In *The Oxford Handbook of Governance*, edited by David Levi-Faur, 730-744. Oxford: Oxford University Press.

INDEX

I